What people are s

Kabbalistic Pan

We have all heard of the similarities between the Upanishads, Hermeticism, Sufism, etc., and modern ontologies such as panpsychism, cosmopsychism and analytic idealism. Dr. Schipper now reveals how the Jewish Kabbalah also anticipates, with exquisite and uncanny precision, much of these modern developments. His work addresses a conspicuous gap in the literature, solidifying the notion that the primacy of consciousness in nature is far from a new idea, but one with a very long and robust historical tradition. Hyman's case is sober, scholarly, but also highly enticing and persuasive. His understanding of both Jewish mysticism and modern philosophy and neuroscience is profound, making him the ideal person to rebuild the bridges between us and our forefathers. This book is obligatory reading for anyone interested in philosophy of mind, neuroscience and mysticism.

Bernardo Kastrup, Doctor of Philosophy and Computer Engineering

Dr. Schipper has taken the Kabbalah and science discourse to an entirely new level. The longstanding Eurocentric bias of previous discussions, ignoring the Near Eastern contributions of the Rashash school, has finally been corrected. It is unique that a writer so steeped in Kabbalah also incorporates the profound ontology of Plotinus and Aquinas. It is also gratifying to finally see a thorough examination of the parallels between David Bohm's physics and the Kabbalah. The author has a great gift for rendering the complex accessible, yet redolent with meaning.

Prof. Jonathan Garb, Gershom Scholem Chair in Kabbalah, Hebrew University of Jerusalem

Professor Schipper's erudite monograph on Kabbalistic Panpsychism is a marvelous treasure of lucid insight into what are millennia-long enigmas related to consciousness in Jewish mystical thought. As a theoretical physicist and priest with interests in philosophy of mind, this is just the type of thing I have longed for. A physics of the observer has been delayed because physicists generally wish to avoid anthropic parameters which hint at 'spirituality'. I applaud Professor Schipper for bringing us to the gates of understanding in relation to the imminent paradigm shift.

Prof. Richard L. Amoroso, Noetic Advanced Studies Institute

This book is without doubt the most thorough and interesting discussion of consciousness and the Kabbalah that I have seen. Dr. Schipper has done a masterful job of reviewing the enigma that is consciousness; he is also an expert in Kabbalah and its imagery, and sensitively explains the many spiritual links to consciousness. The book delves into quantum mechanical ideas about consciousness, especially as formulated by later Kabbalists and the ideas of the pioneering quantum physicist, David Bohm. Clear and systematic, and quite detailed, this book is mandatory reading for anyone wanting to understand the essential spiritual nature of human consciousness from a Jewish mystical perspective.

Howard Smith, astrophysicist and author of *Let There Be Light: Modern Cosmology and Kabbalah*

Dr. Schipper presents a rigorous alignment of cutting-edge quantum physics with ancient Kabbalistic metaphysics and deftly brings this juxtaposition to elucidate the nature of consciousness. He shows how these disparate explorations of reality are not just compatible but actually complement each other. This work should touch hearts and open minds.

Sarah Yehudit Schneider, Author, *Kabbalistic Writings on the Nature of Masculine & Feminine*

Kabbalistic Panpsychism is a unique addition to the literature on the problem of consciousness. Hyman M. Schipper examines Jewish mysticism and develops a novel, comprehensive Kabbalistic approach to consciousness that is radically distinct from the conventional materialist approach. I recommend this book to anyone who is interested in learning how ancient Jewish thought may help us solve one of the most profound puzzles of existence.

Yujin Nagasawa, HG Wood Professor of the Philosophy of Religion, University of Birmingham

I can't even begin to describe my feelings—this book is extraordinary! It is a splendidly imaginative work that invigorates the science-religion dialogue in unprecedented ways. It should be studied and not merely read.

Rabbi Reuben Poupko, Spiritual Leader, Beth Israel Beth Aaron Congregation (Montreal)

This book is a serious counterpoint to the materialist model of contemporary science. It demonstrates that the metaphysical structure of Jewish mysticism (Kabbalah) is not only concordant with ideas in quantum physics, but provides a compelling paradigm for understanding consciousness. I strongly recommend this highly original work to professionals and students who are fascinated by the mystery of consciousness and its role in the unfolding of reality.

Nathan Kuperstok, PhD, Chief Psychologist (ret.), St. Mary's Hospital, McGill University

Kabbalistic Panpsychism

The Enigma of Consciousness in
Jewish Mystical Thought

Kabbalistic Panpsychism

The Enigma of Consciousness in
Jewish Mystical Thought

Hyman M. Schipper
MD, PhD, FRCP(C)

IFF
BOOKS

Winchester, UK
Washington, USA

JOHN HUNT PUBLISHING

First published by iff Books, 2021
iff Books is an imprint of John Hunt Publishing Ltd., No. 3 East Street, Alresford,
Hampshire SO24 9EE, UK
office@jhpbooks.com
www.johnhuntpublishing.com
www.iff-books.com

For distributor details and how to order please visit the 'Ordering' section on our website.

ISBN: 978 1 78904 517 8
978 1 78904 518 5 (ebook)
Library of Congress Control Number: 2020938268

Design: Stuart Davies

UK: Printed and bound by CPI Group (UK) Ltd, Croydon, CR0 4YY
Printed in North America by CPI GPS partners

We operate a distinctive and ethical publishing philosophy in
all areas of our business, from our global network of authors to
production and worldwide distribution.

Contents

Acknowledgments   xv

Preface   1

Chapter 1: The Problem of Consciousness   5

Chapter 2: Panpsychism and Panentheism   9

Chapter 3: Quantum Mechanics, Consciousness and
    the Kabbalah   13
    3.1 The Heisenberg Uncertainty Principle   15
    3.2 Kabbalah and the Physics of David Bohm 18
    3.2.1 Hidden Variables and the Implicate Order 19
    3.2.2 The Holographic Universe   21

Chapter 4: Principles of Kabbalah   26
    4.1 Orientation to Jewish Mysticism
    4.2 *Sefirot, Partzufim* and Worlds   36
    4.3 *Ensheathment, Interinclusion* and *Interpenetration* 44
    4.4 *Orech* and *Oivi*—Complementary Modes
    of Awareness   54
    4.5 On the Nature of Paradox   60

Chapter 5: Kabbalistic Panpsychism and Panentheism   63
    5.1 A Hierarchy of Consciousness   64
    5.2 Relativistic Consciousness   68
    5.3 Are Golems Conscious?   83
    5.4 Human Brain Organoids   87
    5.5 *Chaya* Consciousness and the Tower of Babel 88

Chapter 6: Female Intuition   93
    6.1 Ontology of the *Keter-Malchut* axis   94

Chapter 7: Supervenience and Top-Down Causation   98
    7.1 Wheeler's Participatory Universe   102

Chapter 8: *Tefillin* and the Seat of Human Consciousness   108

Chapter 9: Consciousness and the 'Unknowable Head'   120
    9.1 On Prophecy and Free Will   127

Chapter 10. Clinical Models of Kabbalistic Panpsychism   139

Chapter 11: Kabbalah and Process Philosophy   149

Chapter 12: Consciousness and Conscience   152

Chapter 13: The Future of Human Consciousness   156

Chapter 14: Conspectus   163

Epilogue   170

Bibliography   172

Index   203

List of figures and tables in order of appearance

Figure 1: Young's two-slit experiment demonstrating the dual (wave-particle) nature of light. (https://landing.newscientist.com/department-for-education-feature-3/)

Figure 2. The implicate and explicate orders. Represented by Bohm as an ink drop in a rotating, glycerin-filled cylinder. From http://forumserver.twoplustwo.com/137/religion-godtheology/alpha-omega-gravity-order-899479 and [1] with modifications.

Figure 3. Laser holography. From [1] with permission.

Table 1. Glossary of Kabbalistic terms contained in this book.

Table 2. *Gematriya* — **the numerical values of the Hebrew letters.**

Figure 4. A. The ten *Sefirot* (*Da'at* is included when *Keter* is not). **B. Kabbalistic causal hierarchy** (*Seder Hishtalshelut*). Bars indicate potential interactions among the *Sefirot*. Arrows denote standard pathway for the descent of Divine influence. From [1] with permission.

Figure 5. Initial acts of Creation (pre-Genesis 1:1). A. Light of the Godhead (*Ohr Ein-Sof*; unbounded white space). **B.** 'Retraction' of *Ohr Ein-Sof* (*Tzimtzum*) establishing a 'Void' (*Chalal* or *Makom Panoi*; black). **C.** Residual Light (*Reshimu*; red/circumferential) lining the Void. **D.** Ray of *Ohr Ein-Sof* (*Kav*; white) entering the Void. **E.** *Kav* unites with the *Reshimu* forming concentric *Sefirot* (colored/concentric rings). **F.** Arrangement of the *Sefirot* in the image of Man=Creation of *Adam Kadmon* (supernal World).

Figure 6. Descending   hierarchy of Worlds. Spiritual progenitors transduced to physical reality by *Malchut* of *Malchut* of the 'lowest' World, *Asiyah*.

Figure 7. The *Partzufim* comprising each World. *Atik Yomin* can be considered the top *Partzuf* of the World in question or the bottom *Partzuf* of the World immediately above. *Arich Anpin* extends from top to bottom of a World. *Abba* and *Imma* respectively 'dress' (are explicate or superficial to) the right and left arm and hemi-thorax of *Arich Anpin*. The *Nukvah* (Divine Feminine) 'dresses' on the *Netzach–Hod–Yesod* of *Zeir Anpin* (Divine Masculine). *Zeir Anpin*, in turn, receives its 'brains' (*Mochin*; *Chochmah–Binah–Da'at*) from the *Netzach–Hod–Yesod* of *Partzuf Imma*.

Figure 8. **'Signet-ring' metaphor (*Chotem V'nechtom*) for the manifestations and correspondences of things and events across the hierarchy of created Worlds.**

Figure 9. Ensheathment (*Hitlabshut*). Metaphorised by a set of extendable telescopes. **A.** Reference configuration of the Kabbalistic superstructure. Joints of the telescope symbolize degree of 'overlap' (enclothement) among *Sefirot*, *Partzufim* and Worlds. **B.** 'Descent' of Creation into *Orech* (increasing apparent disunity and 'distance' from *Ein-Sof*). **C.** 'Ascent' into *Oivi* (progressive revelation of wholeness and the indivisible Light of *Ein-Sof*). Modified from http://www.gilai.com/ images/ items/1498_big.jpg and [1] with permission.

Figure 10. Interinclusion (*Hitkallelut*). Represented as a deca-*Sefirotic* fractal. From [1] with permission.

Figure 11. A. Simulation of neural network in human brain (Shutterstock). B. Computer simulation of the large-scale distribution of galaxies or cosmic web (Wikimedia Commons), with modifications.

Figure 12. Interpenetration (*Hitkashrut*). Simultaneous co-actualization of like *Sefirot* (e.g. *Chesed*, dark ovals) within and among Worlds (e.g. *Briah*, *Yetzirah* and *Asiyah*). Such 'parallel processing' of homologous parts circumvents the linear, hierarchical flow of Divine influence illustrated in Fig. 4B and represents a greater manifestation of Wholeness (*Shlaymut*). From [1] with permission.

Figure 13. Progressive transduction (revelation) of transcendent consciousness (*Ohr Makif*) into immanent consciousness (*Ohr Pnimi*) by the *G″R*'s of the various domains of Creation. White denotes consciousness space. *G″R=Gimel Rishonim* (three top *Sefirot* or 'brains'/ *Mochin*); *Z″T=Zayin Tachtonim* (seven bottom or 'bodily' *Sefirot*).

Table 3. Homologous constructs or 'dualities' (*Kinuim*) within the Kabbalistic hierarchy.

Figure 14. Artificial Life Forms. A. The Golem of Prague. B. Lt.-Commander Data with positronic brain exposed.

Figure 15. Wheeler's U-diagram of the Participatory Universe. From https://www.designspiration.net/save/10073566899495/

Figure 16. *Tefillin* and the human nervous system. A. Homologies between head-*Tefillin* (*Shel-Rosh*) and the central nervous system (CNS), and between arm *Tefillin* (*Shel-Yad*) and the peripheral nervous system (PNS). **B.** Relationship of the head-*Tefillin* to skull and brain. **C.** Decussation of the pyramids (corticospinal tracts) in the lower medulla oblongata. **D.** Variation in the knotting of the *Kesher Shel-Rosh*. Straps cross to opposite sides in square *end-Mem* (ם; left) and *Ari″ZL's* (middle) knots and remain uncrossed in the *Dalet* (ד) knot (right). **E.** *Tefillin* and acupuncture points in Traditional Chinese Medicine, from [2] with permission.

Figure 17. A model depicting boundaries of human insight into the fabric and workings of the universe imposed by Newtonian (classical) physics, quantum mechanics and the Kabbalah. Modified from [3] with permission.

Figure 18. Wigner's friend paradox.

Figure 19. Markov blankets.

Figure 20. The RADLA as Markov blanket. 'r' denotes individual human consciousness; 'Ψ', universal consciousness (the 'Mind of God'); 'a', active state within Markov blanket allowing human consciousness to interact with Ψ. 's', sensory state within Markov blanket whereby Ψ impacts human consciousness. Thick arrows, permeation of the RADLA membrane (Markov blanket) during prophecy. Modified after [4] with permission.

Figure 21. The Block Universe. Presentism (top) implies that only the present moment is real. The Block Universe or Eternalism (bottom) derives from Special Relativity and posits that all points in time and space are co-extant. The Block Universe is compatible with Kabbalistic notions of space-time as viewed from the holistic perspective of *Oivi*. Modified from https://www.resetera.com/threads/presentism-or-eternalism.107854

Figure 22. Fundamental axes of reality. Science currently acknowledges three revealed dimensions of space (x, y, z) and one of time (t) described by eight (four pairs) of the ten *Sefirot*. The Kabbalah insists that a 'Theory of Everything' will remain elusive pending incorporation of *Keter-Malchut* ($K{\rightarrow}M$), a fifth axis of *Kedushah* (Holiness) originating beyond the physical universe.

This book is dedicated to the memory of my parents, Mendel and Freda Schipper *Z"L*, and my grandfather, Nosson Nuta Perelmuter *Z"L*, who defied *Gehenna* (1939-1945) and embraced righteousness.

About the Author

Dr. Schipper is a professor of neurology and medicine (Geriatrics) at McGill University, a clinical neurologist at the Jewish General Hospital in Montreal and the director of a neuroscience laboratory in the hospital's affiliated Lady Davis Institute. His research focuses on degenerative diseases affecting the brain and mind and he is the author of over 200 peer-reviewed papers on these and related topics. Prof. Schipper has long been interested in the interface between contemporary science and the Jewish mystical tradition (Kabbalah). His research in this area was initially published in Yeshiva University's *Torah u-Madda Journal* (2012-13) and more recently in *Unified Field Mechanics II* (RL Amoroso et al. eds., World Scientific 2018) and Bar-Ilan University's *DAAT*: Journal of Jewish Philosophy & Kabbalah (2019).

Acknowledgments

This work would not have been possible without the thoughtful insights various scholars, both scientific and religious, shared with the author over a period of many years. My understanding of consciousness and the Kabbalah has been shaped by persons too numerous to list, although several individuals deserve special mention. Rabbi Raphael Afilalo, then Chief of Pastoral Services at the Jewish General Hospital in Montreal where I work, introduced me to the esoteric writings of the *Ramchal* which lend themselves to the establishment of cogent parallelisms between the Jewish mystical tradition and contemporary physics. My interest in achieving this synthesis was further bolstered by my primary *'Rebbe'* in *Nistar* ('hidden Torah'), Rabbi Ephraim Goldstein (Safed, Israel), whose sheer knowledge of the breadth and scope of Lurianic Kabbalah is wondrous to behold. Presenting on the sacred Kabbalah in a secular venue is a somewhat 'delicate' matter and so I remain indebted to Rabbi Goldstein for his *Heter* (Rabbinic assent) to undertake this initiative. Words cannot adequately express my gratitude to Prof. Yaakov Brawer (Montreal), my *'Chevrutah'* (study partner) and dear friend of 40-odd years, whose profundity in Chassidic philosophy and science has colored much of my thinking. I thank the *Posek* (adjudicator) Rabbi Yoel Chonon Wenger (Montreal), Rabbi Moshe Schatz (Jerusalem) and Levi Katz (London) for stimulating discussion apropos to this work, and polymath Prof. Richard Amoroso (Oakland, CA) for facilitating my discourse with the physics community. I am also grateful to Adrienne Liberman and Sophie Abergel for assistance with the artwork. To my wife, Dr. Rachel Rubinstein—a woman of valor who edited the manuscript, provided penetrating insights and unflagging support—I consciously proclaim my love and heartfelt appreciation.

Preface

Consciousness and associated notions of free will, top-down causation, qualia, etc., have been largely neglected by the (reductionist) scientific community for many decades as illusions or epiphenomena, 'side effects' of brain physiology and neurochemistry with no impact on the material world. Spurred on in large measure by recent interpretations of quantum physics, such as the inescapable role of the 'observer' in the unfolding of reality, consciousness is now at the forefront of neuroscientific and philosophical inquiry. To my knowledge, a comprehensive treatise on the Kabbalistic understanding of consciousness as it relates to contemporary secular analysis of the phenomenon has never been published. The last hundred years or so have witnessed an expanding literature conflating aspects of mainstream science and philosophy with the Jewish mystical tradition or Kabbalah.[5-11] In prior work we demonstrated robust conceptual parallels between specific Kabbalistic constructs and both Heisenberg's Uncertainty Principle[12] and the physics of David Bohm.[1,13] In those papers, we argued that contemporary science and ancient mysticism display unprecedented degrees of confluence because both systems — one grounded in empirical research, the other revelation-based — may provide legitimate and complementary insights into the nature of reality. The goal of the current work is not to provide sweeping generalizations concerning perceived similarities between Jewish mysticism and contemporary science. Nor will I argue that prescient insight into the underpinnings of physical reality is unique to the Jewish mystical tradition. Indeed, non-Jewish metaphysical systems, e.g. Plotinus's *Enneads* 5,[14] the writings of Thomas Aquinas[15] and various Eastern philosophies,[16,17] contain motifs that resonate with current scientific thinking. Finally, no attempt is made to exhaustively adduce evidence supporting panpsychism over materialism as a legitimate, competitive and parsimonious explanation for the prevalence of consciousness in our universe.

There already exists a compelling literature addressing this topic including Christof Koch's *Consciousness: Confessions of a Romantic Reductionist*,[18] Thomas Nagel's *Mind and Cosmos*,[19] Peter Ells' *Panpsychism*,[20] Henry Stapp's *Mindful Universe*,[21] Gregg Rosenberg's *A Place for Consciousness*,[22] Adrian Nelson's *Origins of Consciousness*[23] and Bernardo Kastrup's *The Idea of the World*,[24] among others.

The present volume contributes to the dialogue between Jewish mysticism and science by expounding the Kabbalistic understanding of consciousness *vis-à-vis* modern accounts of the phenomenon. To develop this theme, I begin by defining the 'problem' of consciousness and broadly describing major historical approaches to its resolution (Chapters 1 and 2). Next, I outline several key advances in physics which lend support to a Kabbalistic explanation of consciousness (Chapter 3). Following an overview of the Kabbalistic infrastructure (Chapter 4), a metaphysic for consciousness is elucidated drawing on classical mystical texts (e.g. *The Zohar* and *Etz Chaim*), the writings of latter day Kabbalistic luminaries such as Rabbi (R') Moshe Chaim Luzzatto (1707-1746), R' Shalom Sharabi (1720-1777) and R' Shlomo Eliyashiv (1841-1926), and several Chassidic masters. I attempt to show, notwithstanding the radically different lexicons naturally invoked by the various disciplines, concordant perspectives on consciousness between the Kabbalah and modern formulations of panpsychism, panentheism (Chapter 5), quantum/Bohmian mechanics (Chapter 3), idealism (Chapter 10) and process philosophy (Chapter 11). Implications of Kabbalistic panpsychism for female intuition (Chapter 6), causation (Chapter 7), neural organization (Chapter 8), free will, prophecy (Chapter 9), clinical states of awareness (Chapter 10), ethics (Chapter 12) and cosmic evolution (Chapter 13) are explored and the epistemological value of such exercises is considered (Epilogue).

I am hoping that exposure to this nascent field will entice and stimulate novel and interdisciplinary thinking among a wide range of academics including neurologists, neuroscientists, biologists, psychologists, psychiatrists, philosophers, physicists, religious scholars and their students. It was also my fervent desire in assembling this monograph to fire the imagination of a more general readership thirsting for an intellectually satisfying framework to integrate the marvels of modern scientific discovery with the immediacy of subjective experience, the primacy of spirit and the efficacy of consciousness.

Chapter 1

The Problem of Consciousness

Consciousness is the biggest mystery... the largest outstanding obstacle in our quest for a scientific understanding of the universe.
David Chalmers[25]

The Oxford Dictionary defines consciousness as "the state of being aware of and responsive to one's surroundings" or "the fact of awareness by the mind of itself and the world".[26] Although easily recognized by all, there is arguably no phenomenon as thorny as consciousness from a scientific and philosophical point of view. So devilishly elusive is the concept that for several hundred years until very recently talk of consciousness was largely expunged from neuroscientific discourse. The facetious definition of consciousness as "those irritating periods between naps"[27] attests to the disdain with which many in the West view the matter. Subject to the prevailing reductive materialism/ physicalism, many to this day consider consciousness and qualia, i.e. what it feels like to have a subjective experience such as seeing blue, tasting chocolate or suffering pain,[28] as illusions or epiphenomena outside the bounds of natural law and thus incapable of 'top-down' causation and exerting influence on the (closed) physical world. Philosopher Peter Ells neatly sums up the physicalist position on consciousness as follows:[29]

- Completed physics gives a complete, objective (observer-independent) description of the ontology of the cosmos.
- The ultimate entities of the universe (e.g. electrons) have no intrinsic, hidden properties... are not sentient.
- The same applies to simple entities such as rocks, water, flashes of lightning and volcanoes.

- The universe in its initial years existed entirely without consciousness.
- Consciousness only exists in small pockets of the universe where life has evolved to a certain degree of complexity.
- Consciousness requires complex structures of matter, such as water, carbon and other chemicals, and can be explained in terms of these complex material structures.

Many theories have been floated to explain the phenomenon of consciousness — not surprisingly, as the number of theories is often a fair metric of how little we know about a subject. Among the various physicalist formulations of consciousness the following four classes are currently receiving significant attention in the neuroscientific community:[30]

1) First-Order Theories: These approaches posit that consciousness arises directly from dynamic interactions among neural impulses within the brain circuitry responsible for the cognitive processing of sensory information.

2) Higher-order Theories maintain that the manipulation of data coded by neural activity within sensory pathways is in and of itself unconscious, and that consciousness only emerges when the sensory stream is subjected to specific analysis by some independent and yet-to-be identified neural network(s).

3) According to the Global Workspace Theory (GWT), consciousness is experienced when information is transiently held in a designated 'neural workspace' — assumed by Stanislas Dehaene at the College de France (Paris) and others to reside within the prefrontal cortex — which then broadcasts the information to brain modules responsible for executing specific tasks and behaviors.

4) The Integrated Information Theory (IIT), championed by Giulio Tononi of the University of Wisconsin-Madison, views consciousness as a graded phenomenon which is critically dependent on the degree to which information traversing cognitive networks of a particular architecture, likely involving posterior brain regions, is capable of feeding back to influence (exert causative power upon) itself. IIT is the first to seek a mathematically-defined quantity, termed *psi*, which may reflect the 'magnitude' to which a given system (be it a biological organism or *in silica* circuit board) is conscious. As this book was being written, the Templeton World Charity Foundation began organizing a series of high-profile conferences where evidence for or against these theories of consciousness will be presented and (likely hotly) debated by their leading protagonists.[30]

But attempting to resolve the neural correlates of consciousness is one thing—understanding the phenomenon's immaterial (mental) nature is quite another. By posing the following queries William E. Seager[31] captures the intractability of conscious experience: "How can mental states cause things (to happen) in the world? How do physical processes generate or underlie consciousness? Why does consciousness exist at all? Should consciousness be understood as an emergent feature of the world or does it somehow stand as a fundamental and irreducible aspect not exhausted by the physical?" In the words of neuroscientist Christof Koch,[32] "consciousness does not appear in the equations that make up the foundations of physics, nor in chemistry's periodic table, nor in the endless molecular sequences of our genes." At the end of the day, reductionists are left intellectually paralyzed by what David Chalmers calls the 'hard problem' of consciousness—how and why physical (neural) matter gives rise to non-material mental states.[33] Many would concur with the opinion of psychologist and philosopher Adrian Nelson that "the (hard) problem seems more than just difficult—it's not clear what a solution would even look like!"[34]

7

In coming to grips with the nature of consciousness it should be pointed out that reductive materialism is not, and never was, the only intellectually viable option (reviewed in [35]). Historically, ideas about consciousness were often inextricably bound to matters of theology and spirituality. Primitive animism and Cartesian dualism insisted on the utter separateness of irreducible matter (Descartes' *res extensa*) and spirit or mind (*res cogitans*). Dualism allows for the existence of immaterial consciousness but provides no logical mechanism for matter-spirit interaction.[36,37] Various iterations of monism posit the existence of a single substance exhibiting matter-like or mind-like properties. Monism may be idealistic (all is fundamentally Mind), materialistic (all is essentially physical) or neutral (co-dominance of mind and matter attributes) and may either be theistic or atheistic. Many monistic frameworks incorporate the principle of 'ontological emergence', i.e. the unpredictable and inexplicable appearance of truly novel properties in the course of physical complexification. An example of this germane to the current thesis, and ostensibly a weakness of many monistic paradigms, is the advent of consciousness from unconscious, inanimate, material precursors.[38] After arguing extensively for the contingency of the modern human mind on brute facts of evolution by natural selection, Harvard psychologist Steven Pinker admits being stymied by "maddeningly simple consciousness... that is somehow pasted onto neural events without meshing with their causal machinery."[39] Indeed, the unfathomability of emergent consciousness from non-conscious precursors has led some philosophers such as Thomas Nagel to conclude that neo-Darwinian materialism is almost certainly a false, or at best incomplete, conception of nature.[19] This realization has prompted hitherto ardent reductive materialists such as Koch and Chalmers to reject pure physicalism in favor of panpsychism.[23,32]

Chapter 2

Panpsychism and Panentheism

Panpsychism, roughly synonymous with *panexperientialism*,[40] is a monist position dating back to pre-Socratic Greece asserting that consciousness or mind is a primordial and ubiquitous feature of all things regardless of size, scale or complexity.[41] According to this theory, all entities manifest an 'exterior' objective phase as well as an 'interior' experiential dimension.[42] As panpsychists are wont to point out,[43] the latter is not to imply that electrons manifest human-like sentience — a crude anthropomorphism — but that they contain a modicum of proto-consciousness allowing them to 'feel' their existence at some rudimentary level. Certain neurobiologically-oriented schools promote the concept of 'neurocognitive panpsychism' whereby all things capable of receiving, processing and transmitting information are construed as conscious to some degree or another.[44-47] Panpsychism resolves Chalmers' 'hard problem' and the existence of qualia by affirming consciousness as fundamental to all things extant in the universe alongside matter, energy and space-time.

The theory is not immune to controversy and raises important questions of its own. How, for instance, does proto-consciousness inhering in atoms and molecules blossom into overt sentience as the molecular assemblies become increasingly organized in nervous tissue and higher organisms — the so-called 'combination problem'?[35] Some offer no meaningful responses to this query but nonetheless regard panpsychism as a more compelling and satisfactory account of the consciousness enigma than positions promulgated by competing theories. In his recent book *Combining Minds* Luke Roelofs offers diverse philosophical, neuroscientific and psychological arguments supporting the feasibility of progressive complexification of consciousness along panpsychist lines.[48] Roger Penrose and Stuart Hameroff look to quantum macro-coherence, non-locality and entanglement at the level of cellular microtubules as potential mechanisms for the emergence of higher-order consciousness in advanced nervous systems.[49-52] Although photosynthesis in plants provided a precedent for the participation of quantum processes in biological functions,[53] skeptics were quick to argue that the quantum states required for consciousness could not be maintained in the warm, wet environs of the mammalian brain. Scientists at the *National Institute for Materials Science* in Japan subsequently garnered evidence that it was indeed possible for the microtubular network to achieve the quantum effects demanded by the Penrose-Hameroff hypothesis.[54] Quantum entanglement within microtubules or other neural subcellular compartments may explain the 'unbroken unity of consciousness'[55] and represent a physical instantiation of the Kabbalistic principle of *Hitkashrut* (Interpenetration) discussed in Section 4.3. Other approaches to resolve the 'combination problem' contend that quantum holographic principles organize information in ways that imbue the universe as a whole with high-level consciousness that can be progressively 'tapped' by nervous systems as they develop and grow increasingly complex.[56,57] There is also a recent idealist position that the combination problem is a mere 'thought artifact' with no basis in empirical reality.[58] In what follows, it should become clear that although the Kabbalistic understanding of consciousness is decidedly panpsychist in nature, any concerns regarding the 'combination problem' are rendered moot by this discipline's panenetheistic underpinning.

Given its fundamentally theological origin and basis, no discussion of Kabbalistic panpsychism could be complete without reference to its defining metaphysical framework. The latter is best captured by *panentheism*, a formulation that informs virtually all aspects of Jewish mystical doctrine including its apprehension of consciousness. Panentheism posits that God both transcends and is immanent in nature.[35] Either assertion alone—that God is solely immanent (pantheism) or transcendent (deism)—is anathema to Orthodox Judaism. A valid Jewish perspective on the relationship of God to the World is succinctly summed up in a phrase from the *Shacharit* (Morning) liturgy: "Blessed is He Who spoke and the World came into being": ברוך שאמר והיה העולם. The centrality of 'speech' in the Creation process is elegantly portrayed in an adaptation by Yanki Tauber of the works of the seventh Lubavitcher Rebbe, R' Menachem Mendel Schneersohn. In his book *Inside Time* Tauber remarks on Scripture's account of Creation based on the Ten Utterances recorded in Genesis 1:3-31. Had God instead decided to *build* the World as a craftsman sculpts pottery, then just as the latter remains extant upon withdrawal of the artisan so might the cosmos persist in perpetuity without requiring further participation of its Creator. This view smacks of deism and is unacceptable to Orthodox Judaism. As a third possibility, the Lord could simply have *thought* the World into being. But just as human thought remains confined to the thinker, a universe existing solely in the Mind of God would deny us any modicum of independent reality (in both *Oivi* and *Orech* modes of awareness—see Section 4.4) and render meaningless the Torah's insistence that we "choose life": ובחרת בחיים.[59,60] *Speech,* on the other hand, 'leaves' the speaker, is audible to an 'outside' listener and dissipates should the speaker fall silent—an apt analogy for Judaism's stance on the Creation's relationship to and contingency on God.[61]

As described below, the Kabbalah assumes the position that just as God's Light or Consciousness at once pervades and envelops the Creation so too does human consciousness, having been formed in God's image (*imago Dei*[62]), register both within and beyond the physical confines of the brain.[35,63-65] This view runs counter to the prevailing wisdom of most contemporary neuroscientists who believe, as Nobel laureate Francis Crick put it, that we "... are nothing but a pack of neurons."[66] To develop this theme we will invoke the writings of leading Kabbalistic visionaries and draw analogies and insights from contemporary science (mainly physics and neuroscience) and philosophy.

Chapter 3

Quantum Mechanics, Consciousness and the Kabbalah

I regard consciousness as fundamental. I regard matter as derivative from consciousness. Everything that we talk about, everything that we regard as existing, postulates consciousness.
Max Planck[67]

The content of consciousness is the ultimate reality.
Eugene Wigner[68]

Quantum mechanics? What relevance might this 'hard science' portend for appreciating Kabbalistic wisdom and unraveling the mystery of consciousness? In this author's view it would have been virtually impossible to elaborate a nuanced Kabbalistic ontology of consciousness 100-120 years ago. Not because of limitations in the scientific formulation of consciousness at that time (as investigation of the latter is in its embryonic stages even to this day) but because concepts emerging from twentieth century physics (relativity, quantum theory, Bohmian mechanics) are proving essential for explicating or analogizing fundamental Kabbalistic formulations at the heart of the consciousness problem. As discussed below, the Kabbalah stands four-square behind philosopher Peter Ells' prediction that "fundamental physics will be found to be inextricably bound up with consciousness."[69]

Since its inception millennia ago, Jewish mystical thought has steadfastly attested to the absolute oneness of the Creator and His Creation in the face of apparent separateness and individuation. This perspective is at face value counterintuitive and outside the purview of classical (Newtonian) physics. The advent of quantum mechanics in the twentieth century provided a novel conceptual framework for resolution of this great paradox thereby breathing fresh life into the dialogue between Torah and science. That all particles and forces comprising the observable universe are blatantly interconnected ('entangled') was the inescapable conclusion which followed a series of intriguing *gedanken* (thought) experiments and the confirmatory bench work of Alain Aspect and colleagues at the University of Paris in 1982.[70,71] In this monograph I have attempted to further underscore the growing reconciliation of Torah and contemporary science by juxtaposing fundamental Kabbalistic principles with mainstream (Copenhagen) and Bohmian mechanics as they pertain to an explication of consciousness.

Quantum mechanics is an enormously successful branch of physics that builds upon and transcends classical notions of physical existence.[3,72] Many have identified its origins with the discovery of 'blackbody radiation' (the delivery of energy in discrete packets or 'quanta') by Max Planck in 1900. A quantum mechanical understanding of matter, energy, space and time unfolded apace with the seminal contributions of Ernest Rutherford, Niels Bohr, Albert Einstein, Erwin Schrödinger and others in the first half of the twentieth century. During the last sixty years input from pioneers such as Murray Gell-Mann, Richard Feynman, Steven Weinberg and Eugene Wigner have enabled further refinements of quantum theory, a marriage of particle physics and cosmology and the advent of numerous 'disruptive' technologies based on this knowledge. Interested readers are referred elsewhere for further details concerning the history of quantum physics and timeline of key discoveries which have punctuated the field.[3,72]

The remarkable accomplishments of quantum mechanics have led to the commonly expressed belief that the fundamental forces governing physical existence are now largely understood and that future efforts in the field will mainly be directed towards achieving more precise measurements of the phenomena already disclosed. Notwithstanding the justification for this claim, the latter in and of itself is no trivial task. As discussed below, the very act of measurement when conducted on an infinitesimally small quantum scale necessarily perturbs and is inextricably linked with the system undergoing observation. This chapter focuses on two seminal developments in quantum physics—the Heisenberg Uncertainty Principle and Bohmian mechanics—because these themes resonate deeply with Jewish mystical tradition and in the author's opinion are indispensable to a Kabbalistic theory of consciousness.

3.1 The Heisenberg Uncertainty Principle

In 1927 Werner Heisenberg published his groundbreaking paper on the 'Uncertainty Principle' in *Zeitschrift fur Physik*.[73] According to the uncertainty principle, paired physical properties of a system cannot both be measured to arbitrary precision; the more accurately one property is known the less precisely the other can be known. Importantly, this imprecision is not contingent upon the skills of the observer or the resolution of the measuring apparatus but is an inherent attribute of physical systems as dictated by the equations of quantum mechanics. While it is true that the very act of measurement affects the physical properties of particles (e.g., its position or momentum), the Uncertainty Principle makes a more profound claim—that we *cannot* know as a matter of principle the present in all its details.[74]

In classical physics it is theoretically possible to ascertain the position and momentum of every particle in the universe and thereby accurately determine the future. In contemporary quantum physics it is fundamentally impossible to predict future events because one can never attain full knowledge of the position and momentum of even a single particle. In the standard (Copenhagen) interpretation of quantum mechanics, e.g. the results of the classical 'two-slit experiment',[75] every possible outcome for an event, represented mathematically as a statistical wave function, exists in the unobserved state. The act of observation elicits a 'collapse of the wave function' whereby one of these many potential outcomes is 'selected' as the reality actually experienced (Fig. 1). And what is observation if not consciousness applied? To David Chalmers the inconceivability of existing in superposition and an ability to collapse wave functions may be the very *definition* of consciousness![76]

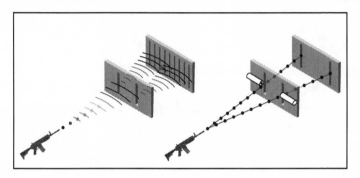

Figure 1. Young's two-slit experiment demonstrating the dual (wave-particle) nature of light. (https://landing.newscientist.com/department-for-education-feature-3/)

The Copenhagen interpretation of quantum mechanics was bolstered after attempts to refute it failed. Examples of such investigations include the *'gedanken* (thought)' experiments of the famous Einstein-Bohr debate of the 1920s and, more tellingly, resolution of the EPR (Einstein-Podolsky-Rosen) paradox which resulted from repeated experimental violation (1972-1982) of 'Bell's inequality' in support of quantum theory.[77] The results of these experiments (especially those of Alain Aspect in 1982) implied that (i) all particles emerging from the Big Bang singularity maintain an indefinite 'connectedness' with one another, (ii) each particle therefore 'knows' about the existence of every other particle and (iii) due to preserved complementarity intrinsic to the Copenhagen interpretation, the properties of one particle (position, momentum, spin, etc.) change instantaneously and commensurate with changes in a 'partner' particle regardless of the extent of their physical separation (Einstein's 'spooky action at a distance'). For the latter to arise by classical causal interaction, information would need to pass from particle A to particle B at impossible supraluminal speeds. Quantum theory dictates that the particles' shared history forever 'locks' them in a reciprocal dance ('quantum entanglement') that does not obligate the transmission of new information between them ('acausality').[1,12]

In this book, reference will be made repeatedly to the classical Copenhagen interpretation of quantum physics and to Bohmian mechanics because pivotal aspects of these disciplines dovetail with Kabbalistic doctrine and emerging conceptualizations of consciousness. To wit, there exist competing variations of the Copenhagen interpretation (e.g., Bohr vs. von Neumann) as well as several non-Copenhagen formulations of quantum behavior. Prominent among the latter are Einstein's Neo-Realism, Hugh Everett's Many-Worlds interpretation and Information Theory.[78]

As one illustration of a distinctly non-Copenhagen interpretation Everett's model of quantum mechanics states that all statistically feasible outcomes actually do become manifest in some version of reality. In this model, observations do not 'collapse' the wave function into a singular reality but generate a multiverse of innumerable parallel, non-intersecting worlds.[79] While the multiverse interpretation may logically resolve the Anthropic Principle conundrum by countering the infinitesimally remote probability of a single universe whose laws just happen to be exquisitely fine-tuned for our existence, it remains untestable in practice and in theory. It thus constitutes a 'belief'; one which curiously many scientists happily cling to rather than acknowledge the possibility of an Omniscient Creator. Adrian Nelson put it this way: "An infinite landscape of other worlds is a compelling and exciting idea... but is it really the explanation for why our choices seem to influence the way the quantum world behaves? It is surely no less incredible than the idea that consciousness may be involved."[80] Of all the non-Copenhagen formulations of nature, none to my mind recapitulates essential Kabbalistic insight and speaks to the unicity of consciousness more cogently than the physics of David Bohm.

3.2 Kabbalah and the Physics of David Bohm

The physics of influential twentieth century physicist David Bohm (1917-1992) cannot be considered 'mainstream' in so far as it deviated from the classical Copenhagen interpretation of quantum mechanics. Yet, Einstein openly acknowledged Bohm as one of his intellectual successors.[81] Indeed, Bohm's imprint not only regarding physics but on many fields of science, philosophy and sociology has endured and even gained in popularity with the passage of time.[82] A synopsis of Bohm's academic development and interests, both scientific and political, was presented elsewhere[1] and readers are referred to the extensive biography by David Peat[81] for more detailed information regarding the life and times of this intriguing personality. At Princeton and beyond the iconoclastic Bohm withdrew from mainstream physics to develop his theory of 'hidden variables' and the 'implicate order'. He was particularly disappointed in the way Niels Bohr and other leading physicists dealt with matters of interconnectedness and causality.[83] His view of nature progressively adopted a holism more reminiscent of Eastern religious philosophies than the prevailing science of his time. The physicist's rich and protracted correspondence with the Indian teacher and mystic Jiddu Krishnamurti[81] and early indoctrination with Chassidic thought at home[1] almost certainly helped shape the emerging Bohmian *umwelt*. Bohm's perspective on Wholeness and of the universe as Hologram signified a startling departure from conventional physics with profound implications for the neurosciences, psychology, religion and consciousness. As I will now illustrate, several key themes of Bohmian mechanics have compelling homologues in the Kabbalistic literature.

3.2.1 Hidden Variables and the Implicate Order

Bohm's theorizing and mathematical platform led him to consider the cosmos and its untold contents and processes as an emergent property of an indivisible Wholeness which he termed the 'holomovement'. Bohm conceptualized the holomovement as manifesting two major incarnations: (i) a familiar reality or 'explicate order' consisting of all things and events which are amenable to our senses directly or via instrumentation, and (ii) an 'implicate order' comprising layer upon layer of 'hidden variables' beyond our perception. He viewed each deeper layer as more abstract than, but ultimately causative for, the dimension mapping immediately superficial to it with the most proximate hidden layer giving rise to the explicate order. Bohm construed every perceptible object and event as rooted in a vast, possibly infinitely regressing, series of causal matrices that ultimately originate from a state of absolute and inconceivable wholeness. Bohm envisioned a highly dynamic interaction between the implicate and explicate orders. In Bohmian mechanics, shifts designated 'enfoldments' periodically make implicate that which was previously explicate while 'unfoldment' of certain hidden variables renders them explicate and within the purview of human awareness.[84,85] In an earlier publication[1] I provided several simple analogies invoked by Bohm that effectively convey his notion of implicate and explicate orders. Several examples are reproduced here *verbatim* inasmuch as they lend a clear scientific voice to the ethereal Kabbalistic principle of *Hitlabshut* ('ensheathment') which, as we will see later (Chapters 4 and 5), must be integrated into any Kabbalistic discourse on the nature of consciousness:

1) Enfoldment and Unfoldment: *Picture two concentric cylinders separated by a translucent viscous material such as glycerin (Fig. 2).*[85] *Add a drop of black ink to the glycerin. While the cylinders are stationary, the ink is clearly visible as a dark spot within the glycerin (explicate order). Rapidly rotate the inner cylinder about its long axis. The black dot first stretches into a thin dark filament (still explicate) but soon disappears from view entirely (implicate order). Although the ink is now implicate, the information 'coding' for the original black spot is not lost. Indeed, if the motion of the cylinder ceases and is then resumed in the opposite direction, the dispersed, imperceptible particles of ink coalesce to re-form the dark filaments and eventually the original ink spot itself (explicate order). Bohm would refer to the initial disappearance of the ink spot/filament as 'enfoldment' within the holomovement and its re-emergence as 'unfoldment'.*

2) Motion: *The standard interpretation of motion is that of an object moving from point A to B within the experiential (Bohm's explicate) realm. In Bohm's model, again drawing on the glycerin cylinder analogy, two drops of ink, A and B, are added to the rotating glycerin separated by time and space, e.g. five seconds and five millimeters apart. The inner cylinder is rotated until both spots become implicate with Spot B disappearing five seconds after Spot A. At this juncture, the myriad particles belonging to Spots A and B are extensively intermingled, although the 'memory' of each particle's trajectory from its original ink spot is conserved as described above. The cylinder is then immobilized and spun at the same rate in the opposite direction. After a defined number of turns, spot B materializes (becomes explicate), followed five seconds later by the appearance of Spot A. As the cylinder rotates further, Spot B now becomes implicate and Spot A remains visible for an additional five seconds until it, too, enfolds. If this experiment is repeated with the reverse rotation conducted at much greater speeds, it will seem as if a single ink spot emerges and moves five millimeters from position B to position A before disappearing. Thus, according to Bohm, the linear motion of objects (be they electrons* *or elephants) we perceive in the experiential world is an illusion resulting from complex cycles of unfoldment-enfoldment between the implicate and explicate orders.*[1]

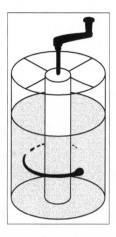

Figure 2. The implicate and explicate orders. Represented by Bohm as an ink drop in a rotating, glycerin-filled cylinder. From http://forumserver.twoplustwo.com/137/religion-godtheology/alpha-omega-gravity-order-899479 and [1] with modifications.

3.2.2 The Holographic Universe

In addition to and incorporating the concept of implicate and explicate orders, Bohmian mechanics posits that the entire cosmos is based on a grand holographic design—with each part containing (enfolding) a miniature replica of the entire universe! Bohm considered the existence of each component to hinge upon its intimate relationship to the whole implying that individuality is only feasible if it unfolds from wholeness. Bohm believed that "the world acts more like a single indivisible unit, in which even the 'intrinsic' nature of each part (wave or particle) depends... on its relationship to its surroundings";[86] that "the inseparable quantum interconnectedness of the whole universe is the fundamental reality, and (the) relatively independent behaving parts are merely particular and contingent forms within this whole."[87] According to Bohm, our conventional notions of space, time, distance and separation apply only to the 'surface' of things as they are revealed within the explicate order. Akin to a hologram (Fig. 3), two physical objects may be separated by enormous expanses of space and time in the linear, explicate order while little or no such separation may exist between their hidden components enfolded within the implicate order.[88]

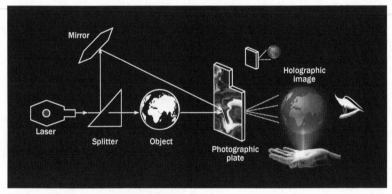

Figure 3. Laser holography. From [1] with permission.

Evidence in support of Bohm's 'holographic universe' has been adduced in fields as disparate as astrophysics, molecular biology and the neurosciences.[83,89-92] One such intriguing report was published in 2007 by Jacob Bekenstein in *Scientific American* based on a theoretical analysis of 'black holes'. A black hole is a region of space-time thought to arise from the collapse of a star with matter so dense and gravitational forces so powerful that nothing—not even light—can escape from inside it. According to Bekenstein, the mathematics underpinning certain behaviors of black holes suggest that all information in the universe, as in a hologram, is encoded on two-dimensional (flat) surfaces and then transduced ('read out') by our minds as four-dimensional (Minkowski) space-time.[93]

Evidence of Bohmian mechanisms at work in the brain is equally provocative and more directly relevant to the study of consciousness. Supported by experimentation in humans, animals and isolated nerve cells in culture,[94-96] the Stanford neuroscientist Karl Pribram concluded, independently of Bohm (whom he later consulted), that aspects of the human brain may operate holographically (the so-called 'holonomic brain theory'). Pribram argued that many functions of the central nervous system (CNS), e.g. memory storage and retrieval, sensory perception and consciousness, are at least partly non-localizing and better understood as enfoldments and unfoldments within a complex implicate neural order.[81,83,85,97-100] Citing the work of Marcer & Schempp,[90] Edgar Mitchell hypothesized that in the act of perception the brain behaves as a "quantum computer which utilizes both quantum and space-time information."[91] Some have even conjectured that human intuition, paranormal phenomena such as telepathy, clairvoyance and telekinesis, and certain neuropsychiatric states (e.g. schizophrenia) may be products of nonlocal quantum neuroholography.[83,91,101-103] Further in this book I elaborate on the implications of Bohmian mechanics for Ensheathment (Heb., *Hitlabshut*), Interinclusion (*Hitkallelut*) and Interpenetration (*Hitkashrut*), three pillars of Kabbalistic metaphysics (Chapter 4). The latter, informed by the tenets of twentieth century physics, offer a powerful and unprecedented perspective on panpsychism (Chapter 5), free will (Chapter 9), process philosophy (Chapter 11) and the nature of human consciousness.

At the interface of these seemingly disparate fields emerge flashes of insight into an ancient Kabbalistic formulation of consciousness which, lacking for serviceable explanatory frameworks and analogies provided by contemporary science, lay encrypted and inaccessible to general scholarship until as recently as one hundred years ago. We will see for example that there is no sacrifice of intended meaning when the jargon used by Bohm to elucidate his innovations in quantum physics is interchanged with homologous Kabbalistic terminology. Where

Bohm speaks of a 'holomovement' to describe Reality's absolute wholeness from which all particulars spring and remain inextricably linked, the Kabbalah will employ the corresponding concepts *Ohr Ein-Sof*, *Shlaymut*, *Klal* and *Oivi* (Chapter 4). Bohm's 'implicate order' will be readily understood as a ladder of spiritual domains 'above' the 'lowest' rung of the Kabbalistic hierarchy (Heb., *Seder Hishtalshelut*). Similarly, Bohm's 'explicate order' will be construed as tantamount to the physical domain amenable to our perception at the very 'bottom' of the Kabbalistic infrastructure. Bohmian mechanics mandate that each domain of the holomovement arises from, clothes and is causally influenced by the layer immediately 'implicate' to it. Similarly, we will see how the concept of Ensheathment (*Hitlabshut*) dictates that each component of the Kabbalistic hierarchy 'dresses' and is controlled by the component immediately 'above' or 'interior' to it. As described in Chapters 4 and 5, the Kabbalah teaches further that the elements comprising its hierarchy are in flux among various states of concealment and revelation. Bohm invokes the terms 'enfoldment' and 'unfoldment' to capture precisely this dynamic, with enfoldment connoting the 'upward/inward' movement into hidden unification (*Oivi*) and unfoldment a 'descent' into apparent disunity (*Orech*; Section 4.4).

Perhaps the most revolutionary idea that Bohm injected into contemporary quantum theory—one that continues to impact scientific disciplines beyond physics and fire the public imagination—is the universe's holographic design. The theoretical and practical implications of a cosmos wherein each and every part enfolds (recapitulates) the entire whole can only be dimly appreciated at this juncture. Yet, this singular concept, termed *Hitkallelut* in Hebrew (Section 4.4), is a fundamental feature of the ancient Kabbalistic landscape and an essential aspect of the intrinsic interinclusiveness of God's Creation. As will be made clear, by linking the principle of Interpenetration

(*Hitkashrut*) to Interinclusion (*Hitkallelut*) the Kabbalah takes the indivisibility of the holographic universe a step further. Interpenetration reinforces the unicity of the Creation by establishing a functional connection between a specific part of one mini-hologram and its doppelgängers within the entire created network of fractal substructures. An appreciation of such intricacies of Kabbalistic 'logic' and the light they shed on the enigma of consciousness presupposes a more general and contextualized familiarity with basic Kabbalistic infrastructure and dynamics, a theme introduced in Chapter 4.

Chapter 4

Principles of Kabbalah

4.1 Orientation to Jewish Mysticism

What is Kabbalah? The Hebrew term קבלה derives from the root קבל which means 'receive'. The classical Jewish tradition, as endorsed by R' Ezra of Gerona and Nachmanides in 13th century Catalonia, defines the Kabbalah as the esoteric aspect (*Sod*, Heb.) of the Oral Law that God transmitted to Moses on Mount Sinai in the year 2448 (1312 BCE) after the creation of Adam.[104] Whereas the Written Torah (Pentateuch) and the exoteric or 'revealed' dimensions of the Oral Torah (the body of legal and homiletic lore) were disseminated by Moses to the entire Nation of Israel, Kabbalistic wisdom was discretely passed on to select sages and their disciples beneath the radar of general Torah scholarship. Superimposed upon this long, covert chain of esoteric indoctrination were periods of intensified mystical fervor, such as the eras of R' Shimon Bar-Yochai (second century CE), the Safed mystics (sixteenth century) and the birth of Chassidism (eighteenth century), when shards of Kabbalistic Light would pierce the darkness of the current and final Exile.

As we gain on the Seventh (Messianic) Millennium, there are signs that we may be at the threshold of something far more profound — an outpouring of Kabbalistic truths, in part nurtured by the sciences, that is more aptly compared to a new dawn after a long night than to brief illuminations of the evening sky by flashes of lightning. The advent of said Messianic age and the ways we commonly mark time can be read allegorically into Genesis 1:1: Rearrangement of the letters of the very first word, בראשית ("In the beginning") yields בא׳ תשרי ("on the first day of the first Hebrew month, *Tishrei*" — the Jewish New Year). The Hebrew verse contains seven words signifying the seven-day week (which despite lacking a celestial counterpart is observed 'arbitrarily' by much of the world). There are 28 letters approximating the lunar month. But what about the future? In this opening verse of the Bible are six instances of the Hebrew letter א (אלף; *Aleph*) that, spelled the same as its cognate *Eleph* (*Heb.*, 'one thousand'), hint at the 6000-year span destined to demarcate the transition zone between the current and Messianic orders. The timing of this long-awaited eruption of esoteric wisdom is anticipated to proceed in lockstep with the blossoming of a 'cosmic consciousness' described in Chapters 5 and 13.

Already we are seeing interest in the Kabbalah burgeoning, with the number of titles available online and on bookstore shelves devoted to this topic accelerating at a rapid pace. The latter can be divided into two major categories: (i) books 'about' the Kabbalah which tend to discuss the subject matter in the context of theological, sociological or literary history and (ii) works 'of' Kabbalah which expound on or develop further principles embodied by this discipline. The current volume may be considered a 'hybrid' of both categories in so far as mainstream Kabbalistic ontologies are solicited to elucidate our current understanding of the phenomenon of consciousness (category 1) while offering novel interpretations or applications of passages from the 'revealed' and 'hidden' Torah (category 2). The latter are invoked in an effort to demonstrate unprecedented alignment of ancient Kabbalistic insight with contemporary innovations in physics, philosophy and neuroscience pertaining to the topic of consciousness.

I would be remiss at this juncture to omit informing readers that the Orthodox Ashkenazi and Sephardi rites imbue the primary Kabbalistic writings with a high degree of sanctity and regard immersion in its teachings (and Torah study in general) as an act of worship. As such, protagonists of the Kabbalah advise that certain 'preparations' be implemented before embarking on such study. While suggestions published by rabbis historically targeted students of the Jewish faith, some clearly have more ecumenical applicability. In his Kabbalistic treatise *Petach Sha'ar HaShamaim*, Rabbi Yaakov Moshe Hillel recommends that students (i) first be well-grounded in Scripture and the 'revealed' aspects of the Oral Law, (ii) enter into study under the guidance of an experienced mentor or teacher and (iii) maintain the strictest code of ethics and purity of spirit.[105] To this list I might add two practical suggestions: (iv) Develop the knowledge in an orderly, spiral fashion beginning with a bird's-eye view of the 'field' sacrificing depth for the sake of scope. Then there should follow recursive study at ever-deepening levels of analysis. "In Kabbalah, you need to know everything before you can know anything" is a whimsical tautology expressed by R' Ephraim Goldstein to underscore the holistic nature of the subject (*personal communication*). To plunge directly into mid- or higher-echelon material is like trying to ascertain the strategy of chess grandmasters before understanding the initial board positions and permissible moves of the various pieces.

A logical progression of study may, for example, begin with R' Shalom Ullman's *Da'at Elokim*[106] augmented by R' Ephraim Goldstein's 133 online lessons providing a lucid English explication of this work.[107] This may be gainfully followed by the *Ramchal's Klach Pitchei Chochmah*, a more elaborate and well-organized text available in Hebrew[108] and English.[109] Thereafter students may elect to engage the seminal work of Lurianic Kabbalah, the *Etz Chaim* again supplemented if necessary by R' Goldstein's extensive series of web-based readings in English.[110] More advanced students may discover the spectacularly comprehensive writings of the *Leshem*,[111,112] the intricate Kabbalah of the *Rashash*[113] and his disciple R' Chaim De la Rosa,[114] the Chassidic teachings of R' Sholom DovBer Schneersohn of Lubavitch,[115] and the 'Prophetic' or 'Ecstatic' Kabbalah of the thirteenth century mystic R' Abraham Abulafia[116,117] to be particularly inspiring (although many of their works still await translation). Finally, (v) gain familiarity with advances at the leading edges of science and their philosophical implications, a deeply rewarding initiative in its own right. This can often be achieved to a very satisfactory degree by thoughtful laymen absent formal professional training. It is my overarching conviction that basic knowledge of contemporary physics (in particular quantum and Bohmian mechanics), cell and organismal biology and neuroscience allow for an appreciation of Kabbalistic wisdom not universally attainable by earlier generations. I hope to prove convincing on this point by the end of the monograph.

On account of its rarefied nature the Kabbalah often employs the term 'light' (*Ohr*, in Hebrew) as metaphor to connote spiritual influences which emanate from, and mediate the Will of, the Creator. When employed in this context throughout the manuscript, 'Light' is capitalized to distinguish it from conventional, physical light. Similar uppercase lettering or quotation marks are used for 'Before', 'After', 'Above', 'Below', etc. when purely metaphysical constructs best conveyed by such terms are intended. Students of the Kabbalah take great pains to avoid anthropomorphisms—the attribution to God properties that even remotely smack of physicality. This exercise is often more difficult than meets the eye: While few would assign any vestige of corporeality to metaphors such as the 'finger' of God, arcane concepts invoking 'light', 'time', 'sequence', 'space', or 'movement' pre-Genesis 1:1 demand unconventional, nonlinear thinking and are exceedingly prone to unwarranted concretization.

Several additional pointers concerning Torah scholarship are worth mentioning here. The first relates to a definition of 'proof'. In the context of science and philosophy proof typically implies direct or circumstantial evidence based on experimentation, mathematics or logical inference. In Torah study, including its mystical tradition, 'proof' connotes support for a given statement or opinion based on surface or deeper interpretations of verses from the five books of Moses, the Prophets and the Writings (the 'TaNaCh'); the legal decisions and homiletics recorded in the

Talmud, the Responsa and the Codes; and the classic Kabbalistic texts (see Preface). Novel thinking is paramount to Torah study but there can be no frank contradiction or break with earlier authoritative sources. In this sense Scriptural precedence is an anchor or 'strange attractor' (to borrow a mathematical metaphor from chaos theory[118]) which stimulates productive thinking within set boundaries that limit the potential diffusion of focus through the ages. Far from curtailing creativity, Torah-imposed constraints on thought and behavior, much like the boundary conditions imposed by the equations of connected Julia sets,[119] perpetuate novelty and heightened states of psychological 'flow'[120] which might otherwise stall in cognitive space afforded unbridled degrees of freedom. This brings us to a fundamental and fascinating difference between scientific and Torah epistemology. In science, new knowledge is generally deemed the more credible as it invariably alters or replaces antiquated notions. The opposite is true of Torah—the more ancient the source (i.e. the closer to Revelation at Mount Sinai), the more authoritative and compelling the evidence.

The Torah is a *corpus symbolicum* which divulges its truths on four planes of interpretation: (i) *Pshat*—the literal meaning or storyline of the text; (ii) *Remez*—homiletics or allegory; (iii) *Drash*—legal (*Halachic*) ramifications; and (iv) *Sod*—esoteric or mystical dimension (the Kabbalah). At the same time, Orthodox Judaism insists that the Torah is the seamless Word of God and accepts these diverse perspectives on Scripture to be complementary and never mutually contradictory. In addition to these four seminal approaches to Biblical exegesis there are said to be 'seventy faces (facets)' to Torah[121] and readers may legitimately gravitate to some which may challenge the main theses of this volume. Key passages citing Jewish literary sources in this work are therefore reproduced in the original Hebrew or Aramaic to encourage readers knowledgeable in these languages to offer their own interpretations. Certain Kabbalistic descriptors cited repeatedly in the text and figures are presented in transliteration. A glossary of the relevant Kabbalistic terms is provided in Table 1.

Three hermeneutical tools commonly employed by the Kabbalah are *Gematriya*, *Notarikon* and *Temurah*. *Gematriya* is an alphanumeric code that assigns numerical values to Hebrew words, names and phrases derived by summation of the values of their constituent letters (Table 2). Novel nuances of meaning are often adduced by the juxtaposition of Hebrew words and sentences bearing equivalent *Gematriyas*. Here's an example my grandfather Nosson Perelmuter *z"l* taught me as a young child (in part, I suspect, to bolster my proficiency in arithmetic): The great Torah commentator *Rashi* informs us that the Patriarch Jacob left his family and returned across the River Jabbok to recover some overlooked פכים קטנים "small jars"[122] which fatefully brought him into conflict with the Angel of Esau. Upon prevailing, Jacob's spiritual stature was raised and God bestowed upon him the exalted name, Israel. As if to underscore the often subtle ways of Providence (as opposed to mere happenstance), the *Gematriya* of the seemingly trivial "small jars" פכים קטנים (=150+209=359) when added to that of Jacob יעקב (=182) yields the numerical value of Israel ישראל (=541). As another example, some are of the opinion that a synthesis of wisdom חכמה (=73) and prophecy נבואה (=64) is prerequisite to mastery of Kabbalah קבלה (=137) knowledge.[123] *Notarikon*, derived from the Greek νοταρικόν and Latin *notarius* or "shorthand-writer",[124] refers to acronyms or abbreviations which may be used to convey additional insight or as simple mnemonic devices. The author once heard the following *Notarikon* from the previous Radziner Rebbe, R' Yaakov Lainer *z"l*: Among other reasons, the Torah refers to the Israelites as *Bnei Yisrael* (בני ישראל, "the children of Israel") because the letter י of ישראל (Israel) stands for יצחק and יעקב (Isaac and Jacob); the ש for שרה (Sarah); the ר for רבקה and רחל (Rebecca and Rachel); the א for אברהם (Abraham); and the ל for לאה (Leah)—the three Forefathers and four Matriarchs of the Jewish people. *Temurah* means "exchange" and is a method of interchanging Hebrew letters based on specified algorithms (e.g. substituting the first for the last letter of the Hebrew alphabet, the second for the penultimate letter, etc.) in order to reach a deeper understanding of Torah verses. The saintly Kabbalist R' Shimshon of Ostropol (Poland), martyred in the infamous Chmielnicki massacres of 1648-9, employed an interesting *Temurah* in support of the Talmud's dictum[125] that 'eye-for-an-eye' compensation is effected monetarily: He indicates that the salient Torah statement עין תחת עין[126] translates literally as "eye *under* an eye" and that the Hebrew letters "under" (after) each of the three letters of עין (eye) — פ-ס-כ — rearrange to spell כסף, money.[127] We will occasionally invoke these hermeneutical instruments to sharpen the intended meaning of key phrases or concepts.

Reverberating in my mind as I worked on this project is the following oft-cited quotation attributed (correctly or not) to Albert Einstein: "Everything should be made as simple as possible, but not simpler."[128] In this spirit I endeavored to simplify many esoteric and abstract concepts of the Kabbalah by leaning heavily on analogies and metaphors drawn from the sciences, Western cultural practices and normative life. At the same time certain Kabbalistic constructs and logic streams relevant to this work were recapitulated from original sources in relatively 'undiluted' fashion whenever I felt that the tone or force of the intended message would dissipate or be misconstrued by attempts at further 'clarification'. Examples of this are the metaphysical intricacies described in Section 6.1 (Ontogeny of the *Keter-Malchut* axis) and Chapter 7 (Supervenience and Top-Down Causation). In many instances contemporary English language references are provided alongside classical Hebrew and Aramaic citations to facilitate tracking of original sources by a wider readership.

The Kabbalah elaborates a hierarchy of interlocking spiritual domains which originate within the unfathomable Godhead, 'descend' progressively in holiness through a system of 'coarsening' immaterial worlds and culminate in the creation of the physical universe. Kabbalistic doctrine provides an ontogeny for all existence and explicates, often allegorically, the hidden ways by which God engages and informs the unfolding reality. The latter is mediated by a fractal-like (self-similar) network of interacting 'Lights' or forces which establish causal, often reciprocating, associations among God, humanity and the cosmos.[3,129] Central to the perspective of the Kabbalah, and Judaism in general, is the absolute unity of the Creation at its core, with all semblances of separateness and distinction rendered apparent only after 'filtration' of the one Infinite Light of God (*Ohr Ein-Sof*) through the various *Sefirot* (defined below).

Table 1. Glossary of Kabbalistic terms contained in this book.

Abba: Father; a Partzuf

Adam Kadmon (A"K): Primordial Man; a World

Arich Anpin (A "A): Long Countenance; a Partzuf

Asiyah: the World of Action

Atik Yomin (A"Y): Ancient of Days; a Partzuf

Atzilut: World of Emanation

Bayit (Batim,pl.): house; Tefillin box containing parchments

B'chira Chofshit: free will

Bilti-Gvul: boundless, infinite

Binah: Understanding; a Sefirah

Briah: the World of Creation

B'Tselem Elokim: in God's image

Chotem V'nechtom: seal-upon-seal (signet ring metaphor for trans-World correspondences)

Chaya: second highest manifestation of Soul

Chaye: animal life

Chesed: Lovingkindness/Expansiveness; a Sefirah

Chalal: empty "space" (also Makom Panoi)

Chiluf: switches, exchanges or crossings

Chochmah: Wisdom; a Sefirah

Chomer: substance

Chush (Chushim,pl.): sense

Da'at: Knowledge; a Sefirah

Dalet: fourth letter of the Hebrew alphabet; shape of one type of Kesher Shel-Rosh

Domem: inanimate objects

Drush: Legal (Halachic) interpretation (as of Scripture)

Ein-Sof: the Infinite (Godhead)

Elokut: Godliness

Emunah: belief

Etz Ha'chaim: Tree of Life; Kabbalistic
   superstructure
Gematriya: sum of numerical values of
   letters comprising a Hebrew word or
   phrase
Gevurah: Strength/Restriction; a Sefirah
Gilui: revelation
Gimel Rishonim (G"R): top three Sefirot
   ('brains) of deca-Sefirotic system
Golem: animated humanoid made of
   clay, wood or metal
Gvul: boundary, finite
Halacha: law
Ha'orah: reflection [of Godliness]
Hashgacha Pratit: Divine Providence
Havdalah: concluding Sabbath blessings
   (Jewish liturgy)
He'elam: concealment
Hitkallelut: interinclusion
Hitkashrut: interpenetration
Hitlabshut: enclothement;
   ensheathment; overlap
Hod: Splendor; a Sefirah
Imma: Mother; a Partzuf
Kav: line or ray (of the Ohr Ein-Sof)
Kedushah: holiness
Keli: vessel of a Sefirah that holds its
   share of Ohr (Light)
Kesher: knot; as in Tefillin
Keter: (pl.,Ketarim): Crown/Divine Will;
   a Sefirah
Kinui (pl.,Kinuim): homologue
Klal: whole/wholeness; generality
Kohen Gadol: High Priest

L 'vush: clothing
Makom Panoi: empty "space" (also
   Chalal)
Makar (Makorot,pl.): source
Malchut: Kingship; a Sefirah
Mashpiah: donor; connotes masculine
   influence
Mati V'lo Mati: oscillation of Light into
   and out of a Keli
M'daber: human life (literally, 'speaker')
Memutak: sweetened
Mezuzah: case affixed to doorposts of
   Jewish dwellings containing
   parchment bearing Scriptural passages
Midrashic: homiletic
Mispar Katan: numerical diminutive of a
   Gematriya
Mitzvah (Mitzvot, pl.): positive deed/
   command
Miyut Ha'yareach: diminishment of the
   Moon
Mochin: "brains"; three upper Sefirot of
   Partzuf which confer 'consciousness'
Nefesh: fifth and lowest manifestation
   of Soul
Nefesh Ha'bahamit: lower, animal Soul
   (of humans)
Nefesh Ha'Elokit: higher, Godly Soul (of
   humans)
Nekudah: point, singularity
Neshama: third highest manifestation
   of Soul;
   also used more generally to connote
   Soul

Netzach: Victory/Eternity; a Sefirah

Nevu'ah: prophecy

Nukva: Feminine; a Partzuf

Ohr: Light (metaphysical)

Ohr Makif: transcendent Light

Ohr Pashut: undifferentiated Light

Ohr Pnimi: immanent Light

Oivi: "horizontality", implying 'ascent'
into greater wholeness

Orech: "verticality", implying 'descent'
into greater separateness

Parsha (Parshiot, pl.): Biblical passage
written on parchment contained
within Tefillin boxes

Partzuf (Partzufim, pl.): face/visage/
countenance; a configuration of
Sefirot

Pirud: divisiveness/separateness

Prat (Pratim, pl.): part/particular

Pshat: literal meaning of Scriptural text

Raisha D'lo Ityadah (RADLA): The
Unknowable Head; aspect of A "Y in
Keter

Remez: homiletical or allegorical
interpretation (as of Scripture)

Reshimu: residue (of the Ohr Ein-Sof)

Retzuot (Retzuah, sing.): Tefillin straps

Ruach: fourth highest manifestation of
Soul

Ruach Hakodesh: Divine inspiration

Ruach Shtut: spirit of folly

Seder Hishtalshelut: causal hierarchy
within the Kabbalistic superstructure

Sefirah (Sefirot, pl.): metaphysical Force

or Attribute of the Ein-Sof

Shlaymut: wholeness

Shvirat Hakelim: shattering of the
vessels

Sod: esoteric or mystical interpretation
(as of Scripture)

Tefillin: phylacteries; leather boxes
containing parchments bearing
Scriptural passages worn by Jewish
men during morning prayer

Tefillin Shel-Rosh: phylacteries worn on
the head

Tefillin Shel-Yad: phylacteries worn on
the arm

Tiferet: Beauty/Harmony/truth; a
Sefirah

Tikun (Tikunim, pl.): rectification

Tikun Olam: rectification of the World

Tzomeach: plant life

Tzimtzum: retraction (of the Ohr Ein-
Sof)

Tziur: form

Yechida: highest of five manifestations
of Soul

Yesh M'ayin: arising ex nihilo

Yesod: Foundation; a Sefirah

Yetzirah: the World of Formation

Zayin Tachtonim (Z"T): lower seven
('unconscious') Sefirot of deca-
Sefirotic system

Ze'ir Anpin (Z"A): Small Countenance;
a Partzuf

Zivug: union

100 = ק	10 = י	1 = א
200 = ר	20 = כ	2 = ב
300 = ש	30 = ל	3 = ג
400 = ת	40 = מ	4 = ד
500 = ך	50 = נ	5 = ה
600 = ם	60 = ס	6 = ו
700 = ן	70 = ע	7 = ז
800 = ף	80 = פ	8 = ח
900 = ץ	90 = צ	9 = ט

Table 2. *Gematriya* — the numerical values of the Hebrew letters. The Hebrew alphabet consists of 22 letters (right to left), five of which (כ,מ,נ,פ,צ) change form and may take on new values (boxed) when present at the end of a word.

4.2 *Sefirot, Partzufim* and Worlds

The Hebrew word ספירה *Sefirah* (pl., *Sefirot*) is etymologically cognate to, and shares nuances of meaning with, the Hebrew terms for sphere, number, boundary, book or text, expression or story, and sapphire.[130] Although the Light (emanation) of the *Ein-Sof* is an undifferentiated unity, each of ten *Sefirot* (Fig. 4A) behaves as a 'lens' or 'filter' that transforms a certain part of this Light into a particular force, attribute, action[131] or information packet.[132] The ten *Sefirot* are:

1–*Keter* כתר: Crown/Divine Will
2–*Chochmah* חכמה: Wisdom
3–*Binah* בינה: Understanding
(*Da'at* דעת: Knowledge — included when *Keter* is not)
4–*Chesed* חסד: Lovingkindness/Expansiveness

5–*Gevurah* גבורה: Strength/Restriction

6–*Tiferet* תפארת: Beauty/Harmony/Truth

7–*Netzach* נצח: Victory/Eternity

8–*Hod* הוד: Splendor

9–*Yesod* יסוד: Foundation

10–*Malchut* מלכות: Kingship

Each *Sefirah* is composed of a Vessel (*Keli*) which retains its portion of Light (*Ohr*). There is no differentiation of the Light within the Vessel as it is part and parcel of the original, undivided Light; differences arise from the nature or 'position' of the *Sefirah's* Vessel. The 'substance' of the Vessel is itself derived from Light which may be construed as having 'coarsened' or 'congealed'. A useful way to think about the *Ohr-Keli* relationship is to envision liquid water contained in a mug made of ice.[110] Both the water and the ice are composed of the same fundamental material—H_2O. Ice is less energetic than water and capable of conferring form to the otherwise shapeless liquid. By the same token, the Vessel diminishes the 'wattage' of the incoming Light and imparts to the latter certain qualities unique to that particular Vessel. In this vein, the obscure phrase from Psalms "In Your light we will see light": באורך נראה אור[133] is readily comprehensible as revelation made possible by the intervening Vessel of features hitherto ensconced within the undifferentiated Light of the *Ein-Sof*.

Relative to the 'lower' *Sefirot* (e.g. *Yesod*), those positioned 'higher' on the Tree of Life (e.g. *Tiferet*) are 'closer' to the Godhead, exhibit greater causal potency and lean more to the 'right' (the 'masculine' side dominated by *Chesed* or expansiveness) than to the 'left' ('feminine' side biased towards *Gevurah* or restriction). These relationships only hold *within* a given reference frame; clearly the 'lower' *Sefirot* of a 'higher-echelon' World or *Partzuf* (see below) manifest more sublime attributes than do 'higher' *Sefirot* of a 'lower' stratum. The Kabbalah construes the ten *Sefirot* as the blueprint of all things created; and everything that exists ultimately comprises these ten 'forces'.[3,106,108,129,134]

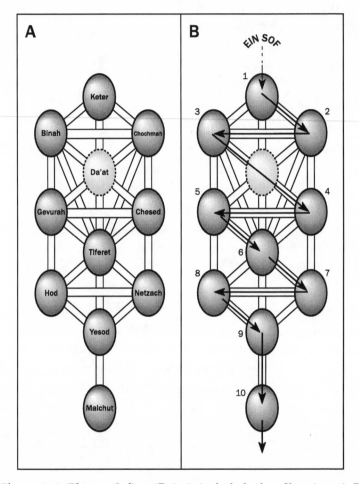

Figure 4. A. The ten *Sefirot* (*Da'at* is included when *Keter* is not). B. Kabbalistic causal hierarchy (*Seder Hishtalshelut*). Bars indicate potential interactions among the *Sefirot*. Arrows denote standard pathway for the descent of Divine influence. From [1] with permission.

A *Partzuf* (*Heb.*, face, visage or countenance) is a configuration of one or more *Sefirot* acting in coordination or towards a defined purpose.[135] By analogy, the information content of a specific human face exceeds that conveyed by the sum of its individual parts. The six main *Partzufim* in 'descending' spiritual order are:

1–*Atik Yomin (A"Y)* עתיק יומין: Ancient of Days
2–*Arich Anpin (A"A)* אריך אנפין: Long Countenance
3–*Abba* אבא: Father
4–*Imma* אמא: Mother
5–*Zeir Anpin (Z"A)* זעיר אנפין: Small Countenance
6–*Nukva* נוקבא: Divine Feminine

To enable the Creation and its spiritual and material constituents, the *Ohr Ein-Sof* (Fig. 5A, unbounded white space) 'retracted' in a process known as *Tzimtzum* thereby establishing a 'void' or 'empty space' (Heb., *Chalal* or *Makom Panoi*; Fig. 5B, black). The Kabbalah teaches that a faint glimmer of residual Holiness deemed the *Reshimu* remained within the 'interior' of the Void (Fig. 5C) and served as the primordial Feminine (*Malchut/Nukvah*) component of all things destined to be created. A shaft of Divine Light (*Kav*) emanating from the surrounding Light of the *Ein-Sof* penetrated the womb-like Void[136] to unite with the *Reshimu* (Fig. 5D). From this union (*Zivug*) emerged all *Sefirot* (Fig. 5E,F), Worlds (Fig. 6) and *Partzufim* (Fig. 7). The first, most diaphanous and cognitively least accessible World arising within the Void is termed *Adam Kadmon* אדם קדמון (Primordial Man). 'Below' *Adam Kadmon* and growing increasingly more remote from God's Essence is *Atzilut* אצילות (the World of Emanation), *Briah* בריאה (the World of Creation), *Yetzirah* יצירה (the World of Formation) and עשיה *Asiyah* (the World of Action) collectively abbreviated as *ABY"A*. The names of these Worlds derive from a verse in Isaiah: כל הנקרא בשמי ולכבודי בראתיו יצרתיו אף-עשיתיו: "Everyone that is called by My Name (*Atzilut*), whom I have created (*Briah*) for My Glory, whom I have formed (*Yetzirah*) and I have made (*Asiyah*)".[137] Each World possesses unique qualities but only those properties relevant to the current thesis will be elaborated here. The following six concepts are fundamental to an appreciation of the Kabbalistic worldview and are relevant to the central theme of this volume:[106,108,134]

1) Each World comprises the six aforementioned *Partzufim*; each *Partzuf* is composed of the ten *Sefirot*; and each individual *Sefirah* is itself made of ten 'miniature' *Sefirot* in a recursive, fractal-like manner (עשר שאין להם סוף "Their measure is ten, yet infinite"[138]).

2) The *Partzufim* overlap one another such that the three lower *Sefirot* (*Netzach-Hod-Yesod*) of the 'Higher' *Partzuf* (e.g. *Abba*) constitute the 'brains' (*Mochin* or *Chochmah-Binah-Da'at*) of the immediately 'subjacent' *Partzuf* (i.e. *Imma*). The *Mochin* animate the *Partzuf* analogous to the relationship of brain/mind to body and convey Divine Guidance from 'higher' spiritual realms.

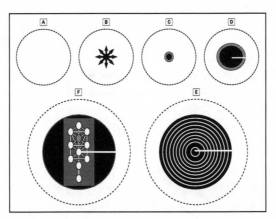

Figure 5. Initial acts of Creation (pre-Genesis 1:1). A. Light of the Godhead (*Ohr Ein-Sof*; unbounded white space). B. 'Retraction' of *Ohr Ein-Sof* (*Tzimtzum*) establishing a 'Void' (*Chalal* or *Makom Panoi*; black). C. Residual Light (*Reshimu*; red/circumferential) lining the Void. D. Ray of *Ohr Ein-Sof* (*Kav*; white) entering the Void. E. *Kav* unites with the *Reshimu* forming concentric *Sefirot* (colored/concentric rings). F. Arrangement of the *Sefirot* in the image of Man=Creation of *Adam Kadmon* (supernal World).

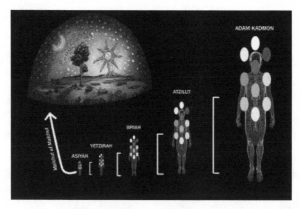

Figure 6. Descending hierarchy of Worlds. Spiritual progenitors transduced to physical reality by *Malchut* of *Malchut* of the 'lowest' World, *Asiyah.*

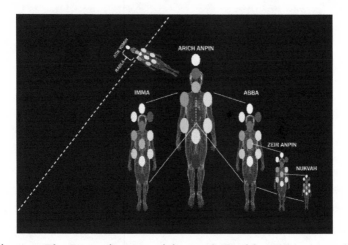

Figure 7. The *Partzufim* comprising each World. *Atik Yomin* can be considered the top *Partzuf* of the World in question or the bottom *Partzuf* of the World immediately above. *Arich Anpin* extends from top to bottom of a World. *Abba* and *Imma* respectively 'dress' (are explicate or superficial to) the right and left arm and hemi-thorax of *Arich Anpin*. The *Nukvah* (Divine Feminine) 'dresses' on the *Netzach-Hod-Yesod* of *Zeir Anpin* (Divine Masculine). *Zeir Anpin*, in turn, receives its 'brains' (*Mochin*; *Chochmah-Binah-Da'at*) from the *Netzach-Hod-Yesod* of *Partzuf Imma.*

3) *Atik Yomin* can be considered the 'top' *Partzuf* of a given World (e.g. *Asiyah*) or the 'bottom' *Partzuf* of the World immediately 'above' (*Yetzirah*). As such, it serves to 'bridge' Worlds akin to the connecting role of *Mochin* between 'adjacent' *Partzufim* (Fig. 7).

4) Physical reality (space-time, matter and energy) comes into being at the very 'bottom' (*Malchut of Malchut*) of *Asiyah* (Fig. 6). Everything in Creation 'above' this level consists of a hierarchy of purely spiritual domains that, via intricate chains of causation (*Seder Hishtalshelut*), ultimately regulate the affairs of material existence.[3,108,134,139]

5) Each created thing and event 'exists' in all four Worlds concomitantly. Although the manifestations of each differ substantially among the Worlds, there nonetheless remains a one-to-one correspondence (or isomorphism[140]) between, say, item *I* in the World of *Asiyah* and its manifestations in *Yetzirah* and *Briah*. Any change in *I* in the World of *Briah* implies corresponding, albeit radically different, alterations in the spiritual and physical characteristics of *I* in the lower realms. The Kabbalah employs the metaphor of a signet ring and a process referred to as 'seal-upon-seal' (*Chotem V'nechtom*) to illustrate this concept[141,142] (Fig. 8): Imagine a ring containing a true-to-life insignia of a tiger. Let the near-perfect image of the tiger stamped in colored ink upon a white sheet of paper signify item *I* as it manifests in the World of *Briah*. While the latter blot is still wet carefully appose it to a second sheet of paper. The resulting insignia of the tiger now appears degraded and 'washed out' relative to the source image representing item *I*'s reality in the World of *Yetzirah*. Although distorted the latter retains a strict mathematical correspondence to its counterpart in *Briah*. Repeat the process again using the moist tiger blot of '*Yetzirah*' to create a third-generation image denoting item *I* as it

manifests in the World of *Asiyah*. The final image may no longer be recognizable as a tiger; yet mathematical symmetry between it and its predecessors persists. Any change in the source insignia necessitates corresponding alterations in the tiger image across all iterations. By the same token, every change or event originating On High reverberates down the cascade of created Worlds in signet ring-like fashion—with the greatest instantiations of apparent disunity registering in the lowermost realms.

6) A pivotal motif of the Lurianic Kabbalah is the so-called 'Shattering of the Vessels' (*Shvirat Hakelim*).[106,112,134] In the first instance when the lower Lights of *Adam Kadmon* arranged themselves to form the ten *Sefirot* of the subjacent World *Atzilut*, the Vessels (*Kelim*) of the bottom seven of these *Sefirot* were incapable of supporting their measure of Light (*Ohr*) and therefore 'shattered'. The broken shards of these seven Vessels 'fell' from *Atzilut* thereby creating the lower Worlds of *Briah*, *Yetzirah* and *Asiah*. A new Light subsequently emanated from *Adam Kadmon* to re-establish the ten *Sefirot* of *Atzilut* in a stable configuration, and the Torah was granted to Mankind as a 'standard operating procedures' manual to assist in the repair of the three lower fragmented Worlds (*Tikkun Olam*). The critical consideration here *vis-à-vis* consciousness is this: Throughout the vast fractal substructure of the Creation, the seven lower *Sefirot* (*Chesed-to-Malchut*) of every deca-*Sefirotic* assembly represent the latter's 'body' whereas the three top *Sefirot* (*Keter-Chochmah-Binah* or *Chochmah-Binah-Da'at*) constitute the assembly's 'brain', 'mind' or 'consciousness' (*Mochin*). During the Shattering of the Vessels, only the Vessels of the 'bodily' *Sefirot* 'broke'; the Vessels of the *Mochin* (three top *Sefirot*) were blemished or descended into lower recesses of *Atzilut* but did not shatter. For this reason, *although the 'body' of every deca-Sefirotic system may consist of innumerable parts (homologous to the*

seven shattered Sefirot), consciousness in all of its myriad forms and regardless of its level of complexity manifests exclusively as a unified whole. This concept is consistent with empirical impressions regarding the state of the healthy human mind and figures centrally in the Kabbalah's understanding of the hierarchical and relativistic nature of consciousness described in Chapter 5.

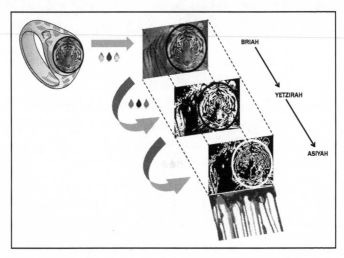

Figure 8. 'Signet-ring' metaphor (*Chotem V'nechtom*) for the manifestations and correspondences of things and events across the hierarchy of created Worlds.

4.3 *Ensheathment, Interinclusion* and *Interpenetration*

The 'flow' or manifestation of Divine Light within the *Etz Ha'chaim* (Tree of Life; the Creation) is dynamic, nonlinear and often counterintuitive. It is informed by three fundamental principles that pervade the classical Kabbalistic literature (*Sefer Yetzirah, Sefer Ha'Bahir, Zohar, Etz Chaim*) and are fleshed out more fully in the writings of R' S. Sharabi (the *Rashash*[113]), R' Moshe Chaim Luzzatto (the *Ramchal*[108]) and R' Shlomo Eliashiv (the *Leshem*; 1841-1926[111]). Familiarity with these principles is essential for understanding the Kabbalah in general and, as discussed in Chapters 6-13, the 'dissemination' of consciousness throughout the universe. The principles are described at length and illustrated with examples adduced from wide-ranging Judaic and scientific sources in an earlier publication (1). The crux of the principles sufficient for current purposes is recapitulated here:

1) **Ensheathment.** 'Ensheathment' or 'enclothement' is translated from the Hebrew *Hitlabshut* (התלבשות) derived from the root *L'vush* ("clothing"). It connotes a system whereby the 'bottom' aspect of a World, *Partzuf* or *Sefirah*, is 'dressed within' or 'enclothed by' the uppermost aspects of its immediately subjacent counterpart. We have already encountered an instantiation of *Hitlabshut* in the case of the *Mochin* (Section 5.1). This relationship can be metaphorized as a partially extended telescope pointing downwards (Fig. 9[1]). The upper rungs indicating more refined levels of spiritual reality nearer to the Godhead (*Ein-Sof*) are interior to and partially overlapped by the lower, progressively more 'mundane' rungs. The overlapping joints function as conduits through which Divine Influence originating in the upper strata 'descends' to guide events within

Figure 9. Ensheathment (*Hitlabshut*).
Metaphorized by a set of extendable telescopes. **A.** Reference configuration of the Kabbalistic superstructure. Joints of the telescope symbolize degree of 'overlap' (enclothement) among *Sefirot*, *Partzufim* and Worlds. **B.** 'Descent' of Creation into *Orech* (increasing apparent disunity and 'distance' from *Ein-Sof*). **C.** 'Ascent' into *Oivi* (progressive revelation of wholeness and the indivisible Light of *Ein-Sof*). Modified from http://www.gilai.com/images/ items/1498_big. jpg and [1] with permission.

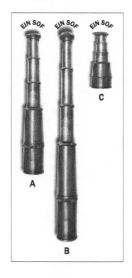

45

the lower realms. Each lower stratum by virtue of the overlap serves to conceal from our direct perception the 'higher'/'inner' domain while revealing by inference the latter's existence and role. In an earlier publication[1] we demonstrate a remarkable concordance of insight between Kabbalistic ensheathment and the physical construct of an 'Implicate Order' proposed by David Bohm (Chapter 3). In Chapter 5 *Hitlabshut* is operationalized in the context of the hierarchical arrangement and relativistic nature of consciousness.

2) The Hebrew term for *interinclusion, Hitkallelut* (התכללות), stems from the root *Klal* connoting 'wholeness', 'cohesiveness' or 'generality'. *Hitkallelut* is tantamount to the notion that the whole is recapitulated or contained within each of its parts: כל מה

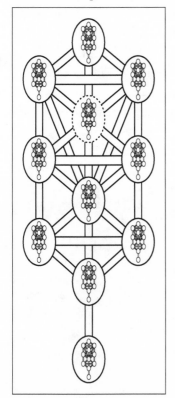

להיות כל [143]שהוא בכללות כן הוא בפרטות ההנהגה בכל חלק.[144] Thus are contained within each *Sefirah, Partzuf* and World miniature versions of all the others (Fig. 10).

Interinclusion is incarnate in the mathematics of fractal geometry, the recursive images of the Mandelbrot set (https://www.youtube.com/watch?v=0jGaio87u3A), the 'Holographic Universe' of Bohmian mechanics, the genetic makeup of cellular nuclei and possibly aspects of normal and pathological brain physiology.[1] The Interinclusion principle may lie at the heart of the extraordinary self-

Figure 10. Interinclusion (*Hitkallelut*).
Represented as a deca-*Sefirotic* fractal.
From [1] with permission.

similarities encountered across vast spatial scales. A jarring example is the unprecedented structural congruity between the filamentous cosmic web of galaxies (the largest structure known) and the cytoarchitecture of the human cerebral cortex as determined by state-of-the-art computer simulations (Fig. 11).[145] Authors Franco Vazza and Alberto Feletti note that despite a difference of about 27 orders of magnitude (10 followed by 27 zeroes), the architecture of the cosmic web resembles the human brain far more than it does each of its roughly 100 billion constituent galaxies; and the brain mirrors the large-scale topography of the Cosmos to a far greater extent than it does any of its estimated 100 billion individual neurons! Might this celestial-neural homology tell us something about the *function* of the cosmic web? Given the intimate interplay of structure and function in mechanics and biology,[146,147] and the perceived role of the brain in the manifestation of human sentience, could it be that the filaments of the cosmic web are the 'circuitry' enabling the expression of consciousness by the physical universe as a unified whole?

That each *Sefirah* contains within it a complete set of ten mini-*Sefirot* is exemplified in the Jewish liturgy by the daily 'Counting

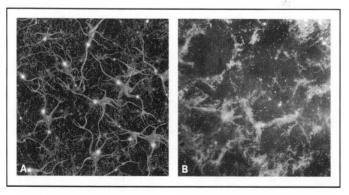

Figure 11. A. Simulation of neural network in human brain
(Shutterstock). B. Computer simulation of the large-scale
distribution of galaxies or cosmic web (Wikimedia Commons),
with modifications.

of the *Omer'* ritual between the festivals of Pesach (Passover) and Shavuot (Weeks): We first count *Chesed* of *Chesed*, then *Gevurah* of *Chesed*, *Tiferet* of *Chesed*, etc. until *Malchut* of *Malchut* on the 49ᵗʰ day. The principle is further underscored by a homiletic stipulating that the bush wherein God revealed Himself to Moses on Mount Sinai (whole; *Klal*) was recapitulated, in miniature form, within each stone (part; *Prat*) hewn from the mountain.[148,149] Both Jewish mystical tradition and Bohmian mechanics posit the mind-bending idea that embedded within each wave and particle is all of the energy and matter in the Universe; that the distant past and remote future are etched within every present moment (note *Rashi* commentary to Scripture[150] that "All things currently in existence have always existed and will continue to exist in the future": שכל דבר ההוה תמיד כבר היה ועתיד להיות; *see* also reference to the 'Block Universe' in Section 9.1); and that enfolded within each thought is the totality of human cognition and consciousness![1] In the words of William Blake:

> *To see a World in a Grain of Sand*
> *And a Heaven in a Wild Flower,*
> *Hold Infinity in the Palm of your Hand*
> *And Eternity in an Hour.*[151]

The seminal principle of *Interinclusion* explains why those who observe a single *Mitzvah* (commandment) to full capacity are rewarded as if they fulfilled all 613 *Mitzvot* of the Torah;[152] why Sabbath blessings inadvertently pronounced by a disoriented traveler on a weekday are, by dint of the mini-Sabbath enfolded within it, not uttered in vain;[153,154] why punishment meted out for each and every transgression effects atonement for the inhering sin of the Golden Calf;[155,156] why the statement "All of Israel are connected one to the other": כל ישראל ערבים זה בזה[157-159] is as much a metaphysical truth as it is a moral imperative; and why the saving of a single life is tantamount to rescuing the entire world.[160]

Although all is subsumed within all, the differential expression (revelation; *Gilui* in Hebrew) of the myriad facets of Creation within each item or event ensures that the world we inhabit is richly textured with seemingly-endless diversity and complexity. The exploration of a Mandelbrot set (see above) brings this dynamic to life beautifully, as novel patterns perpetually emerge at ever-increasing magnifications in the face of an underlying unity reflected in the thematic recurrence of the original fractal infrastructure. When in Chapter 5 the Kabbalah speaks of the 'emergence' of higher consciousness in the Creation hierarchy it does not imply the unprecedented development of *de novo* mental properties as the term is generally understood in the mainstream scientific and philosophical literatures. Rather, it connotes the *progressive revelation of mental attributes hitherto concealed within the very fabric of the Creation at its most fundamental (pre-physics) level.* Here we again see close alignment of the Kabbalah with Bohmian thinking which construes the unfolding of consciousness as a primitive of the Implicate Order ('holomovement') rendered explicate.[161]

3) **Hitkashrut** (התקשרות), Hebrew for *interpenetration*, derives from *Kesher* and connotes 'binding', 'connection' or 'amalgamation'. It is a mechanism that operates in conjunction with the principle of Interinclusion (*Hitkallelut*) to engender a grand underlying unification of the Creation. Interpenetration dictates that intimate bonds exist not merely among the ten *Sefirot* comprising any given particular but also among 'like' *Sefirot*, e.g. *Chesed*, across *all* of the cosmos' individual parts. Interpenetration ensures that the *Chesed* (or any *Sefirah*) component of each and every part of the universe may be actualized concurrently (Fig. 12) thereby circumventing the 'domino effect' behavior of the Kabbalistic hierarchy (*Seder Hishtalshelut*; Fig. 4B). Russian physicist Eduard Shyfrin must have had something similar in

mind when he alluded to the vast fractal network of the *Sefirah Chochmah* as the "intellectual skeleton of the system of spiritual worlds".[162] *Hitkashrut* may be the spiritual correlate or origin of the quantum mechanical principle of 'entanglement' — the non-local, acausal synchronization of the behavior of sister particles irrespective of their degree of separation in space-time (see Section 3.1). Indeed, as if intimately familiar with the notion of quantum entanglement the twelfth century Provençal Kabbalist R' Abraham ben David remarked that the *Sefirot Chesed* and *Gevurah* originated as a single entity in order to facilitate their future interactions![163]

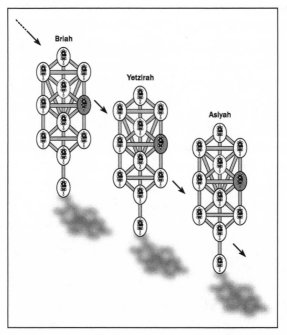

Figure 12. Interpenetration (*Hitkashrut*). Simultaneous co-actualization of like *Sefirot* (e.g. *Chesed*, dark ovals) within and among Worlds (e.g. *Briah, Yetzirah* and *Asiyah*). Such 'parallel processing' of homologous parts circumvents the linear, hierarchical flow of Divine influence illustrated in Fig. 4B and represents a greater manifestation of Wholeness (*Shlaymut*). From [1] with permission.

This shift from the sequential mobilization of *Chesed* within each branch and leaf of the *Etz Ha'chaim* (Tree of Life; the Creation) to the simultaneous 'parallel processing' of *Chesed* throughout the entire cosmos would be construed by both the *Rashash* and Bohm as an enhanced expression of the universe's latent wholeness.[1,113] One may read *Hitkashrut* (Interpenetration) into the words of the Psalmist:[164] מלכותך מלכות כל עולמים. Commonly translated as "Your Kingdom is a Kingdom for all ages", a Kabbalistic rendering might proceed as follows: מלכותך... the grand unified expression of the *Sefirah, Malchut...* מלכות כל עולמים... is the coalescence of the countless mini-*Malchut*s strewn across all the Worlds of Creation.[165] A final, Biblical instantiation of Interpenetration, adduced from the inanimate domain, is the miraculous splitting of all bodies of water concomitant with the partition of the Red (Reed) Sea at the Exodus from Egypt.[166]

Students of the Kabbalah construe the Torah as the 'blueprint' of the universe in accord with the dictum הסתכל באורייתא וברא עלמא: "[God] looked into the Torah and created the World."[167] As such, they fully expect that the esoteric doctrines of Ensheathment, Interinclusion and Interpenetration not be confined to the musings of mystics and Bohmian physicists but rather prove discernible across the entire landscape of Creation. In a previous paper[1] we showed how these principles may pertain to the operations of basic biology:

The human body is a hugely complex system of discrete organs and tissues, each discharging unique duties for the health and welfare of the organism as a unified whole. Brain cells express proteins indispensable for the regulation of diverse physiological functions, sensory perception, movement and cognition; liver cells synthesize very different sets of proteins for the maintenance of the body's energy requirements and detoxification of harmful substances. Yet, in accord with the principle of Hitkallelut (Interinclusion), each brain cell contains within its nucleus all the DNA required to generate the full gamut of liver (and indeed all other human) proteins, and vice versa for liver cells: ...כל מה שהוא בכללות 'everything contained within the whole...' — in this case the body — כן הוא בפרטות... '...is recapitulated in each of its parts' — brain, liver, etc.[143] Our ability to clone an entire organism from a single cell is a pragmatic realization of this principle. In the example invoked, neuronal genes (DNA) coding for liver and other non-brain proteins, albeit present in latent form (Hitkallelut), are repressed (He'elam/concealed or made implicate in Bohm-sprache) and only those proteins necessary for the maintenance of normal neurological function are actually produced (Gilui/revealed or rendered explicate). In his Sparks of the Hidden Light, Rabbi Moshe Schatz broadens the anatomical analogy further to implicate the principle of Hitkashrut (Interpenetration). He intimates that achievement of absolute biological integrity and optimal component performance presupposes a functional 'bonding' (Hitkashrut) of, say, the right eye with some aspect of 'right eyeness' inherent to every limb and tissue.[168] Along similar lines, but now operating inter-personally, Hitkashrut would explain the Midrashic (homiletic) account of sudden and widespread fecundity among hitherto childless women that coincided with the birth of a child to the previously barren Matriarch, Sarah.[169] In the examples cited, Hitkashrut would imply, respectively, that the right eye per se is but the fullest expression of an attribute distributed throughout the organism as a whole, and that Sarah's abrupt fertility is microcosmic of a property permeating the community at large. Such top-down organization and regulation of biological systems is in harmony with an emerging antireductionist viewpoint which maintains that, to intuit deepest levels of 'meaning' (a concept dismissed a priori by most contemporary molecular biologists but gaining in respectability in quantum mechanics circles[57]), living and conscious processes are more profitably understood in their own right rather than in terms of any deconstructing physics or chemistry.[170]

The examples cited above illustrate the principle of *Hitkashrut* as it plays out within and among the organs and tissues of a single organism. The same metaphysic was also noted to manifest interpersonally within society as a whole. The Kabbalah intimates that whenever Alice befriends, empathizes with or loves another, call him Bob, she is in fact connecting with (Interpenetration) the mini-version of herself embodied as a hidden fractal (Interinclusion) with the object of her affection. If Bob reciprocates in kind then he similarly bonds with the mini-Bob within Alice. On a spiritual plane, the result of this mutual interaction is an 'exchange' (Heb., *Chiluf*) of Alice's mini-Bob for Bob's mini-Alice thereby promoting the unification ('strengthening') of both Bob and Alice.[110] What if Alice and Bob were to reiterate this 'bonding' process with their cosmos-wide network of fractal counterparts? The unfolding of such bonding, according to Kabbalistic reasoning, is essential to the revelation of a state of 'cosmic consciousness' in and beyond the Seventh (Messianic) Millennium.

It is noteworthy that analogous deliberations have recently been surfacing on purely secular grounds. On the basis of *psi* (telepathy) data accruing from 'Ganzfeld' sensory deprivation experiments and the principle of quantum mechanical non-locality (entanglement), psychologist Adrian Nelson posed the following: "To what extent do our inner mental landscapes interpenetrate during everyday life? To what degree might we be subtly exchanging information with others and our environments? If consciousness reflects an intrinsic aspect of all reality, it invites us to consider ourselves... as part of a single, evolving experiential system".[171] We will revisit Alice and Bob in Chapter 13 to flesh out in more detail the metaphysical implications of these principles for Messianic era consciousness.

The overarching theme of this volume is that the Kabbalah's position on consciousness is panpsychist in essence. To the extent that this is so, the end-of-days interpenetration of 'minds' can be anticipated to impact both the animate and inanimate domains culminating in a grand self-awareness of the Creation *in toto*. The inevitability of this transition, heralded by the advent of a Messianic era, is an unshakeable pillar of the Jewish faith—a message of hope for eternal peace when the unified Name of God will be revealed and glorified: "On that day God and his Name will be One": ביום ההוא יהיה ד' אחד ושמו אחד.[172] In Chapters 5 and 13, Kabbalistic impressions concerning the evolution of human consciousness and its putative end-game are examined further.

4.4 *Orech* and *Oivi*—Complementary Modes of Awareness

The propensity for Divine influence to descend from one level to the next, which we took to be proportional to the extent of 'overlap' (*Hitlabshut*) among Worlds, *Partzufim* and *Sefirot* (Section 4.3), varies as a function of time and position within the Kabbalistic superstructure (*Etz Ha'chaim*). The 'overlap' diminishes and divisiveness (*Pirud*) within the Creation grows with increasing 'distance' from *Ein-Sof* (e.g. among the *Partzufim* of *Briah* relative to those of *Atzilut*; or when *Pirud* is exacerbated by the sins of humankind). The 'downward stretch' of reality into states of greater disunity is regarded by the *Rashash*[113,173] and others[110] as movement into *Orech* (אורך) or 'vertical' descent. This can be conceptualized as the downward extension of the inverted telescope depicted in Fig. 9B. This is the natural 'top-down' unfolding of the Creation necessary for the advent of apparent separateness, evil and free will (*B'chira*).[106,108,139,174] Contrariwise, 'Ensheathment' (*Hitlabshut*) is progressively realized as one 'ascends' the *Etz Ha'chaim* (Kabbalistic hierarchy) or as a consequence of the *Mitzvot* or *Tikkunim* (positive deeds, rectifications) performed by humanity. This is equivalent to movement from *Orech* (*Pirud*; disunity) into states of increasing unification (*Shlaymut*) or *Oivi* (עובי; 'horizontality') as depicted by upward retraction of the telescope in Fig. 9C. In extreme conditions of *Oivi*, in opposition to *Orech*, the Creation's hierarchical scaffolding dissolves and all things are perceived as spiritually equidistant from ('horizontal to' or united with) the Godhead. We encountered an example of movement from *Orech* into *Oivi* in our discussion of Interpenetration (*Hitkashrut*) in Section 4.3 where far greater unity was achieved by the simultaneous co-mobilization of the *Sefirah Chesed* in every nook and cranny of the cosmos. Additional examples drawn from *Midrashic* literature and common life experience illustrating the relationship of *Orech* and *Oivi* were originally presented elsewhere[1] and are further developed here:

1) From the hierarchical standpoint of *Orech* we would ordinarily attribute greater intrinsic value to humans than to fleas or pebbles. However, in so far as the three fulfil the mandate of the Creator, they are when viewed from the angle of *Oivi* equally 'proximate' to the supernal *Sefirah* of *Keter* (Divine Will) and therefore equally essential to God's Plan:

כי מצד בריאת השי״ת כל הברוים שוים. מאחר שעל ידי כלם נעשה רצונו בעולם.[175]

2) On *Orech's* ladder-like scale, a seminary student who previously studied ten hours a day but now only commits to eight hours is still held in higher esteem than a peer who increased his daily learning from one to two hours. Not so in *Oivi*—by shifting the ground 'horizontally' ('leveling the playing field') student *A* has lost momentum and receded from God's Will (*Keter*) into increasing disunity (*Pirud*) whereas student *B* has entered a more profound state of wholeness (*Shlaymut*).[110]

3) Employing the symbolism of mathematics, we move from *Orech* to *Oivi* and towards greater expressions of wholeness whenever we collapse a *Gematriya* (sum of numerical values

of the letters comprising a Hebrew word; Section 4.1, Table 2) to its numerical diminutive (*Mispar Katan*). Thus are the 613 *Mitzvot* (Torah commandments/duties) grounded in the more fundamental Ten Commandments (6+1+3=10) which in turn branch out from the singular Will (*Keter Elyon*) of the One God (1+0=1). Perhaps to convey this truth did our sages indicate that the Ten Commandments were initially uttered as a 'single word'.[176] Let us take up a second example in the 'opposite direction' *viz.* evolving from wholeness to partition: As alluded to earlier in this chapter the primordial acts of Creation can be conceptualized as a 'movement' from *Oivi* into *Orech*. At the outset is the unified Light of the Godhead, the *Ohr Ein-Sof* symbolized by the number '1'. Prior to the creation of 'things', God withdrew his Light (act of *Tzimtzum*) from a 'central point' thereby giving rise to the first Void (*Makom Panoi*). The *Etz Chaim* (seminal work of Lurianic Kabbalah) states that this Void "was in the shape of a perfect circle": היה עגול מכל סביבותיו בהשוואה גמורה.[177] Why specify this (or any other) geometry in 'spiritual space' when there is no inkling yet of physical shape or dimension? The *Ari"ZL* offers an explanation having to do with the 'equidistance' of the incoming ray of Light (*Kav*) to all points bounding the Void which need not preoccupy us here (*ibid.*). One may conjecture that the circle denotes 'zero' and the novel absence of Light within the Void—the inception of 'nothingness'. From God's point of view and from the holistic slant of *Oivi* adding zero to one (1+0=1) complies with the dictum "regarding the Creator, no change occurred from before the Creation to after": שלגבי הבורא לא חל שום שינוי בין קודם הבריאה ואחריה[178] explicating the passage in *Malachi*, "I am the Lord, I do not change": אני ד' לא שניתי.[179] But from our mundane or 'bottom-up' perspective of *Orech* deployment of a zero after a one yields ten, not one! In other words, *Orech*-consciousness in contradistinction to *Oivi* perceives multiplicity or divisiveness (*Pirud*)—ten *Sefirot* to be exact—emerging from unity through the medium of an intervening nothingness (much as a prism diffracts white light as a spectrum of colors). This idea of 'something emerging from nothing' is succinctly expressed by the Izhbitze-Radziner Rebbe as על ידי הצמצום תזכה להרחבה: "the Contraction merits the Expansion"[180,181] and is spiritually homologous to the spontaneous materialization of particles as vacuum fluctuations in quantum mechanics.[182] One may claim that the historical assignment of the symbol '0' to connote nothingness was arbitrary and therefore of little relevance to (or retro-fitted onto) the 'topology' of the Void (*Makom Panoi*). But such argument would be at odds with Kabbalistic reasoning which denies random coincidence and sees all physical reality, especially that which concerns humankind, as a point-to-point reflection of deeper spiritual truths (see discussion of *Chotem V'nechtom* and Fig. 8 in Section 4.2). Just as our single bodies branch into ten fingers[183] and ten toes in symbolic recapitulation of Celestial Design (ten *Sefirot* emanating from the singular *Ohr Ein-Sof*) so too may the iconic '0' have been 'selected' (purposefully or unwittingly) by humanity to signify the 'shape of nothing' within the Primordial Void. Also, given that the virtually endless permutations and combinations of the ten *Sefirot* ultimately comprise everything in the known universe, it should come as no surprise to the Kabbalist that (i) Egyptian hieroglyphics dating back to 3000 BCE already provide evidence of the ubiquitous base-10 or decimal number system;[184] (ii) the computer age adopted binary code—chains of '1's and '0's—to register information; (iii) the 'de Sitter'-like geometry of the expanding universe described by inflationary cosmology is a sphere-like space with ten symmetries or ways it can be reconstructed without changing;[185] and (iv) several of the leading superstring theories describing physical reality at its most fundamental level are 10- or 11-dimensional (the latter ostensibly corresponding to the Tree of Life in rare situations when both *Keter* and *Da'at* are reckoned).[186] The Kabbalah is rife with examples of 'inverted causality' along these lines. In Chapter

8 for instance we demonstrate interesting similarities between *Tefillin* (phylacteries) worn by Jewish males during morning prayer and human neuroanatomy. The point is then made that the design of *Tefillin* seemingly preceded knowledge of nervous system structure by millennia suggesting, counterintuitively, that *Tefillin* was God's 'blueprint' for the human nervous system and not *vice versa*—another instantiation of the passage **הסתכל באורייתא וברא עלמא**: "[God] looked into the Torah and created the World".[167] This is the kind of 'nonlinear' thinking readers were encouraged to engage (Chapter 4) in order to appreciate Kabbalistic logic. Regardless of one's position on this admittedly controversial topic, both believer and skeptic alike may find tantalizing the cosmology of the *Sefer Yetzirah*—that most ancient and cryptic of Kabbalistic texts—wherein we find inscribed: **עשר ספירות בלימה, עשר ולא תשע, עשר ולא אחת עשרה** "Ten Sefirot of Nothingness; ten and not nine; ten and not eleven".[187]

4) According to Jewish tradition, the orbs of the sun and moon were initially created on par with one another (state of *Oivi*). God subsequently diminished the moon (*Miyut Ha'yareach*) and rendered it a passive recipient (*Keli*) for the light of the sun—a 'descent' from *Oivi* into *Orech*. In the Messianic era the moon will regain its original stature: **וקיימא סיהרא באשלמותא**—"the moon will be established in its completeness",[188] a reversion to (better, augmented revelation of) *Oivi*, and function in harmony with the sun as **שני מלכים משתמשים בכתר אחד**: "two monarchs sharing a single crown".[189] Have you ever wondered why it is that the silhouette of the moon superimposes so precisely on the sun's disk in the course of a total solar eclipse? Is the exquisite offsetting of the sun's ~400-fold greater diameter than the moon by the former's ~400-fold greater distance[190] a mere cosmic fluke? Or might this 'co-incidence' hint at a deeper spiritual equivalence of these heavenly bodies as intimated in Jewish Aggadic (homiletic) writings and as glimpsed through the lens of *Oivi*?

The dynamic tension between the sun and moon is but one special case of the Kabbalistic relationship of masculine (*Mashpiah*-donor) and feminine (*Keli*-recipient) which pervades all aspects of the Creation[191,192] and is considered further in Chapter 6.

5) Finally, let us revisit Alice and Bob whom we encountered in our earlier deliberations on Interpenetration (*Hitkashrut*; Section 4.3). From the viewpoint of *Orech*, Alice is a circumscribed individual who upon sharing positive experiences with Bob begins to identify with (*reveals* or 'makes explicate' in Bohmian terminology) the mini-Alice present in Bob. The emphasis here is on the word 'reveals' because from the vantage point of *Oivi* there never was nor can there be any interruption of her entanglement (Interpenetration) with the countless mini-Alices disseminated as fractals throughout the entire cosmos (including the one within Bob). From the holistic perch of *Oivi* as in Bohm's Implicate Order, Alice *is* the sum total of all her scattered 'selves', period. Only in *Orech*-consciousness (or Bohm's explicate order) is there the semblance of *differential* bonding, with Alice manifesting greater Interpenetration with relatives and friends than with acquaintances and strangers.

A 'healthy' Torah outlook demands attention to both sides of the *Orech-Oivi* dialectic as enlistment of either perspective alone is insufficient. Exclusionary adherence to an *Orech*-consciousness, as practiced by many physicalists, is unacceptable to Orthodox Judaism because it denies or marginalizes God and numbs the practitioner to the wonder of the Creation's unified underpinning. Overindulgence in *Oivi*-consciousness is similarly inadequate given Judaism's emphasis on *Tikkun Olam* — humankind's obligations to actively engage and repair the numerous 'deficiencies' inherent to material existence (a consequence of the 'Shattering of the Vessels' described in Section 4.2). Lawyer and poet Allen Afterman alluded to this *Oivi-Orech* dynamic as a "running towards God [which] is inevitably followed by a fall into ordinary consciousness... part of the natural spiritual rhythm in which transcendent experience is integrated into the routine of daily life."[193] The counterintuitive nature of this dual *Orech-Oivi* perspective and of paradox in general are outlined in the following section. Implications of the latter *vis-à-vis* Kabbalistic panpsychism and the nature of human consciousness will become apparent later in this volume.

4.5 On the Nature of Paradox

In the previous section we encountered two seemingly disparate approaches to comprehending the organization and unfolding of reality: a familiar hierarchical arrangement (*Orech*) emphasizing progressive diversification and distinctiveness and a less-intuitive 'cross-cutting' mode (*Oivi*) hinting at the Creation's underlying cohesion. But at any given instance which system does the Creator employ to weave the fabric of the universe and regulate its workings? The answer according to the Kabbalah is both. At a more fundamental level of understanding the Kabbalah insists that there really are no 'moving parts' and that the flow of Divine Light along serial (*Orech*) and parallel (*Oivi*) tracks is *concomitant* and contingent more on *shifts in conscious awareness* than any realignment of the underlying metaphysics. Plainly spoken, both the unified and the particularized dimensions of the Creation are *co-extant*. The significance of this *Orech-Oivi* simultaneity for inculcating genuine and often penetrating Kabbalistic insight into the nature of reality cannot be overemphasized. It is a powerful intellectual tool capable of resolving, or at least providing a useful paradigm to assimilate and analyze, numerous scientific, philosophical and theological conundra. Take for example Adrian Nelson's perplexing statement that

the Big Bang and the ultimate destiny of the universe are

really one primordial singularity of existence, and that our relative spatiotemporal reference frame is what creates their apparent duality.[194]

This is certainly true in the Kabbalistic sense as we shift our consciousness from the *gestalt* perspective of *Oivi* (the perception of '... one primordial singularity...') to that of *Orech* ('...their apparent duality'). Kabbalistic paradoxes of the *Orech-Oivi* type are legion, a fact which has undoubtedly hindered mass appreciation of this knowledge over the centuries. It is my opinion that dramatic developments in twentieth century scientific thinking, especially in the realm of physics, have opened unprecedented gateways to the proper assimilation of Kabbalistic wisdom. A most striking example apropos to the current discussion is the quantum physicist's embrace of the paradoxical nature of light. Contemporary science has grown comfortable with the notion that light exists simultaneously as *both* a wave and a particle — energy *and* matter — with one or the other facet revealed by the consciousness of an observer. The *Oivi-Orech* dialectic can be illuminated by rephrasing this account of the physical duality of light in Kabbalistic terms: "The Creation exists simultaneously as *both* a seamless whole (*Oivi*) and as a collage of countless particulars (*Orech*), with one or the other facet revealed by the consciousness of an observer." In a very real sense, *Oivi* and *Orech* respectively describe a 'wave function' — conceivably a spiritual counterpart of the Schrödinger equation — before and after its 'collapse'.

Another material example of inherent paradox is time. A strain of quantum mechanics posits that time is only experienced as linear, unidirectional and dynamic by observers *inside* the physical universe. This experience of emergent temporality is ostensibly predicated on the observation of, and interaction with, photons in states of non-local entanglement. The Italian physicist Marco Genovese and others conjectured that a hypothetical 'super-observer' stationed *outside* the Universe would not engage entangled photons and would therefore view time as static.[195,196] Einstein's theory of Special Relativity teaches further that even within the confines of the universe time is not absolute inasmuch as its perceived rate of flow varies in relationship to the velocity of the observer.[196,197] I will have more to say on this in Section 9.1 when the so-called 'Block Universe' is considered.

I tried to demonstrate how a contemporary physicist's understanding of light and time is in many ways analogous to the Kabbalah's conceptualization of the *Orech-Oivi* paradox and its contingency on consciousness. Importantly, both the physical and Kabbalistic paradoxes described herein are 'ontological' (as opposed to 'epistemological') in so far as they point to the *intrinsically* self-contradictory character of the underlying reality and not merely the limitations of our cognitive faculties. As such, better mathematics, logic and instrumentation may help us further *define* the nature of such paradoxes but cannot *resolve* them.

That ontic paradoxes of the kind described above fall squarely within Judaism's comfort zone is reflected in the etymology of ancient Hebrew. Take for example the Hebrew word עולם (*Olam*). The term may connote both space (e.g. *Ha'olam* = the World) and time (e.g. *L'olam Va'ed* = forever)[198]—a prescient allusion to the counterintuitive notion of 'space-time' predating Einstein by millennia! The word עולם (*Olam*) is also cognate with העלם (*He'elam*) which means 'hidden' inferring that God's presence is at once revealed and concealed by the physical universe. A similar idea is conveyed by פנים (*Panim* = face) and פנימיות (*Pnimiut* = interiority) whereby stirrings in the deepest recesses of a person's mind are projected as facial expressions for all to see.

Chapter 5

Kabbalistic Panpsychism and Panentheism

Based on the general principles provided in Chapter 4, a set of conclusions germane to a Kabbalistic understanding of consciousness can be drawn. The emerging ontology will then be further fleshed out upon demonstration of its unique hierarchical and relativistic infrastructure. Thereafter, implications of the latter for a nuanced appreciation of specific facets of human and other consciousness will be considered.

The following five ramifications stem directly from 'first principles' outlined in the previous chapter:

1) Consciousness is not the product of, 'secreted' by, emergent within, or the exclusive domain of neural tissue. Nor is it an epiphenomenon bereft of any causal action within the material world. Rather, consciousness is primordial to, transcends, lends existence to ('vivifies'), is immanent within and impacts all aspects of reality both spiritual and physical. This view is compatible with 'cosmopsychism'[199] and the 'idealistic panpsychism' of Peter Ells which posits an 'experiential layer' *beneath* completed physics which comprises the elementary particles "as they are in and of themselves".[20]

2) The Kabbalistic perspective is panpsychist in so far as all things created, be they animate or inanimate,[200] comprise ten *Sefirot* of which the 'top' three (*Chochmah-Binah-Da'at* or *Keter-Chochmah-Binah*) represent the construct's 'brains' (*Mochin*) or conveyors of 'consciousness'. In accord with the Copenhagen interpretation of quantum mechanics, the *Mochin* of every deca-*Sefirotic* system may collapse the superposition of the associated seven 'bodily' *Sefirot* into discrete entities or events much as the

consciousness of human observers effects the reduction of probabilistic wave functions into palpable realities. Whereas the Kabbalah endows each particular with a 'proto-mind' capable of triggering self-materialization, Ells would argue that particles in close proximity 'experience' ('observe') one another resulting in mutual wave function collapse.[20] Biophysicist Stuart Kauffman suggested similarly that "quantum variables... measure one another in what is called phase information which is acausally lost from the system to the measuring quantum environment in decoherence."[201] With either the Kabbalistic or these quantum mechanical accounts, we have here a satisfactory explanation for the congealment of probability waves into tangible entities and the evolution of a classical universe eons before the appearance of life, brains or human observers.

3) Kabbalistic doctrine is panentheistic inasmuch as it underscores the existence of a single Deity that is both transcendent and immanent in nature.[202]

4) Invoking the doctrine of *imago Dei*[62] and Moltmann's *analogia relationis*,[203] it follows from #3 that the human mind/Soul at once transcends (*Yechida-Chaya* components of the Soul), is immanent within (*Neshamah-Ruach-Nefesh* aspects of Soul) and is inseparably bound to the physical body (*Guf*) in life.[131,204]

5) Espousing panentheistic panpsychism the Kabbalah rejects any formulations of human (or other) consciousness devolving from mainstream reductive materialism, Cartesian dualism, Eastern and Berkeleyan idealism, Spinozan pantheism or deism.

5.1 A Hierarchy of Consciousness

A closer look at the Kabbalistic portrayal of consciousness reveals features that appear paradoxical and largely irreconcilable with dominant scientific accounts of the phenomenon. As discussed in Chapter 4 each rung of the Kabbalistic infrastructure be it a World or a *Partzuf* within a World is composed of ten *Sefirot* and each deca-*Sefirotic* system is spearheaded by consciousness-mediating *Mochin*. *Ergo*, the entire physical cosmos and its spiritual progenitors are imbued with and regulated by a vast assemblage of consciousnesses which together convey the Will (*Ratzon*) of the Creator in hierarchical fashion. Not unlike a major-general issuing commands that filter down the ranks of a military or justice proportionately meted out by a system of higher and lower courts, a point of consciousness 'situated' close to the Godhead (*Ein-Sof*) conveys 'sweeping' influences which are progressively parcellated, compartmentalized and delegated to a network of lower-ranking *Mochin* ('brains') for their implementation. The latter may include instances of novel creation *ex nihilo* (*Yesh M'ayin*), the natural or supra-natural (miraculous) unfolding of earthy events and the doling out of rewards and punishments to worthy recipients. The concept of 'hierarchical' Will (*Ratzon*; *Sefirah* of *Keter*) and *Mochin* (consciousness) can be illustrated with the following simple example:

Stage 1. A woman has a desire (*Ratzon=Keter*) to live in a house.

Stage 2. A *gestalt*, undifferentiated image of the kind of house she fancies (cottage, duplex, etc.) comes to mind (*Chochmah*).

Stage 3. Architectural plans are drawn (*Binah*) for each component of the residence infrastructure (design, dimensions, materials, etc.).

Stage 4. After the details of the project have been thoroughly fleshed out by the *Mochin* (*Chochmah-Binah-Da'at* or *Keter-Chochmah-Binah*), a construction company representing the first six of seven lower ('bodily') *Sefirot* (*Chesed-Gevurah-Tiferet-*

Netzach-Hod-Yesod) is recruited to physically build the house.

Stage 5. Upon completion of the house, representing the final *Sefirah* of *Malchut*, the woman inhabits the edifice thereby satiating her initial desire (*Keter*). The latter establishes a critical *Keter-Malchut* axis (see Chapter 6) and is an instantiation of the passage from the Sabbath liturgy סוף מעשה במחשבה תחילה: "last in deed, first conceived".

Stage 6. Having settled in her new home the proprietor now focuses on decorating the living room. This desire manifests as its own *Keter* which activates in sequence nine lower *Sefirot* necessary to furnish a living room according to her specifications. This and other sub-*Keters* are nested hierarchically or in parallel within the overarching Will (*Keter Elyon*) to own a house of her liking. Although minutiae of the living room decor may not have entered consciousness at the outset, the former once conceived do not contradict and indeed extend her *uber-Keter* desire for the perfect home.[205]

Consistent with the Kabbalistic principle of Interinclusion (*Hitkallelut*; Section 4.3), the deca-*Sefirotic* network of 'consciousness-body' dipoles is scalar-invariant and holds true for any and all constructs perceived as individual entities by the human mind. When we consider a World as a whole, its constituent ten *Sefirot* naturally divide as *Gimel Rishonim* (*G"R*), translated as "the three first (*Sefirot*)" or consciousness-conveying *Mochin*; and *Zayin Tachtonim* (*Z"T*) or "seven lower (bodily) *Sefirot*".[106,108,134] The bottom *Sefirah Malchut* always denotes the final manifestation or revelation of that particular World as intended by that World's *Keter*—hence, a *Keter-Malchut* axis.[206,207] As soon as we shift our attention away from the World as a unified whole towards a constituent part—e.g. an individual *Partzuf* or in the special case of our physical world an ocean, human or subatomic particle—we acknowledge that each of the latter, too, comprises ten *Sefirot* arranged in identical *G"R-Z"T* (3-brain/7-body) format. Within a multipartite World the *G"R* (mini-consciousness) dimension of each nested dipole (entity) filters from the dominant *Mochin* of that World the precise quality and intensity of Light (*Ohr*) necessary for the actualization of its unique *Z"T* component (which acts as a Vessel for the *G"R's* Light). Along similar lines many quantum physicists and investigators of *psi* ('paranormal') phenomena have come to recognize consciousness as a pivotal "ordering principle... rooted deeply in the organization of nature".[208] The Kabbalah's hierarchy of consciousness guarantees that the narrow objectives of the individual parts do not contravene and indeed help bring to fruition the general Will (*Keter Ha'klali*) pertaining to that particular World. The *Keter Ha'klali* of any given World when viewed from the vantage point of the entire Creation is but a cog in the boundless and ultimately unfathomable Will of the Creator (*Ratzon Elyon*).

This branching tapestry of 'top-down' consciousness has held profound meaning for practitioners of Judaism throughout the ages: Judaism abides by the principle that deeds, more so than beliefs or pronouncements, are the essential determinants of Divine reward and punishment and the ethical fabric of the universe. The 613 *Mitzvot* (statutes) prescribed by the Torah are construed as the final distillate and physical embodiment of God's Will (*Ratzon Elyon*). As such, the *Mitzvot* provide a vehicle by which specified actions appropriately committed or resisted enable human consciousness to 'partner with' and deploy Divine Intent for rectification of this base World (*Tikkun Olam*). The deduced or intuited awareness of the cascading nature of Divine consciousness instils belief (*Emunah*) that the *Mitzvot* still beyond our ken (termed *Chukim*; e.g. the Red Heifer purification rite[209]) are no less essential to God's Plan than those appealing to our sense of reason (*Mishpatim*; such as the injunction against murder[210,211]). The concept of transcendent consciousness (i) undergirds the Torah principle of נעשה ונשמע "we will do and (then) we will hear"[212] imploring prioritization of *Mitzvah* performance over intellection (with the latter often proving attainable only by dint of the former); (ii) informs Ben-Azzai's directive, הוה רץ למצוה קלה כבחמורה "Run to perform a 'simple' Mitzvah as you would a (seemingly more) important one";[213] and (iii) addresses the theodicy problem[214] by transforming the Hebrew proclamation גם זו לטובה "even this is for the good"[215] from a hopeful sigh uttered in times of despair to a sublime conviction that *all* circumstances decreed by the Benevolent One, including those beyond our current comprehension, are ultimately in humanity's best interest.[216]

5.2 Relativistic Consciousness

In 1905 Albert Einstein published his landmark Special Theory of Relativity.[217] In so doing, he upended the world of physics and our understanding of reality by proposing the inviolate nature of the speed of light in a vacuum and the variability of spatial magnitude and the flow of time relative to the velocity of the observer — highly disruptive notions amply supported by over a century of experimentation. As mentioned previously, Einstein's revolutionary conflation of space and time into a unified four-dimensional space-time continuum, a counterintuitive insight of stunning proportions, is hinted at by ancient Hebrew's dual usage of the term "*Olam*" to connote both space (e.g. *Ha'olam* = the World) and time (e.g. *L'olam Va'ed* = forever)!

The very concept of relativity is no stranger to the Written Torah. In 2016, Russian theoretical physicist Alexander Poltorak[218] showed how Special Relativity can be deduced from analysis of the Miracle of Manna (a food that descended from Heaven) recounted in Exodus 16:18. In this passage, God instructs the Israelites to gather one *Omer* of Manna per capita daily. Although some individuals gathered more or less than this amount, Rashi[219] informs us that the quantity of Manna tallied by each individual upon returning to his tent was precisely one *Omer!* God set the *Omer* quantity as a universal constant—one that could be defined by the following formula:

$$m' = (m1 + m2)/[1 + (m1m2/M^2)]$$

where M is the amount of Manna each man was commanded to collect (one *Omer*); m' is the final quantity of Manna remaining with an individual after his harvest is counted; m1 is the quantity he collected in fulfilment of God's instruction (= M); and m2 is the excess (+ m2) or deficient (- m2) amount he gathered deviating from M. If after collecting the commanded one *Omer* zealous Bob gathered an additional two *Omers* how many *Omers* would he have at the end of the day? Plugging these values into the equation we get:

$$m' = M + 2M/[1 + (M \bullet 2M/M^2)]$$
$$m' = 3M/[1 + (2M^2/M^2)]$$
$$m' = 3M/3 = M \text{ (one Omer)}$$

So regardless of how much or how little Bob gathered, he remained with the one *Omer* decreed by God. This is precisely the formula of Special Relativity employed to portray the speed of light as a universal constant:

$$v' = (v1 + v2)/[1 + (v1v2/c^2)]$$

where c is the constant speed of light in a vacuum; v' is the actual velocity realized; v1 is, say, light speed (= c) of a beam of photons emitted from a stationary laser; and v2 is additional speed of the laser itself in the same (+ v2) or opposite (- v2) direction of the photon beam relative to c. In strict analogy to the situation of the Manna, the observed velocity of the radiating photons (v') remains locked at the constant speed of light (c) irrespective of the additional motion of the laser.

The Lurianic Kabbalah intimates that the consciousness hierarchy pervading the Creation (Section 5.1) is, like space-time, relativistic. The metaphysical basis of this assertion resides in the fact that the 'bottom' *Sefirot, Netzach-Hod-Yesod* and *Malchut* of a given World or *Partzuf* are enclothed within (*Hitlabshut*; Section 4.3) their 'subjacent' counterparts where they respectively serve as the latter's *Chochmah-Binah-Da'at* and *Keter*. In other words, the 'lower', 'non-conscious' aspects of a superior construct are the 'brains' (*Mochin*) of, and impart 'consciousness' to, the immediately inferior entity. In essence, this is a special case of the more general *Ohr-Keli* relationship where the *Keli*-recipient of a system (e.g. *Partzuf Imma* in *Adam Kadmon* receiving from *Abba*) behaves as the *Ohr*-donor for the next lower level (*Partzuf Zeir Anpin* in *Adam Kadmon* in the example cited) of the system.

The panentheistic structure of the Kabbalah argues further that the relationship between the transcendent and immanent influences coursing through the system is fluid, relativistic and contingent on the 'observer's' frame of reference. The *Ohr Ein-Sof* (Divine Light/Consciousness) relates to all things created in one of two ways: First as an immanent Light (*Ohr Pnimi*) which fills the created Vessel (*Keli*). The Immanent Light acts as the 'brains' (*Mochin*; *Chochmah-Binah-Da'at*) of the Vessel. It vivifies/ animates the Vessel and is its consciousness. Second, a transcendent Light (*Ohr Makif*) signifying the *Sefirah Keter* surrounds the Vessel. It influences the Vessel remotely and subliminally. The Transcendent Light (*Ohr Makif*) represents a level of consciousness/intelligence/knowledge beyond that Vessel's capacity to assimilate.

By analogy, material presented by a teacher which the student comprehends and is then able to transmit to others is Immanent Light (*Ohr Pnimi*). Those dimensions of the teacher's presentation which remain beyond the student's grasp and which the latter cannot therefore pass on to others is Transcendent Light (an *Ohr Makif* or *Keter*—a Crown 'outside the system' that is on, but not in, the head of the student). With time and effort, this material may eventually come to be understood by the student at which point that aspect of the Transcendent Light is converted to Immanent Light. For those classmates who still cannot absorb the gist of the lesson the teacher's Light remains transcendent.[220,221] So one person's *Ohr Pnimi* may be another's *Ohr Makif* (relativity). For the teacher, the entire lesson is Immanent Light inasmuch as she is in full command of, and is able to effectively convey, the knowledge. This transmission is mediated by the teacher's *Netzach-Hod-Yesod* which becomes the *Chochmah-Binah-Da'at* of the comprehending student. For the perplexed student, the teacher's *Malchut* (lowest of the *Sefirot*) manifests as the student's *Keter*,[206] surrounding but not penetrating his or her head.

We stated earlier that every *Sefirah* is comprised of Light (*Ohr*) and Vessel (*Keli*). But what about *Keter*? Does it or does it not have a Vessel? The answer is *both*, again depending on perspective: From the point of view of humankind (metaphorized above by the non-comprehending student) *Keter* by definition remains 'outside the system' and therefore has no Vessel. From God's omniscient perspective (represented by the teacher) nothing is 'outside the system' and even *Keter* (Divine Will or *Ratzon*) has a Vessel. (On one level of analysis, the Kabbalah intimates that *every* Light no matter how lofty must have some sort of Vessel in order to preserve its identity and permit it to 'radiate'.[111]) As described below, identical Light-Vessel dynamics may be invoked when considering the hierarchy of consciousness manifested by the four domains of material existence.

Let us see how the concept of 'relativistic consciousness' plays out when applied to representatives of the familiar world transduced by *Malchut* of *Malchut* of *Asiyah*, the lowest rung of the Kabbalistic ladder (*Etz Ha'chaim*). The Kabbalah speaks of four physical domains which progressively ascend in order of complexity and consciousness:[108,111,134]

- *Domem* דומם: Inanimate objects (consciousness informing existence)
- *Tzomeach* צומח: Plant life (consciousness informing growth and reproduction)
- *Chaye* חי: Animal life (sentience)
- *M'daber* מדבר (literally, speaker): Human beings (self-awareness and rationality)

The Kabbalah also describes a future Messianic era when human consciousness will transcend the confines of self and begin embracing the Creation *in toto*—a fifth state or 'cosmic'

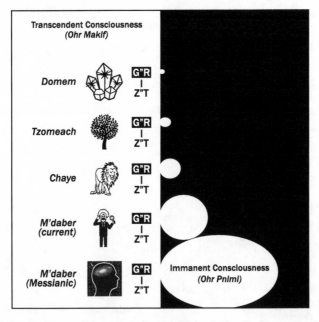

Figure 13. Progressive transduction (revelation) of transcendent consciousness (*Ohr Makif*) into immanent consciousness (*Ohr Pnimi*) by the *G"Rs* of the various domains of Creation. White denotes consciousness space. *G"R=Gimel Rishonim* (three top *Sefirot* or 'brains'/ *Mochin*); *Z"T=Zayin Tachtonim* (seven bottom or 'bodily' *Sefirot*).

consciousness. This transitioning is slated to begin in the Seventh ('Sabbath') millennium, with the year of this writing being 5780 according to the Hebrew calendar. The progressive transduction/revelation of transcendent consciousness (an *Ohr Makif*—the 'mind of God') by the *G"Rs* (three top *Sefirot*) of the *Domem-Tzomeach-Chaye-M'daber* domains into ever-deepening pockets of immanent consciousness (*Ohr Pnimi*) is depicted in Figure 13.

The four stages of physical development and their associated five levels of consciousness intimately correspond to, share fundamental properties with, and may at times be conceptually interchangeable with the five Worlds, six *Partzufim*, ten *Sefirot* and five components of the Soul[204,222] (Table 3).

Domain	Soul-part	Sefirah	Partzuf	World
Domem	Nefesh	Malchut	Nukvah	Asiyah
Tzomeach	Ruach	Chesed-Gevurah-Tiferet-Netzach-Hod-Yesod	Zeir Anpin	Yetzirah
Chaye	Neshama	Binah	Imma	Briah
M'daber (current)	Chaya	Chochmah	Abba	Atzilut
M'daber (Messianic)	Yechida	Keter	Atik Yomin-Arich Anpin	Adam Kadmon

Table 3. Homologous constructs or 'dualities' (*Kinuim*) within the Kabbalistic hierarchy.

Many subtle layers of intended meaning can often be gleaned from the Kabbalistic literature by mentally shuffling these homologous constructs or *Kinuim*. In this sense *Kinuim* are reminiscent of the 'dualities' in physics (e.g. wave-particle nature of light; anti-de Sitter space/conformal theory, etc.) which on the basis of mathematical equivalence foster creativity by enabling the transitioning among disparate reference frames.[223-226]

An examination of the *Sefirotic* makeup of, and interrelationships among, the four physical domains brings to light the relativistic nature of their associated states of consciousness. The lowest physical manifestation *Domem* (e.g. a rock) is, akin to all other entities, composed of ten *Sefirot*. The top three *Sefirot* or *G"R* constitute the *Mochin* (consciousness) which impart existence (Section 5.1) and form (*Tziur*) to the proto-substance (*Chomer*) of the lower seven *Sefirot* (*Z"T*).[227,228] Ascending in complexity, the ten *Sefirot* of the rock (*Domem*) are 'compacted' as the *Z"T* ('body') of *Tzomeach* (e.g. a tree). No surprise then that botanical life is composed of the myriad elements and minerals which characterize the inanimate world. But to complete their own deca-*Sefirotic* dipoles plants are endowed with novel *G"R* providing life-affirming properties of cellular growth and reproduction, an emergent (revealed) form of consciousness unavailable to the *Domem* class. As outlined in Section 5.2, the 'bottom' *Sefirot*, *Netzach-Hod-Yesod* and *Malchut* of a given entity are incorporated (*Hitlabshut*) as the *Chochmah-Binah-Da'at* and *Keter* of the entity immediately 'below'. In this model consciousness is patently relativistic as the very same *Sefirot* which mediate consciousness (as *Mochin*) when part of an isolated mineral are concomitantly unconscious (a component of the 'bodily' *Z"T*) when the mineral is a constituent of a tree. In his opus *Mei Hashiloach* the Izhbitzer Rebbe alludes to this relationship with the following remark:[229,230] שהדומם מכניס כחו בצומח וצומח בחי וחי במדבר "... that the *Domem* (inanimate) class inserts its 'strength' within the *Tzomeach* (plant) domain, and the

Tzomeach (plant) within the *Chaye* (animal) domain and the *Chaye* (animal) within the *M'daber* (human)." In 1990, physicist David Bohm expressed a strikingly parallel conviction that "each mental side (of every physical-mental dipole) becomes a physical side as we move in the direction of greater subtlety."[231] The Kabbalah is quite clear on why this should transpire: Recall from Section 4.2 that while the seven lower 'bodily' Vessels of the primordial World of *Atzilut* 'shattered' (*Shvirat Hakelim*), the top three Vessels mediating 'consciousness' remained intact. This ensured that while the 'body' of every deca-*Sefirotic* system may consist of innumerable parts, consciousness only manifests as a unified whole... with lower 'mineral-consciousness' eclipsed (rendered implicate) by higher 'plant-consciousness' in the case of a tree.

It is important at this juncture to take stock of the fact that the foregoing description of 'relativistic' consciousness is accurate solely from the 'vertical' or bottom-up perspective of *Orech* (Section 4.4). It is only from this reference frame that we can speak of the 'emergence' of 'novel' *G"R* (consciousness) in transitioning from the category of inanimate objects (*Domem*) to botanical life (*Tzomeach*). Viewed from the holistic, 'horizontal' perspective of *Oivi* (Section 4.4) and the holographic principle of Interinclusion (*Hitkallelut*; Section 4.3), the sum total of consciousness is omnipresent but differentially concealed in all branches of the Creation. In this light the appearance of 'new' *G"R* in plants manifesting as growth and reproduction is but the partial *revelation* of the totality of consciousness latent ('hidden') within the inanimate world (see Section 4.3). In Bohm-speak (Chapter 3) we might say that properties of growth and propagation which are concealed in the Implicate Order unifying all of existence (the holomovement) are 'unfolded' and rendered explicate in biological organisms.

Returning now to the consciousness hierarchy we see that an identical dynamic holds when ascending from *Tzomeach* (plant life) to *Chaye* (animal life). The entire deca-*Sefirotic* *G"R-Z"T* ('three top-seven bottom') span of the plant is compressed as the *Z"T* ('seven bottom') of the animal and the latter is bestowed with new *G"R* ('three top') conveying unprecedented animal consciousness. The capacities for growth and reproduction empowered by the conscious *G"R* of the plant persist within the animal kingdom but are subsumed within compactified *Z"T* which relative to the new *G"R* are unconscious. The novel (newly-revealed) *Mochin* confer sentience, emotion and other neurological/behavioral features to the animal not observed in plants.

Upgrading from *Chaye* to *M'daber*, the ten *Sefirot* of animal life are compressed as the *Z"T* of humans and endow us with a broad spectrum of animalistic traits. These *Z"T* mediate the physiological and psychological functions necessary for human survival and are roughly equivalent to the *Nefesh Ha'bahamit* or lower, 'animal Soul' described in the seminal Chassidic work, the *Tanya*.[232,233] Superimposed on these *Z"T* and completing the deca-*Sefirotic* system are novel (newly revealed) *G"R* which confer attributes of language, reason, self-consciousness, morality, free will and creativity unique to our species. Implemented appropriately (i.e. according to Torah Law) this higher level of consciousness expresses the *Nefesh Ha'Elokit* or Godly Soul which subjugates the Animal Soul (*Nefesh Ha'bahamit*) thereby channeling Divinity into the lowermost realms.[232,233]

The above can be understood mechanistically and the role of humankind in Creation intuited when we consider the aforementioned homologues (*Kinuim*) of *M'daber* (Table 3): The domain *M'daber* (humankind) maps onto the *Chaya* component of the Soul, the *Partzuf Abba*, the *Sefirah Chochmah* and the World of *Atzilut*. In contradistinction to the lower Worlds of *Briah-Yetzirah-Asiyah* (*Kinuim* of animals, plants and inanimate objects, respectively) which represent progressively diminishing reflections (*Ha'orah*) of Godliness, the World of *Atzilut* is

Godliness itself. Hence, humans but not other forms of life were created in God's image (*B'tzelem Elokim*[62]) and tasked with consciously preparing the Earth for Divine rule.

The association of *M'daber* with the *Sefirah Chochmah* provides further insight into the special nature of human consciousness. Among the *Sefirot*, *Chochmah* is the paradoxical interface between the infinite, transcendent Light of *Keter* (*Ohr Makif*) and the finite realm (immanent *Ohr Pnimi*) of the Kabbalistic causal hierarchy (*Seder Hishtalshelut*). Just as the *Sefirah Chochmah* arises *ex nihilo* (*Yesh M'ayin*) from *Keter* (termed *Ayin*, 'nothingness'[234]), so do spontaneous and creative ideas ('eureka! moments') arise in the human mind as if out of nowhere. Cosmologically, *Chochmah* appears as a singularity—a unified, infinitesimal whole devoid of any form or structure yet encapsulating all facets of reality destined to erupt forth. As such, *Chochmah* relates to (is a *Kinui* of) the World of *Atzilut* which as mentioned above is absolute Godliness (*Elokut*). The 'drop' from *Chochmah* into *Binah* (the *Sefirah* homologue of the World *Briah*) is the origin of separateness (*Pirud*), space-time and the possibility of Evil. *Ergo*, by virtue of its affiliation with *Chochmah* human consciousness is well poised to propel the world into higher states of unification, transcend time and space (e.g. prophecy) and aspire to righteousness.

The link (*Kinui*) between human consciousness and the *Chaya* component of the Soul is equally intriguing: The three lower aspects of Soul, the *Nefesh*, *Ruach* and *Neshama*, relate to the domains of *Domem*, *Tzomeach* and *Chaye* as immanent projections (*Ohr Pnimi*). The *Neshama* capably bestows animal life with sentience. Manifesting as an *Ohr Pnimi* (Immanent Light) within the confines of the body (*n.b.* the *Leshem* describes a transcendent dimension to the *Neshama*[235] which need not concern us here), the *Neshama* component confers awareness but largely precludes *self*-awareness. Not so the *Chaya* component which links most specifically to the human Soul and was deemed necessary for the creation of Adam.[236] Unlike the three lower aspects of Soul, the *Chaya* is a 'local' Transcendent Light (*Ohr Makif*) that oscillates (a process designated *Mati V'lo Mati*[134]) between the outside and inside of the Vessel (*Keli*) or body. The immanent phase (*Mati*) confers awareness or consciousness akin to the outcome of the *Neshama-Chaye* (animal domain) association. The transcendent phase (*Lo Mati*) of the oscillation 'observes' the awareness generated by the immanent phase yielding *self*-awareness or *self*-consciousness, a characteristic fairly unique to humans and possibly several nonhuman species.[32,237] For those who regard quantum wave function collapse as the *sine qua non* or very definition of consciousness,[238] *self*-awareness may be a natural consequence of the transcendent *Chaya* 'observing' and concretizing its own immanent (*Pnimi*) phase.

The biography of Sigmund Freud offers an oblique but illustrative example of this *Mati V'lo Mati* conjecture: Freud partly credited his penetrating analysis of the human psyche to anti-Semitism which prevented him from establishing a 'comfort zone' among Vienna's professional elite. By weaving inside (*Mati*) and outside (*Lo Mati*) his guild, Freud felt he could engage his work to advantage with a level of detached objectivity and introspection denied to his Gentile colleagues.[239]

From the above considerations we see that humans are endowed not only with a highly sophisticated form of consciousness but also with a level of *self*-awareness fairly unique in the known universe. Allen Afterman reminds us that despite our sense of personal unity "ordinary awareness cannot grasp the undivided oneness of reality... The mind's rational and analytic powers break unities into dichotomies, and then into sub-concepts and elements",[240] a perceptual 'limitation' also firmly underlined by David Bohm.[161]

Why should there be this 'disconnect' between our perception of self and surround? We learned in Chapter 4 that consciousness is always experienced as a unity because, in contradistinction to the seven 'bodily' *Sefirot* (the *Z"T*), the three top *Sefirot* conveying 'consciousness' (the *G"R* or *Mochin*) 'fell' in the primordial World of *Atzilut* but did not 'shatter'. At the same time, the principle of Interinclusion (*Hitkallelut*) described in Section 4.3 informs us that true to their fractal nature, the 'mindful' top *Sefirot* are each composed of ten mini-*Sefirot* (Fig. 10) of which the seven lower ones are by definition 'bodily'. The latter, although part and parcel of the 'big three' conscious *Sefirot*, 'broke' during the Shattering of the Vessels (*Shvirah*) along with the seven *general* 'bodily' *Sefirot* (Section 4.2). This has two important ramifications operating in parallel: (i) We experience our personality and consciousness as fully integrated because the overarching three top *Sefirot* (the *G"R*) remained intact and (ii) we fail to assimilate within our consciousness the unity underlying the rest of existence (Bohm's holomovement) because the iterative seven lower ('bodily') mini-*Sefirot* contained within each of the general *G"R* shattered. The latter may well be responsible for our strong tendency to perceive the world through the 'fractured' lens of *Orech* rather than the holistic one of *Oivi* (Section 4.4).

According to the *Ramchal*, even the unicity of consciousness can be considered in starkly relativistic terms. A major theme taken up by authors of many pivotal Kabbalistic and Chassidic texts (e.g. the monumental *B'Shaa Shehikdimu* by the fifth Lubavitcher Rebbe[115]) concerns the subtle, often paradoxical, relationships of finite parts (*Pratim*) to the infinite whole (*Klal*) and of heterogeneous *Sefirot* to the singular *Ohr Ein-Sof*. Germane to the notion of consciousness the *Ramchal* in his classic work *Klach Pitchei Chochmah*[108] elaborates on the sequential 'flow' of Divine consciousness after the *Tzimtzum* ('Contraction', Section 4.2) from the surrounding *Ohr Ein-Sof* to the proto-Vessels of the *Reshimu* (residual Light after the First Withdrawal) within the Primordial Void (*Makom Panoi*): (i) The Ray (*Kav*) projected by the transcendent *Ohr Ein-Sof* into the Void is the source of consciousness intended to vivify and actualize all future Vessels

(*Kelim*) fated to emerge from the *Reshimu*. (ii) The Ray like its source in the *Ohr Ein-Sof* is an absolutely undifferentiated Light (*Ohr Pashut*). In this sublimely unified state it would overwhelm and fail to actualize the specific potential of any limited Vessel receiving its Light. To circumvent this conundrum (iii) the Light of the Ray is enclothed (*Hitlabshut*, Section 4.3) within *Mochin*, the conscious *G"R* ('top three') of all deca-*Sefirotic* dipoles (Chapter 5). In contrast to the invariant Ray, the *Mochin* vary qualitatively among the myriad Vessels (*Sefirot*) and quantitatively within any given receptacle as a function of state. As such, the *Mochin* are ideally poised to interact effectively with each Vessel according to the latter's unique constitution while simultaneously delivering to each recipient the interiorized, undifferentiated Ray (*Kav*). The *Ramchal* thus refers to the *Mochin* ('Brains') as the *Neshama* (Soul) of the Vessels, and the *Kav* as the *Neshama* of the *Mochin* or *Neshama*-of-the-*Neshama* (Soul-of-the-Soul) of the Vessels.[241] The relativistic nature of this arrangement is such that the *Mochin* are for all intents and purposes unified (*Klal*) with respect to the Vessels they 'inhabit', but differentiated (*Pratim*) *vis-à-vis* the Ray (*Kav*).

An identical scheme captures the relationship between human body and Soul: Undifferentiated Light of the Ray emanating seamlessly from the *Ohr Ein-Sof* must be ensheathed by the *Neshama* (Soul) in order to vivify and operate appropriately within each organ and limb of the body. Thus do the Souls—but not the underlying Ray—differ from one person to the next. Relative to the body, the Soul is a unified whole—we don't compartmentalize our 'selves' to move muscle while digesting food; and the pain of a stubbed toe albeit localizable in space and time is experienced holistically by the entire person. Yet, contrasted with the pure Light of the Ray enclothed within (the *Neshama*-of-the-*Neshama*), Souls vary in their proclivities, sensitivities, idiosyncrasies and revealed degrees of Holiness.[241] Two additional analogies which may help drive home the

relativistic nature of Kabbalistic panpsychism are presented in
Box 1.

Box 1. The relativistic nature of Kabbalistic panpsychism.

Analogy 1: The Kabbalistic perspective on relativistic consciousness can be analogized in reference to Einstein's Special Theory of Relativity. Set velocity of the observer proportional to the complexity of the creature's consciousness. Let *Domem* consciousness, the lowest level, equal space-time as perceived by an observer at rest. Just as space contracts and the passage of time slows as a function of increasing velocity, so lesser consciousnesses are diminished and recede from view in the presence of more advanced consciousness. Thus, akin to contracting space-time experienced by an observer accelerating to half the speed of light relative to a stationary observer, the proto-consciousness of an isolated mineral (*Domem*) is obscured by the supervening consciousness associated with growth and reproduction when the mineral is absorbed within the biomass of a plant (*Tzomeach*). In turn, the growth properties previously defining plant consciousness are demoted to the non-conscious $Z"T$ (seven bottom *Sefirot*) of animals (*Chaye*) in the face of novel animal sentience, the new $G"R$ (three top *Sefirot*). Given the homologues (*Kinuim*) of humankind (*M'daber*) to the World of *Atzilut/Sefirah Chochmah* and the latter's transcendence of space-time, our analogy to Special Relativity would conflate human self-awareness with light speed, collapsing space-time to a point (relative to the observer at rest) and eclipsing all consciousness associated with the inferior realms. Beyond self-awareness is a future

---

Cosmic consciousness, an all-encompassing $G''R$-$Z''T$ dipole mapping to the supernal World of $A''K$, the *Sefirah Keter* and the *Yechida* aspect of Soul. In this sublime state supraluminal velocities, non-locality and time reversals invoked by our analogy would render utterly imperceptible, or even call into question, the existence of individual consciousness (human or otherwise). Chapter 13 elaborates further on this point.

Analogy 2: Consider two individuals sparring. Take Bob's lack of training in physical combat technique to represent a creature possessing a low form of consciousness. Let Alice's martial skills as a seventh dan black belt in karate denote a being with advanced consciousness. Not unlike the relative experience of space-time in *Analogy 1*, a punch moving at velocity V thrown by Bob is perceived by Alice as near-frozen in time and is easily side-stepped. Bob, unfortunately, is unable to fend off Alice's identical retaliatory strike which, from his perspective, took virtually no time to find its target.

In this section we observed the hierarchical and relativistic organization of consciousness across the four specified domains of physical being: the inanimate (*Domem*), plant (*Tzomeach*), animal (*Chaye*) and human (*M'daber*). The holographic principle of Interinclusion (*Hitkallelut*) teaches that each domain has within it representations of all the others. Of course within *Domem*, e.g. a rock, the 'higher' manifestations of plant, animal and human consciousness are entirely concealed (Bohm would say 'implicate') and virtually undetectable from the mundane perspective of *Orech* (*Section* 4.4). In contrast, aspects of 'lower-echelon' consciousness are revealed (rendered 'explicate') in creatures occupying upper rungs of the Creation hierarchy.

Thus are archetypes of mineral-like existence, plant-like growth and animalistic drives readily recognizable within humankind. The various gradations of consciousness are not only reflected in humankind but evidence of their hierarchical arrangement is retained, at least symbolically. The Kabbalah 'assigns' the three immanent phases of the Soul, the *Neshama* (representing animal consciousness), the *Ruach* (equivalent to plant consciousness) and the *Nefesh* (dual to mineral consciousness), respectively to the left side of the brain, the thorax (heart and lungs) and the liver.[242] Man's erect stature brings these three dimensions of Soul into vertical alignment with the *Neshama* 'atop' or superceding the *Ruach* and the *Ruach* overriding the *Nefesh*. Note also the progressive diminution of voluntary control, an instantiation of the will, as one descends from the head to the abdomen: the brain housing the *Neshama* thinks and decides epitomizing higher consciousness; breathing accomplished by the lungs embodying the *Ruach* is partly voluntary (conscious) and partly involuntary (unconscious); and the abdominal viscera (including the liver, abode of the *Nefesh*) are digestive organs mainly under autonomic nervous system and hormonal control which are almost entirely unconscious. This scheme does not consider the *Chaya* and *Yechida* aspects of Soul. Although associated with the right hemisphere of the brain, the *Chaya* is an oscillating *Ohr Makif* (partially-transcendent Light) which cannot be fully sequestered within a bodily organ. All the more so the *Yechida* which is isomorphic with the *Sefirah Keter* and is categorically transcendent.[243]

5.3 Are Golems Conscious?

In Section 5.2 I outlined four major classes of physical being recognized by the Torah—the inanimate, plant life, animal life and humankind—and demonstrated a hierarchical and relativistic ontology Kabbalistic panpsychism ascribes to the revelation of consciousness among these groups. But these are at best general categories and there exist 'intermediate' forms and 'outliers' whose consciousness defies simple classification. For example, although he did not comment on consciousness *per se* the eighteenth century Chassidic master, R' Pinchas Shapira of Koretz, considered *'adanei sadeh'* (an organism described in Midrashic sources that was tethered to the ground by a cord) to be part-plant/part-animal and the apes as 'transitional' between animals and humans.[244] How consciousness is expressed in these 'inter-grades' is unclear in so far as they cannot be easily pigeon-holed within the above classification scheme.

Perhaps even more intriguing and relevant to ongoing controversy around artificial intelligence (AI) is the nature of consciousness, if any, in the ersatz 'life form' known as the Golem (Fig. 14). The term Golem derives from the Hebrew word, גלמי *(Galmi)*, which first appears in the Book of Psalms[245] and connotes something imperfect or unformed. Surfacing time and again over the long course of Jewish history, the Golem is essentially a humanoid (usually male) derived from clay or mud (sometimes wood) which was brought to 'life' by means of sacred incantations (combinations of the various Names of God) originating with the primordial Kabbalistic text, *Sefer Yetzirah* (The Book of Creation),[246] and recited by individuals versed in the mystical arts.

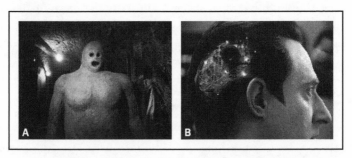

Figure 14. Artificial Life Forms. A. The Golem of Prague (Shutterstock). **B. Lt. Commander Data with positronic brain exposed** (*Star Trek: The Next Generation*, Paramount Domestic Television).

The creature's purpose was most often to protect Jewish communities from persecution, as was the case for the famous Golem conjured by Rabbi Yehuda Loew (the 'Maharal of Prague'; 1512-1609), although some served as domestic laborers or even concubines!

But are Golems conscious? The trivial panpsychist response is 'sure', on par with everything else. We've seen how the Kabbalah understands all things and events to consist of ten *Sefirot* of which the first three, *Keter-Chochmah-Binah* or *Chochmah-Binah-Da'at*, confer consciousness. But what level consciousness are we talking about in the case of Golems? *Domem* (inanimate existence)? *Tzomeach* (plant growth)? *Chaye* (animal sentience)? *M'daber* (self-awareness)? Rabbinic discourse in Talmudic and other sources assist us in narrowing the range of possibilities. The deliberations may be ancient but the concerns raised and conclusions drawn are starkly relevant to modern debate surrounding robotics and AI.[247] First and foremost: Is the Golem, and by extension sophisticated androids, cyborgs and automatons, ever sufficiently human (*M'daber*) to warrant protection by basic human rights? Although still the stuff of science fiction when it comes to robots (see *Star Trek*'s Data (Fig. 14) and the 2015-2018 television series, *Humans*), it is not uncommon for animal activists and others to pose challenges along these lines regarding highly sentient organisms like dolphins and chimpanzees. There is fair Rabbinic consensus, if not unanimity, that despite its outward appearance and anthropoid behavior the Golem is *not* human and therefore undeserving of any special moral or legal dispensations. Most Golems apparently understood simple commands (which some 'chose' to disobey[248]) but could not speak.[249] The latter cannot be relied on in isolation to ascertain whether Golems are or are not human. Although the Hebrew term for 'speaker', *M'daber*, is used with reference to people, it is not the sole arbiter of the designation 'human' (see also Section 5.5). Parrots after all speak and some people are unfortunately mute. The Torah defines 'human' as someone 'born of woman'[250,251] clearly disqualifying the Golem and with the same brush Frankenstein's monster[252] and any AI regardless of their performance on the Turing test or other measures of sapience.[253] The Talmud informs us that a Golem is not tallied in the assembly of a *Minyan* (quorum of ten men required for Jewish public worship). Neither does destruction of a Golem constitute a capital offense because only one who intentionally kills a person 'formed within another human being' is liable for murder.[254] This latter definition is tantamount to insistence on a natural biological origin and should not be taken literally. It would certainly not, for example, absolve one of homicide in cases where the victim was a cloned human being or whose embryonic and fetal ontogeny transpired entirely *ex utero*—hypothetical situations today perhaps but plausible scenarios in the not-too-distant future.

Several prominent adjudicators[255,256] citing Kabbalistic texts[257,258] opined that whereas only God can endow persons with human Souls, the power of the *Sefer Yetzirah* wielded appropriately may sustain Golem consciousness at the level of an animal Soul (*Chaye*). This may have several significant ramifications in Jewish law (*Halachah*) regarding 'Golem rights' and by extrapolation how we might ideally interact with sentient AI in a futuristic society. If human beings indeed have the wherewithal to create Golems with animal-like consciousness, then this knowledge or skill may carry over to the development of our most advanced robotics. *Ergo*, Jewish legislation concerning the treatment of animals may be a useful guide to our, some would say inevitable, interactions with sentient AI. Relevant injunctions to consider are *'Eiver Min Ha'chai'* —the prohibition against consuming the flesh of a limb torn from a living animal[259]—and *'Tzaar Ba'alei Chaim'* —the command against causing unnecessary suffering to animals.[260] That the latter entails not only physical but also emotional anguish is made clear by additional prohibitions against removing eggs or chicks from a nest in the presence of the mother bird ('*Shiluach Hakan*'[261]) and the yoking together of beasts of burden of unequal strength.[262]

Whether teaching by experience or allegory (as the Torah is wont to do) the Golem lore cautions that we should not dismiss out-of-hand the possibility that artificial neural nets (be they electronic, positronic or something beyond our current imagination) may one day confer to machines a sense of what it is like to feel pain, joy or frustration—qualia shared by many nonhuman species as any dog owner will attest to. If this proves to be true it would behoove us at the very least to treat any potentially sentient products of our own design with the same sensitivity and respect we courteously afford our most cherished life forms.

5.4 Human Brain Organoids

In the previous section, we explored some of the ethical concerns surrounding our burgeoning relationship with AI and suggested possible approaches to the matter based on a Kabbalistic understanding of Golem consciousness. But situations may be envisioned where, barring any obvious precedent or analogy in Torah scholarship, novel configurations of biology and consciousness may utterly defy preconceived schemes at classification. Absent the latter, it may prove difficult or impossible to properly foresee and safely navigate the ethical byways that will inevitably accompany such developments. The advent of human brain organoids in 2008 is a fine case in point. Scientists are now capable of generating pea-sized clumps of human embryonic cerebral tissue which can be studied for weeks at a time in culture dishes or after transplantation into living rodent brains. Remarkably, the stems cells within cortical organoids differentiate into mature neurons which elaborate various neurotransmitters and their receptors, establish highly intricate synaptic networks and, albeit the source of much controversy, exhibit electrical activity (brain waves) likened to patterns recorded from human newborn babies![263]

Few doubt the potential of such organoids to provide vital information concerning normal brain embryology and function. A number of laboratories are already engaging cerebral organoids to study human neurodevelopmental conditions such as autism, schizophrenia and microcephaly (small head and brain) resulting from Zika virus infection.[263] But alarms have been sounded to ensure that the science does not outpace the stark moral obligations demanded by this line of inquiry. The overarching worry here is: given rapid refinements in the field, will human cerebral organoids achieve sentience either *in vitro* or after implantation and integration within host animal brains? Are there limits to the complexity of consciousness such organoids may attain? Were they to experience pain and suffering might not such experimentation be tantamount to torture? These concerns would be the same regardless of whether the organoids generate consciousness *de novo* in the physicalist sense or whether they channel consciousness—antenna-like— from an über-conscious surround as inferred by the Kabbalah and other panpsychist positions. Prudently, sophisticated bioethics consortia have been assembled in the United States and elsewhere to address these reservations moving forward. But until consciousness can be effectively 'diagnosed', quantified and monitored in brain organoids and chimeras, a healthy dose of caution should remain *de rigueur*.

5.5 *Chaya* Consciousness and the Tower of Babel

In Section 5.3 I drew evidence from Kabbalistic and Rabbinic sources that Golems and androids may attain levels of consciousness on par with animal sentience (*Chaye*) and that it may be reasonable therefore to afford such beings legal rights commensurate with that stature. Governments the world over enact far more stringent laws to protect the rights and well-being of humans reflecting a widespread belief in the special sanctity of the human condition above and beyond the rest of Creation. If we truly feel that way, why do we treat each other so poorly? Why is our history littered with relentless bloodshed and self-inflicted suffering? What compels us to "imbibe racism and xenophobia with our mother's milk" as Yitzhak Shamir, former prime minister of Israel, graphically intimated? One could surmise that inferior education and cultural deprivation are to blame, but then one would be wrong. The unspeakable brutality of ancient Rome and Nazi Germany, nations steeped in the arts and sciences of their time, makes short shrift of that theory. We may never delineate a 'root cause' for this malevolent side to our nature.

An analysis of the Tower of Babel narrative in light of humanity's 'position' within Kabbalah's consciousness hierarchy offers an interesting perspective. According to Biblical tradition all of humanity repopulated after the Great Flood[264] shared a single language. After migrating to the land of Shinar (Babylonia) humanity arrogantly challenged God's supremacy with the symbolic construction of a city boasting a 'tower reaching Heaven', the Tower of Babel.[265] God confounded their plan by introducing a multiplicity of languages to stymie their ability to communicate effectively and by dispersing them over the face of the globe.

That humans at the Tower of Babel were simply limited in their ability to understand their neighbors' spoken word may be too narrow a reading of Scripture. Indeed, the relevant verse in Genesis 11:1 states: ויהי כל־הארץ שפה אחת ודברים אחדים Many authoritative sources, both Jewish and Christian, translate the passage along the lines of "Now the whole Earth had one language and one speech (or vocabulary)".[266] The phrase 'one language and one speech (or vocabulary)' in this context seems redundant or nearly so. I find more tantalizing the minority renderings of **ודברים אחדים** as 'united matters, causes or purpose'[266,267] which allude to commonalities of disposition, mindset and practice among the inhabitants of Shinar beyond language. Divine interference with these latter characteristics, in addition to or as a result of language diversification, would certainly have the desired effect of thwarting the people's rebellion. I submit that the breakdown of linguistic communication and social harmony experienced at the Tower of Babel, and its dire repercussions throughout human history, can be metaphysically traced to a 'flaw' or 'demotion' in *Chaya*-level consciousness.

As detailed above, humankind is classified as *M'daber* ('speaker'), the loftiest of the four domains of Creation. But the category *M'daber* encompasses a set of unique traits apart from mere speech. *M'daber* corresponds to the *Chaya* component of Soul which, on account of its partially transcendent nature (an oscillating *Ohr Makif*), endows human beings with an unprecedented degree of *self*-awareness (Section 5.2). Pre-Babel humanity was able to confront God in unison because they shared identical self-perceptions and cause in addition to a common language. God disrupted their ability to communicate by diversifying not only language but the content and meaning of subjective experience. While maintaining their capacity for introspection, individuals could no longer fathom the impact of qualia on the psyche and ethos of others.

By singling out speech the Torah informs that the 'disruption' specifically affected the aspect of Soul (*Chaya*) unique to the *M'daber* ('speaker') domain. As the *Nefesh* corresponding to inanimate matter—the lowest level of Soul—was spared, post-Babel Bob had no difficulty identifying with the physical nature of Alice's existence—he understood that her flesh and blood were no different than his own. Neither was there any 'disconnect' at the level of the plant-like *Ruach* aspect of Soul— the phenomena of biological growth and development were appreciated equally by all. Similarly, the animalistic traits, basic cognition and raw emotions attributed to the *Neshama* component of Soul—isomorphic to animal sentience—could still be accurately discerned in others by observing the behavioral correlates of such sentience. In other words, interpersonal dynamics generally connoted by the terms 'empathy' and 'theory-of-mind'[268] persisted.

But a very different picture emerged with the variegation of *Chaya* consciousness. For now Bob and Alice could no longer intuit the nuances and psychosocial impact of each other's subjective experiences. Common cause started disintegrating as the symbolic meaning of events diverged and minds began growing apart. Individuals could now have overt and hidden enemies as readily as friends; furtive competitors alongside trustworthy allies. It is easy to envision how misinterpretations of the 'inner stirrings' of our compatriots and blindness as to their motives might engender suspicion, misapprehension and fear. The latter would, in turn, devolve to alienation, misanthropy, racism, xenophobia and, in worst cases, persecution and genocide. The wide dispersion of humankind after the Tower of Babel incident[265] would exacerbate the polarizations within civilization by deepening ethno-cultural fault lines and facilitating the proliferation of irreconcilable beliefs, communication strategies and social mores. The Judeo-Christian tradition intimates that this sorry geopolitics will persist until the coming of the Messiah. According to the Kabbalah's timeline the advent of the Seventh (Messianic) Millennium will spur a dramatic transition from *Chaya*-consciousness to *Yechida*, or 'cosmic', consciousness when the psychological and social barriers separating us from one another and from the rest of Creation will begin to dissolve. Implications of this future 'enlightened' state of affairs are discussed further in Chapters 12 and 13.

In this and the previous chapter I attempted to assemble a

cogent framework of Kabbalistic principles germane to the understanding of consciousness from the Jewish mystical perspective. Many of the concepts elaborated are of a significantly general nature providing a flavor for Kabbalistic reasoning with wide applicability beyond the consciousness problem. Scant or no attention was paid here to many additional topics central to Kabbalistic doctrine but of lesser relevance to the phenomenon of consciousness. Among the latter are the 'inhabitants' of the five Worlds (*Adam Kadmon* and *ABY"A*), the 'embryology', 'anatomy' and 'physiology' of the various *Partzufim* within each World, the *Heichalot* ('Celestial Palaces'), the *Maaseh Merkavah ('Account of the Chariot'), the ten Angel castes (Kitot Hamalachim)* and the *Sitra Achra* ('Side of Unholiness'). Albeit relevant to the topic of consciousness I felt that Jewish mystical teachings concerning the transmigration of Souls (*Gilgulei Haneshamot*) were overly esoteric and best treated under separate cover. Interested readers can learn more about these subjects by consulting the classical mystical texts, e.g.[108,111,113,114,134,139,269] or compendia on this material published by modern-day scholars including Gershom Scholem,[270,271] Aryeh Kaplan,[246,272] Moshe Idel,[273,274] Daniel Matt,[275,276] Jonathan Garb[277] and Joseph Dan.[278]

The principles of Kabbalistic panpsychism delineated thus far in this volume will, in the forthcoming chapters, serve as a foundation or scaffold for exploring discrete facets of consciousness as they relate to female intuition, prophecy, free will, clinical states of altered awareness and process philosophy.

Chapter 6

Female Intuition

'Intuition' has been defined as "the ability to understand something instinctively without the need for conscious reasoning". The term is roughly synonymous with a hunch, a feeling, an inkling, an impression or a suspicion. In Late Middle English it signified in a narrower sense (but *apropos* to the current thesis) "spiritual insight or immediate spiritual communication".[26] 'Female intuition' implies a set of cognitive and neuropsychological characteristics considered to be more developed, on average, in women than men. It generally entails a heightened sense of empathy, attunement to nonverbal cues, interpretation of facial expressions, body gestures and prosody and theory-of-mind.[279] It has been argued in some scientific circles that women evolved sharpened instincts along these lines to better protect themselves and offspring traditionally in their care from potential threats.[280]

The Lurianic Kabbalah amply acknowledges these unique female traits and elaborates a cogent metaphysic to explain them. At the heart of this knowledge is the *Keter-Malchut* axis alluded to in Chapter 6. Recall that *Keter* is the supernal *Sefirah* of any deca-*Sefirotic* system, a *Sefirah* encompassing the Will of God (*Ratzon Elyon*) antecedent to the faintest hint of intellection (which originates in the *Sefirah Chochmah*) or emotion (*Chesed* and 'below'). Viewed from our perspective *Keter* has no Vessel (*Keli*), it *surrounds* the system under consideration as a transcendent Light (*Ohr Makif*) implied by its name ('Crown'). At the very 'bottom' of the Tree of Life is the *Sefirah Malchut*. It is the ultimate Vessel representing the Divine Feminine (*Partzuf Nukvah*) which receives the effulgence of immanent Light (*Ohr Pnimi*) cascading down in sequence from *Chochmah* via the intervening *Sefirot* to *Yesod* (see Fig. 3B). Concomitantly and in contradistinction to the other *Sefirot*, a direct pipeline between the surrounding Light of *Keter* and *Malchut* bypasses the entire Kabbalistic hierarchy (*Seder Hishtalshelut*) to influence *Malchut*.[206] Whereas the immanent Light (*Ohr Pnimi*) descending from *Chochmah* through *Yesod* vivifies and empowers *Malchut*, the transcendent Light (*Ohr Makif*) of *Keter* ensures that the final 'product' or outcome of the cascade conforms perfectly to the Will of God (*Ratzon Elyon*)[281] in fulfilment of the verses, סוף מעשה במחשבה תחילה 'Last in deed, first conceived' (Sabbath liturgy) and נעוץ סופן בתחילתן ותחילתן בסופן 'the end is wedged in the beginning, and the beginning in the end'.[282] A 'technical' metaphysical foundation for the *Keter-Malchut* axis is outlined in Section 6.1.

Women, as the human counterpart of *Malchut/Nukvah*, are an ultimate Vessel (*Keli*) similarly 'connected' to *Keter* and influenced by its surrounding Light. Inasmuch as *Keter* irradiates from 'outside the system' the intuition it provides women is transpersonal, instinctual and often subliminal—a "spiritual insight or immediate spiritual communication."[26] Direct links between *Keter* and the other (donor/masculine) *Sefirot* do not exist as such and so the intuitive acumen of men may often appear wanting relative to that of women—hence God's admonition that Abraham best heed his wife Sarah's voice.[283] For more in-depth analysis of the Divine Feminine, Moshe Idel's *The Privileged Status of the Divine Feminine in Theosophical-theurgical Kabbalah*[274] and Sarah Y. Schneider's *Kabbalistic Writings on the Nature of Masculine & Feminine*[192] are recommended.

6.1 Ontology of the *Keter-Malchut* axis

Insight into the function and significance of the *Keter-Malchut* axis can be attained by considering its metaphysical origin in the course of Creation. The latter can be conceptualized in the following series of 'stages':[108,134]

Stage 1: The Infinite Light of God (*Ohr Ein-Sof*) pervades all (*Hitpashtut-Rishon*, First Expansion) and is signified by the loftiest numerical name of God, *Ayin-Bet*. (The derivations of these numerical Names are unimportant for present purposes and are elucidated throughout the classical Kabbalistic literature.)

Stage 2: In a process referred to as the *Tzimtzum* (Contraction or Retraction), the *Ohr Ein-Sof* pulls away (*Histalkut-Rishon*, First Withdrawal) from a 'central point' establishing the Primordial Void (*Makom Panoi*); the latter is destined to harbor the five Worlds of Creation (*Adam Kadmon* and *ABY"A*). A residue of the receding *Ohr Ein-Sof* termed the *Reshimu* remains within the interior of the Void (Chapter 4). Absent this *Reshimu*, the surrounding *Ohr Ein-Sof* is now represented by the next-to-highest numerical name of God, *Samech-Gimel*.

Stage 3: From the surrounding *Ohr Ein-Sof* a thin Ray (*Kav*) of Godliness penetrates the Void (*Hitpashtut-Sheni,* Second Expansion). As a diminutive of the surrounding Light (*Samech-Gimel*), the *Kav* assumes a 3rd numerical name of God, *Mem-Heh*. Upon entering the Void, the Ray combines with the *Reshimu*. From this union (*Zivug*) are 'born' the ten *Sefirot* which are to assemble into the *Partzufim* of the first World *Adam Kadmon*. The Ray (*Kav*) is the precursor and sum total of all the Light (*Ohr*) 'pumped' into the Void and distributed to the entire fractal infrastructure of the Creation.

While the Ray serves as the ultimate 'donor' (masculine) within the Void, the *Reshimu* is the quintessential *Malchut* or *Nukvah*—the precursor and totality of the myriad Vessels (*Kelim*) which contain the Light parsed to each and every *Sefirah, Partzuf* and World. As passive recipient of the incoming Ray the *Reshimu* is designated the fourth and 'lowest' of the names of God, *Bet-Nun*. Thus, throughout the Creation (until the Seventh Millennium), *Malchut/Nukvah* (the Divine Feminine) occupies the 'lowest' rung of the Kabbalistic hierarchy (*Seder Hishtalshelut*) in subservience to the 'upper' (donor or masculine) *Sefirot*. The actualization of this relationship in our world is captured by the verse ואל אישך תשוקתך והוא ימשל בך "Your desire shall be your husband, and he shall rule over you".[284] But lest male readers wax overly smug on this point, note that the *Reshimu* has its *source* in *Histalkut-Rishon* (First Withdrawal) on par with the name *Samech-Gimel*, an encompassing Light that transcends the Void (*Makom Panoi*) in its entirety. The *Malchut/Nukvah* manifesting *within* the Creation as the 'lower' name *Bet-Nun* never severs its link with its origin '*outside the system*' in the Light of the name *Samech-Gimel*. The latter is the transcendent *Sefirah* of *Keter* relative to the Light within the Void. Thus, the *source* of *Malchut* (in *Keter*) is 'higher' than the Immanent Lights (*Ohr Pnimi*) cascading down the Kabbalistic hierarchy (*Seder Hishtalshelut*) from *Chochmah* to *Malchut*![285] It is for this reason that the Vessel (*Keli*) of *Malchut/Nukvah* can sequester the superior masculine Lights without 'shattering'. It is also the mechanism which establishes the immutable *Keter-Malchut* bond responsible for (i) guiding the unfolding Creation (transduced by *Malchut*) in strict accord with Divine Intent (*Keter*), (ii) imbuing all facets of the Creation—each speck of dust, every moment of time—with immeasurable vitality and purpose[202] and (iii) the mystery of transcendent female intuition. Indeed, the *Halachic* (legal) principle exempting Jewish women from time-bound positive commandments[286] may hint at this special *Keter-Malchut* connection inasmuch as *Keter* transcends space-time which only materializes upon transition from the *Chochmah* 'singularity' to *Binah*.

Parenthetically, I have heard some Jewish women take umbrage that their pronouncement of the *Shacharit* (Morning Liturgy) blessing, שעשני כרצונו... "... Who fashioned me according to His Will" reads like an afterthought. Yet, were they to associate "Will" with the *Sefirah Keter* how proud they should be of the exalted status implied by the blessing's hidden invocation of the *Keter-Malchut* axis (R. Rubinstein, personal communication)!

The Kabbalah would predict that consciousness as a fundamental force of nature will continue to defy human intellect and Chalmer's 'hard problem' will remain hard as long as *Keter* operates 'outside' our current frame of reference. In the Seventh (Messianic) Millennium the innate source of *Malchut* in *Keter* will be revealed. The moon representing the Divine Feminine (*Malchut/Nukvah*) will then be "established in its completeness" וקיימא סיהרא באשלמותא[188] and function in harmony with the sun (denoting the masculine *Zeir Anpin*) as שני מלכים משתמשים בכתר אחד "two monarchs sharing a single crown".[189] Our understanding of consciousness should then be rendered tractable (Chalmers' 'hard problem' will soften) on par with our appreciation of space, time, matter and energy today. Adrian Nelson, contemplating the premonitions of futurist Raymond Kurzweil, posed the following:

> Does mind and consciousness satisfy a form of cosmic imperative?
> Could it be that the ultimate destiny of intelligence in the universe is in some way connected to its origin?[287]

The Kabbalah is emphatic in its affirmative response to these queries; and the *Keter-Malchut* axis is in place to ensure that the evolution of human consciousness proceeds 'according to schedule'.

Chapter 7

Supervenience and Top-Down Causation

As outlined in Chapter 2 it is not at all settled whether consciousness is constructed piecemeal and is entirely dependent on lower-level physical properties (supervenience) as the reductionists would have it, or whether it inheres as an intrinsically complex, pre-material attribute of the universe capable of downward causation. Although the Kabbalah is evidently panpsychist in outlook (Chapter 5), this fact alone is insufficient to decide the matter as panpsychism *per se* can entail both bottom-up supervenience and top-down causation.

An analysis of the Lurianic Kabbalah as elucidated by the *Leshem*[111] suggests that the cause-effect relationships among higher consciousnesses and the physical cosmos are dynamically bidirectional. In Section 5.1, we noted that each phase of Creation consists of four sequential 'epochs': An initial Expansion of the *Ohr Ein-Sof* (*Hitpashtut-Rishon*); a First Withdrawal (*Histalkut-Rishon*) creating the Primordial Void (*Makom Panoi*) 'lined' with residual Light (*Reshimu*); and a Second Expansion (*Hitpashtut-Sheni*) whereby a Ray (*Kav*) derived from the surrounding *Ohr Ein-Sof* penetrates the Void, combines with the *Reshimu* and engenders all the particulars of the Creation—conscious and non-conscious.

We also determined that consciousness is relative and that the *G"R* (top three *Sefirot* or *Mochin*) conveying consciousness in a lower system is compactified within the unconscious *Z"T* (seven lower 'bodily' *Sefirot*) of the next higher system (Chapter 5). In a Second Withdrawal (*Histalkut-Sheni*), the fourth epoch of each creation cycle, the Light constituting 'lower' aspects of formed Worlds or *Partzufim* (e.g. the *Netzach-Hod-Yesod* triad) is 'raised' (withdrawn) to respective 'higher' levels (e.g. *Chesed-*

Gevurah-Tiferet) as a mini-*Tzimtzum* which stimulates the perpetuation of the Creation process at progressively smaller fractal sub-scales.[143] The 'obstetric' analogy drawn by the Kabbalah to illustrate this dynamic is that of a fetus with its legs (representing *Netzach-Hod-Yesod*) pressed up against its trunk (*Chesed-Gevurah-Tiferet*).[288]

The *Leshem* citing the *Ari"ZL* states that the deca-*Sefirotic* constructs established in the course of First Expansion and Withdrawal are erected in bottom-up fashion beginning with *Nukvah/Malchut* and ending with *Atik Yomin-Arich Anpin/Keter*. The *Leshem* queries how this can occur inasmuch as higher *Partzufim* (e.g. *Abba* and *Imma*) are generally understood to 'give birth' to lower *Partzufim* (e.g. *Zeir Anpin* and *Nukvah*) and not *vice versa*. The *Leshem* resolves the matter by indicating that the rarefied dimension of *Hitpashtut-Rishon* (pre-Genesis 1:1) differs from the 'natural order' witnessed in the cosmos of Second Expansion (*Hitpashtut-Sheni*), the subject of the familiar Creation account of Genesis 1:1-2:3. Specifically, in First Expansion each rung of the deca-*Sefirotic* hierarchy is realized by the Will of the Creator (*Ratzon Elyon*) directly and independently of the actions of any neighboring constructs.[289] The *Leshem* provides a metaphysic to explain this bottom-up construction based on the general Kabbalistic concept that in the course of First Expansion the further the Light (*Ohr*) emanates from its Source (the Godhead), the more it 'coarsens'. *Ergo*, as the Light recedes (First Withdrawal), the 'lower' Lights 'congeal' into Vessels (*Kelim*) first and the order of Creation proceeds in bottom-up fashion from *Malchut* to *Keter*.[290] As such, the establishment of *Nukvah/Malchut* 'prior to' *Abba* and *Imma* poses no difficulty. In First Expansion we see a progressive ascent of complexity from the unconscious (*Z"T*) to the conscious (*G"R*) in accord with the tenets of supervenient panpsychism. ('Supervenient' and not strictly 'emergent' as the Interinclusion of, say, 'conscious' mini-*Binah* within the 'unconscious' *Chesed* renders the advent of consciousness from the insensate somewhat predictable.[291])

With Second Expansion the 'mechanism' of Creation shifts to one of top-down causation whereby Light 'descends' (in the *Kav*) to sequentially fill Vessels (*Kelim*) established by the First Withdrawal. Thus, the higher *Sefirot* mediating consciousness now precede and give rise to the lower, unconscious *Sefirot* and their various manifestations. While the *Keter-Malchut* axis (Chapter 6) ensures that the final products of Creation ultimately align with the Will of God (*Ratzon Elyon*), the immediate contingency of each created particular on Divine Will characteristic of First Expansion is replaced in Second Expansion by a systematic, hierarchical framework of influences largely operating in top-down fashion within each deca-*Sefirotic* fractal. We note therefore that Kabbalistic panpsychism incorporates both bottom-up *and* top-down causation in its ontology.

Viewed from the perspective of *Orech* (Section 4.4), it may be surmised that top-down causation reflecting the current dominance of Second Expansion is the revealed state (*Gilui*) whereas the revelation of First Expansion in and beyond the Seventh (Messianic) Millennium will bring bottom-up panpsychism (and more intimate proximity of Creator and creation) to the foreground. From the holistic viewpoint of *Oivi* (Section 4.4), which conflates the timelines of the First and Second Expansions, the flow and influence of consciousness is construed at all times and everywhere as 'bidirectional'.[292]

What might the significance be for the switch from bottom-up supervenience (in First Expansion) to downward causality (in Second Expansion)? The answer may be grounded in the fundamental Judeo-Christian belief that the reality we experience is a 'work-in-progress' and that mankind (human consciousness) was created in God's image[62] so as to 'partner' with the Deity in completing the Creation (*Tikkun Olam*[293]). Thus, in First Expansion proto-consciousness (the *G"R* of each ten-*Sefirah* system) was established and progressively rendered more

complex in anticipation of, and to serve as a higher source
(*Makor*) for, the advent of people. At the apex of Creation on Day
Six of Second Expansion, human consciousness was empowered
with downward causation (beyond that bestowed upon lower
beings) to assist in the 'proper' unfolding of reality. This
sequence of events is hinted at in Genesis 2:5 which states that
the "grass of the field (albeit created) had not yet sprouted for
God had not sent rain upon the earth and there was no man to
work the soil":

וכל עשב השדה טרם יצמח כי לא המטיר ד' אלקים על הארץ ואדם
אין לעבד את האדמה.

On this verse, the Torah elucidator *Rashi* comments: "the
vegetation did not emerge from the earth but stood at the
entrance (surface) of the ground until the Sixth Day. For God
had not sent rain. And why? Because there was no man to work
the soil and none who could recognize the goodness of the rains.
When Adam came and realized the necessity of the rains for the
World, he prayed for them and they descended and the trees and
vegetation sprouted":[294]

עדיין לא צמח ובשלישי שכתוב ותוצא הארץ על פתח הקרקע עד יום ששי. ומה
טעם לא המטיר? לפי שאדם אין לעבוד את האדמה ואין מכיר בטובתם של גשמים,
וכשבא אדם וידע שהם צורך לעולם התפלל עליהם וירדו, וצמחו האילנות והדשאים.

This passage alludes to the role assigned to humankind in
perfecting the Creation and the top-down potency of human
consciousness (efficacy of prayer in this example). In most
general terms, throughout First Expansion God alone established
the *G"R* (*Mochin* or 'brains') and *Z"T* ('bodies') of every deca-
Sefirotic system. In Second Expansion God again created all
the *Z"T* but tasked humanity to 'bring down' through Torah
learning and observance of *Mitzvot* — i.e. conscious exertion —

the corresponding $G''R$ required to cement various facets of the Creation (*Tikkun Olam*).

The Kabbalistic formula describing bidirectional conscious influence encompasses George Ellis' notion of hierarchical (top-down) causation.[295] It also exhibits interesting parallels with Erik Hoel's anti-reductionist theory of 'causal emergence' where higher-order scales apply quantifiably more causal power over ("wrest control of") the future state of a system than the sum of their constituent parts.[296] Both the Kabbalah and Hoel lend support to a 'fringe' opinion in the neurosciences promulgated by psychiatrist Jeffrey Schwartz and physicist Henry Stapp: Based on principles of quantum indeterminacy, a logic stream developed by mathematician John von Neumann and evidence garnered from clinical practice, functional neuroimaging and attention psychology, Schwartz and Stapp concluded that states of consciousness *per se* influence the natural history of mental illness (e.g. obsessive-compulsive disorder) by directly impacting brain structure and function at the synaptic level (neuroplasticity).[297] Confirmation of mind-brain interactions of this kind and downward causation in general would have profound ramifications for the theoretical and clinical neurosciences as well as for the free will conundrum (Section 9.1) and other vexing philosophical issues.

7.1 Wheeler's Participatory Universe

The Kabbalistic doctrine of bidirectional causality may also shed light on a stunning paradox at the heart of the Participatory Universe hypothesis advanced by physicist John Archibald Wheeler (1911-2008). Wheeler was struck by the highly counterintuitive but experimentally robust conclusion that conscious observation is necessary and sufficient for 'collapse' of wave functions, descriptors of the probabilistic nature of the intangible quantum world, into discrete classical realities (see Section 3.1). Extrapolating to cosmology he conjectured that human consciousness as the universe's organ of self-awareness catalyzes the materialization of the cosmos' classical physical properties ('particles') from the spectrum of precursor quantum possibilities ('waves'). In effect, the universe behaves as a closed causal loop which brings itself into existence![298] Wheeler's famous U-diagram depicting this relationship is reproduced in Fig. 15.

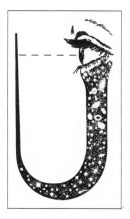

Figure 15. Wheeler's U-diagram of the Participatory Universe. From https://www.designspiration.net/save/10073566899495/.

But if human (and possibly other) consciousness is a prerequisite for transducing 'no-things' into things, and human consciousness/mind presupposes the existence of material brains as reductionists would have it, how do brains arise in the first place to enable observation and kick-start wave function collapse—a 'Catch-22' of breathtaking proportions? In 1978, Wheeler proposed a clever *Gedankenexperiment*, the Delayed Choice paradigm, which addresses this conundrum. In a variation of Young's original two-slit design demonstrating the impact of observation on the wave-particle duality of light, he reasoned that *delayed* knowledge of the trajectory of photons in a two-slit paradigm is capable of *retroactively* converting the previously unobserved and therefore wave-like behavior of light into well-defined particle streams. In essence, conscious observations made in the present (and future) are able to alter past world lines! The Universe is regarded by Wheeler as 'participatory' in so far as it creates itself through auto-observation within a self-excited closed loop circuit.[298] It is as if the mere potential for emergence of human consciousness sometime in the distant future guarantees the retroactive crystallization of quantum waves into classical particles at the most primordial stages of existence.

Full implications of the Wheeler hypothesis for the Anthropic Principle—the (outrageously) exquisite fine-tuning of the universal constants of physics for consciousness and sapient life—are beyond the scope of this book and are considered elsewhere.[298] It is sufficient to state here that to Wheeler[299] and British astrophysicist Martin Rees[300] the universe we know could only have materialized under physical law enabling 'observer participation'. Needless to say any support for the Anthropic Principle should be of great interest to the Kabbalah. Not because the former presents a novel approach to deciphering reality—an anthropocentric ('Goldilocks') universe has been the Judeo-Christian view all along—but because it is exhilarating to witness a significant segment of the scientific community including many secular thinkers converge on this same realization.

The Kabbalah views the implied 'fine-tuning' to extend beyond cosmogony to encompass biological evolution and the providential unfolding of each and every human life (regarded in Rabbinic literature as an *Olam Katan* or world-in-miniature[142,301]). Look for example at the Biblical narrative detailing the life of Joseph:[302] Only after assuming power as the viceroy of Egypt and its repercussions for rescuing the House of Jacob was he able to fathom the purpose of the unrelenting hardships (family discord, political intrigues, imprisonment) that punctuated his formative years. This pattern of Divine Providence is encrypted in the Hebrew spelling of his wife's name, Asenath (*Osnat*) = אסנת.[303] The name read from right to left begins with the first letter of the Hebrew alphabet, א (*Aleph*) and ends with the last of the 22 Hebrew letters, ת (*Taf*). Let *Aleph* allegorically represent the beginning of one's life and *Taf* the end. Moving *forward* in life from *Aleph* to *Taf* Joseph experienced incomprehensible turmoil symbolized by the two intervening letters of *Osnat*'s name, ס (*Samech*) and נ (*Nun*). The combination of these letters *Samech-Nun* is meaningless in Hebrew. Having reached the end of his journey, a life review from *Taf* to *Aleph* brought Joseph to re-engage the two intervening letters of *Osnat*'s name but this time in reverse order, *viz. Nun-Samech* (נס), the Hebrew word for miracle! What initially amounted to Joseph as a series of random and unfortunate events devoid of meaning in linear time took on great significance when considered in retrospect. And thus he consoled his brothers saying "you intended evil against me (but) God designed it for good to bring to pass this day that a great populace be kept alive" ואתם חשבתם עלי רעה אלקים חשבה לטבה למען עשה כיום הזה להחיות עם־רב.[304]

For such is the nature of Divine Providence (*Hashgachah Pratit*). Every experience is 'tailored' to the particular individual and replete with spiritual meaning, although the full impact of the latter may only be disclosed after the fact. The story of Purim commemorating deliverance of the Jews from Persian oppression makes this point emphatically.[305] As a more contemporary example of the Kabbalah's radical teleology, one may speculate that the decades-long 'concealment' of the Leviathan gas field currently enabling the State of Israel to become an energy exporter was a 'blessing in disguise'. For had an abundance of natural resources been available at the outset (in 1948), the fledgling population may not have been as compelled to innovate the extraordinarily diverse portfolio of intellectual property (scientific, technological, agricultural) which it currently enjoys.[306] Based on the axiom of Interinclusion (*Hitkallelut*; Section 4.3) the Kabbalah apprehends Divine Providence pertaining to the life-history of each person and nation as a microcosm of the 'Anthropic Principle' guiding the Creation at large.

Returning to Wheeler's conjecture, the Kabbalistic ontology described herein does not contradict the notion of staged or progressive evolution of consciousness. There is even precedent for temporal retro-causality in the application of Jewish law under certain circumstances[307,308] and in the spiritual edification of present-day Chanukah and Purim by future manifestations of these holidays.[309] Yet, Wheeler's Participatory Universe can be reinterpreted in the light of Kabbalistic doctrine without recourse to retro-causality as follows: (i) Proto-consciousness is built into the fabric of the cosmos at its inception by the Creator as the $G"R$ ('brains') of every deca-*Sefirotic* dyad. In accord with this panpsychist position (see Chapters 2 and 5), the inhering proto-consciousness ensures the collapse of wave functions and progressive 'crystallization' of reality independently of any future human observation. (ii) In First Expansion (*Hitpashtut-Rishon*) consciousness grows increasingly sophisticated (is steadily revealed) in bottom-up fashion (*Malchut*-to-*Keter*) to serve as sources for the gradations of consciousness destined to become manifest in the *Domem-Tzomeach-Chaye-M'daber* domains (see Chapter 5) of Second Expansion (*Hitpashtut-Sheni*). (iii) In Second Expansion top-down causation (*Keter*-to-*Malchut*) is introduced (revealed) and human consciousness contributes to the Creative process *in real time* — not retroactively as necessitated by Wheeler (Fig. 15) — by drawing 'brain'-*Sefirot* ($G"R$) into 'bodily'-*Sefirot* ($Z"T$) prefabricated by God.[289] Which is the more plausible model: a Divinely-inspired cosmos unfolding in orthogonal (real) time or Wheeler's self-created, retro-causal universe? This we leave for the reader to ponder (although Wheeler's later admission that his Participatory Universe theory may have been "metaphysically extravagant" speaks volumes[20]). Before we move on, let us for a moment examine point (i) above more closely. If intrinsic $G''R$-mediated proto-consciousness effects the concretization of every deca-*Sefirotic* dyad, what wave functions remain for future human (or other) consciousness to 'collapse'? From the holistic perspective of *Oivi* (Section 4.4), absolutely none—all is preordained by God and materialization of the cosmos is on auto-pilot. Contrariwise, the 'earthly' vantage point of *Orech* ensures that the stochastic reduction of probability curves by human conscious intervention (measurement or observation) into tangible realities is what we actually experience. Why this occurs will become apparent from our discussion of the Markov blanket-like properties of a Kabbalistic construct known as the *RADLA* and the so-called Wigner's friend paradox (Chapter 9). The *Orech-Oivi* dichotomy will also be invoked to shed light on the free will paradox and the apparent flow of time in a 'block universe' (Section 9.1).

In the following chapter, further Kabbalistic insight into the nature of consciousness is adduced based on the ancient Jewish ritual of *Tefillin* and the latter's uncanny resemblances to the structure of the human nervous system.

Chapter 8

Tefillin and the Seat of Human Consciousness*

*Rabbi Raphael Afilalo, former Chief of Pastoral Services at the Jewish General Hospital (Montreal), contributed to ideas developed in this chapter.

As documented in Chapters 5 and 7 the Kabbalistic conceptualization of consciousness may be best described as panentheistic panpsychism with an ontology consistent with both supervenience and top-down causation. We saw how consciousness (or rather its revelation) grows increasingly sophisticated as the Creation evolves from the inanimate *Domem* to the rational *M'daber* domains (Chapter 5). It is patently clear from the writings of the Kabbalah and common experience that consciousness as perceived from the ground-level perspective of *Orech* (Section 4.4) is not distributed homogeneously throughout the cosmos as a whole, within each stratum of Creation or within a single organism.

History has variably ascribed the seat of human consciousness to the liver, heart, lungs, pineal gland as well as the brain.[310-312] Although few today would contest the primacy of the brain as the organ most intimately linked to consciousness,[44,313-315] the field remains shrouded in mystery. Sorely lacking are satisfactory responses to the following queries: Which parts of the brain are necessary and sufficient for human consciousness? What is the relationship between brain, mind and consciousness? Commonly referred to as David Chalmers' 'Hard Problem' of consciousness[33] (Chapter 1), how can material neurons obeying purely physico-chemical laws (a 'computer made out of meat') give rise to qualia—the perception of red, the taste of a strawberry, the rapture of love or the memory of pain? Why does synaptic activity in temporal lobe structures conjure up a symphony while similar patterns of electrochemical discharge in occipital cortices are experienced visually? Does the brain 'secrete' consciousness as the liver does bile or is the CNS an antenna for consciousness signals originating extracorporeally?

As described in Chapter 5, the Kabbalah acknowledges five aspects of the Soul, with the second highest component, the *Chaya*, being expressed most prominently in humankind (*M'daber*) prior to the Seventh Millennium. The Kabbalah traditionally associates the *Chaya* and its homologues, the *Partzuf Abba*, the *Sefirah Chochma* and the World *Atzilut*, with the right hemisphere of the brain.[246] This annotation dovetails nicely with the holistic, constructional attributes of right hemispheric function inasmuch as *Chochmah/Atzilut* denote undifferentiated singularities (*Shlaymut*) and unadulterated Holiness (*Elokut*; Chapter 5). The third level of the Soul, the *Neshama* representing the *Partzuf Imma*, the *Sefirah Binah* and the World *Briah*, sources of 'broken symmetry' and individuation, maps appropriately to the left hemisphere where unified percepts and ideas fragment into bits and streams of thought and language. The *Sefirah Da'at* harmonizes the functions of *Chochmah* and *Binah* much as the massive white matter bundle, the corpus callosum interconnects the right and left cerebral hemispheres. The lowest manifestations of Soul, the *Ruach* and *Nefesh*, are most often associated with the heart/lungs and liver/blood, respectively.[316]

As noted in Chapter 5, the *Chaya* manifestation of Soul is a transcendent Light (*Ohr Makif*) that toggles between the outside and inside of its Vessel (*Keli*)—the right brain in this case—a process which may facilitate *self*-awareness or *self*-consciousness (see Section 5.2). Clearly then the Kabbalah recognizes that human consciousness is not confined to the material body (brain) and can be channeled from an über-conscious 'surround' (*Ohr Makif*). Such transmutation of Transcendent Light (*Ohr Makif*) to

Immanent Light (*Ohr Pnimi*) is anticipated to intensify dramatically beginning in the Seventh (Messianic) Millennium with ascendancy (revelation) of the highest level of Soul, the *Yechida* ('cosmic consciousness'; Chapter 13).

The Torah teaches that we are a world-in-miniature (*Olam Katan*[301]) made in God's Image (*B'tselem HaShem*[62]) implying that every human physical attribute signifies some spiritual counterpart and *vice versa*. Job informs us that "from my flesh I will know God"[317] מבשרי אחזה אלוק, i.e. we can learn much about the spiritual realm by contemplating the physical. Leaning heavily on this principle I will attempt to show that Kabbalistic insight into human consciousness is deeply ensconced in the Jewish ritual of donning *Tefillin* (phylacteries). The latter is a cryptic Biblical commandment[318-321] the precise details of which are stipulated in the Oral Tradition (Talmud) where *Tefillin* are mentioned over 500 times.[322] *Tefillin* are small black leather boxes containing the *Sh'ma* (declaration of God's Unicity[323]) and other key scriptural passages (*Parshiot*) which Jewish men strap to their forehead and non-dominant biceps during weekday morning prayers (Fig. 16A).

Although predating published records of basic neuroanatomy and physiology by many hundreds of years,[324] *Tefillin* exhibit remarkable homologies with the structure and function of the human nervous system. The nervous system is divided into two general categories, the CNS consisting of the brain and spinal cord and the peripheral nervous system (PNS) comprising nerve roots and nerves which exit the spinal cord to innervate the muscles and organs. The CNS corresponds to the *Tefillin* worn on the head (*Shel-Rosh*) and the PNS to the *Tefillin* affixed to the arm (*Shel-Yad*). The head-*Tefillin* comprises four chambers (*Batim*), each housing a separate Torah passage (*Parsha*) reminiscent of (i) the four lobes of the brain: frontal, parietal, temporal and occipital and (ii) the four senses (*Chushim*) which gain access to the brain exclusively via the head: sight, sound, taste and smell. In contrast, the four passages of the arm-*Tefillin* are bundled within a single compartment reflecting the one sensory modality, touch, which may first traverse the body before entering the head and brain.

The brain sends commands to lower regions of the nervous system which in turn vivify and activate bodily functions. Conversely, the brain is kept informed and responds to signals which ascend to it from peripheral organs and the environment. In analogous fashion the three top 'conscious' *Sefirot* (the *G"R*) 'energize' the seven lower 'bodily' *Sefirot* (the *Z"T*) of each *Partzuf* (top-down causation) while influences rising from lower *Sefirot* stimulate activity in upper echelons of the *Partzuf* (bottom-up organization).

The Torah specifies that the head-*Tefillin* must be placed within four fingerbreadths above the hairline anterior to the coronal suture (Fig. 16B)[325,326] thereby overlying the prefrontal cortex of the frontal lobe, a region most developed in humans and associated with higher cognition, executive functions and personality. The contents (*Parshiot*) of the head-*Tefillin* correspond to the *Mochin, Chochmah* and *Binah* (and *Da'at* if not reckoning *Keter*). The box (*Bayit*) encasing the *Parshiot* denotes *Keter* and corresponds to the skull or possibly a bioenergy field[327] surrounding the brain. Regardless, *Keter* should never be construed as a mere 'container' as its complement of Light (*Ohr*) is always more rarefied (closer to the *Ohr Ein-Sof*) than that of the *Mochin, Chochma* and *Binah*. Indeed, *Keter* imbues the *Tefillin* box (*Bayit*) itself with Holiness (*Kedushah*) to the extent that, according to Jewish law, a defect in the box invalidates the entire head-*Tefillin* unlike *Mezuzah* scrolls affixed to doorposts which remain valid when their casing is absent or damaged.[328] As in most other frames of reference *Keter* is a surrounding Light (*Ohr Makif*) which transmits influences originating 'outside' the system under consideration (see Chapters 5 and 6). The configuration of *head-Tefillin* implies that *human consciousness rather than being confined to the brain draws upon and establishes itself in dynamic equilibrium with a super-consciousness — the Mind of God — which (panentheistically) pervades and transcends the Creation at large.*[329] Although conceivably a characteristic of human consciousness *per se*, the lucidity of awareness achievable via this trans-corporeal modality is likely commensurate with the genetic, intellectual, psychological, moral and spiritual constitution of the individual. Such non-local, *Keter*-like properties of human consciousness may have substantial implications for our understanding of human intuition (see also Chapter 6), prophecy[3,12] (Chapter 9), near-death experiences, paranormal phenomena such as mind-matter interaction, precognition and telepathy[23] as well as certain neuropsychiatric states (e.g. schizophrenia).[1,23]

Although controversial by their very nature, fairly rigorous experiments performed by psychologist Dean Radin at the *Institute of Noetic Sciences* in California and others not only supported the existence of reproducible *psi* phenomena (e.g. ability of meditators to mentally influence the output of a random events generator) but suggested that the magnitude of the effects was independent of the spatial and temporal proximity between the test subjects and the receivers.[330] The recorded *psi* phenomena appeared to behave in a manner reminiscent of photonic entanglement and the non-locality of *Keter* consciousness.

We have thus far discussed the implications of the *Tefillin* head-box and its contents for trans-corporeal and immanent human consciousness. Other components of the head-*Tefillin* and the arm-*Tefillin* provide further parallels with key aspects of human neuroanatomy related to this topic: The black leather straps (*Retzuot*) extending from the right and left sides of the head-*Tefillin* box towards the back of the cranium (Fig. 16A) respectively represent *Chesed* and *Gevurah*, the first two of the seven 'bodily' *Sefirot* (the *Z"T*): חסד דז"א מסבב בצד ימין של-ראש

112

דז"א.גבורה מסבב בצד שמאל של-ראש דז"א.[174] The straps denote the
pathways whereby the *Mochin* or 'consciousness' (the *Sefirot*,
Keter-Chochmah-Binah or *Chochmah-Binah-Da'at*) communicate
with the 'bodily' *Z"T* (*Chesed*-to-*Malchut*). Anatomically, they
correspond in part to the right and left cortico(bulbo)spinal or
pyramidal tracts which transmit motor commands from the
frontal lobe to the brain stem and spinal cord (Fig. 16C). The *Chesed*
and *Gevurah* straps meet in a knot (*Kesher Shel-Rosh*) just below
the external occipital protuberance near the junction between
the back of the head and neck.[326] The knot corresponds to *Tiferet*,
the *Sefirah* which harmonizes the actions of *Chesed* and *Gevurah*.
It is situated precisely over the lower medulla oblongata where
the corticospinal tracts converge ('decussation of the pyramids').
Here, a majority of corticospinal fibers cross to descend on the
opposite sides of the brain stem and spinal cord while a minority
of the fibers remains ipsilateral (Fig. 16C). This organization of
the corticospinal projections is recapitulated in the three main
types of *Kesher Shel-Rosh*: (i) a knot in the shape of the Hebrew
letter *end-Mem* (ם), a square, worn by most Ashkenazi Jews and
certain Chassidic sects wherein the right-*Chesed* and left-*Gevurah*
straps cross to emerge, respectively, as the left-*Hod* and right-
Netzach straps; (ii) a knot shaped like the Hebrew letter, *Dalet*
(ד), donned by most Sephardic and some Chassidic Jews where
no decussation of the straps occurs i.e. right-*Chesed* continues as
right-*Netzach*, and left-*Gevurah* emerges as left-*Hod*; and (iii) a
'double'-knot consisting of one *Dalet* superimposed on another
in inverted fashion (essentially describing a square) worn by the
Ari"ZL and others in which the straps again cross[326,331] (Fig. 16D).
What might the various permutations of the *Tefillin* knots and
straps and their anatomical parallelisms come to teach us about
human neurological function and consciousness?

First described by the Italian neuroanatomist Domenico
Mistichelli in 1709,[332] it remains enigmatic to this day why
centrifugal motor and centripetal sensory (including visual)

fibers from one hemisphere of the brain cross to communicate with neurons, muscles and organs on the *opposite* side of the body. Although several hypotheses have been advanced,[333,334] no single biologically-based formulation has proved wholly satisfactory in ascertaining what advantage(s) the decussating neural pathways confer to humans (and other organisms) over a seemingly more straightforward, 'non-crossed' design.

Given the aforementioned homologies between *Tefillin* and nervous system organization perhaps some insight into this matter may be gleaned from the Kabbalistic literature. The term *Chiluf*, a type of bonding (*Zivug*), refers to 'crossings', 'switches' or 'exchanges' between two spiritual forces which are brought into close 'proximity'. The *Chiluf* (i) enables the weaker of the two forces to be strengthened (*Memutak*, 'sweetened') by the superior and (ii) facilitates the flow of Divinity from higher to lower realms.

One instantiation of the *Chiluf* concept is the passage הוא ד' האלקים[60] connoting the unity of God as manifested on the one hand by the ineffable Tetragrammaton on the side of *Chesed* (right) and, on the other, the stern manifestation of the name *Elokim* connoting *Gevurah* (on the left). It is said that this juxtaposition of both Names is tantamount to the 'sweetening' of Justice by Mercy, a prerequisite for the redemption of the Israelites from Egyptian bondage.[335]

Another example of right-left integration is the passage הוא אהרן ומשה...הוא משה ואהרן[336] which translates as "He, Aaron and Moses—he, Moses and Aaron". Commentators query the anomalous use of the singular 'he' at the mention of both Moses and Aaron and the significance of the verse's repetition with the names given in reverse order. Aaron is traditionally associated with the *Sefirah Hod* on the left (*Seder Hoshanos, Sukkot liturgy*) and yet he is the High Priest (*Kohen Gadol*) whose Light (*Ohr*) originates in *Chesed* on the right—a 'switch' (*Chiluf*). Similarly, Moses is represented by *Netzach* on the right yet as a Levite receives *Ohr* from *Gevurah* on the left. The 'crossing' (*Chiluf*) ensures that certain strengths characteristic of Moses or Aaron, although latent in both according to the principle of Interinclusion (Section 4.3), are overtly expressed (*Gilui*; or 'unfolded' in Bohmian jargon) in the two leaders for the benefit of the Nation. This 'equilibration' of Moses and Aaron is signified by employment of the singular "he" and the reordering of their names in the cited passage.[335] In the same vein Jacob's crossing of his hands (*Chiluf*) upon the heads of Joseph's sons Ephraim and Manasseh ensured that maximum benefits would derive from the family blessings they received.[337]

Features common to the embodiments of 'crossings' (*Chiluf*) cited here are the empowerment and enhanced measure of blessing bestowed upon those subjected to their influence. To the extent that the head-*Tefillin* reflects neurobiological realities, the Kabbalistic elucidation of *Chiluf* suggests that the ubiquitous decussations of motor and sensory pathways in humans and other vertebrates may serve (in ways yet to be delineated by science) to integrate, strengthen and optimize operations of the CNS as a whole.

Homologies between *Tefillin* and neural organization do not end here. Parallel right-*Netzach* and left-*Hod* straps descend from the knot of the head-*Tefillin* along the torso approximating the course of the bilaterally symmetrical spinal cord (Fig. 16A). The arm-*Tefillin* (*Shel-Yad*) is regarded as both the *Malchut* (tenth *Sefirah*) of the head-*Tefillin* (denoting the masculine *Zeir Anpin*) and as a stand-alone *Partzuf*, the Divine Feminine (*Nukvah*). It is placed on the left biceps (in right-handed persons) attesting to the general inclination of the feminine to the side of *Gevurah* (restraint) as opposed to *Chesed* (expansion; Fig. 4). Conforming to the deca-*Sefirotic* composition of all *Partzufim*, the arm-*Tefillin* entails ten windings of the straps: seven on the forearm (for the seven 'bodily' *Z"T*) and three (for the three 'conscious' *G"R*) on either the upper arm or hand.[326] Anatomically, the box of the arm-*Tefillin* and its securing straps are reminiscent of the morphology and relative positions of the dorsal root ganglion and the spinal roots (Fig. 16A). The sensorimotor and autonomic nerves extending peripherally to innervate internal organs, muscles and skin are represented in the arm-*Tefillin* by the strap encircling the forearm and hand. The strap terminates around the distal phalanx of the middle finger symbolizing the course of the digital nerves (Fig. 16A).

The suggestive homologies between the arm-*Tefillin* and the PNS are relevant to consciousness inasmuch as (i) information transmitted from the environment and internal states via the PNS impact alertness, cognition and mood and (ii) *Tefillin* contact points on both head and arm are congruent with seminal acupuncture sites used for treatment of neuropsychiatric conditions in Traditional Chinese Medicine[2] (**Box 2**). Applying Job's maxim מבשרי אחזה אלוק "from my flesh I will know God (Job 19:26)" *in reverse*, a Kabbalistic analysis of *Tefillin* may provide novel insight into the 'wisdom' of neural organization and the nature of human consciousness.

Box 2. *Tefillin* and Traditional Chinese Medicine. The convergence of *Tefillin* application sites on both the head and arm with specific acupuncture points of Traditional Chinese Medicine establishes a further link between *Tefillin* and consciousness.[2] The knot of the head-*Tefillin* overlies Fengfu DU-16 (Fig. 16E) where the 'Governing Vessel' penetrates and nurtures the brain and spinal cord; stimulation of this point is said to improve concentration and memory and ameliorate headache, aphasia and psychosis. The box of the head-*Tefillin* exerts pressure on Shangxing DU-23 and Shenting DU-24 (Figure 16E); the former treats psychosis, headaches and anosmia (diminished sense of smell) while the latter 'calms the mind', 'balances the spirit' and controls mania and epilepsy. Schramm[2] lists a half-dozen key acupuncture sites on the arm and hand directly impacted by the arm-*Tefillin* (with minor variations among Ashkenazi, Sephardic and Chassidic traditions). These sites allegedly promote cognitive, affective and spiritual well-being and are targeted by acupuncturists in the management of various mental disorders. The specific wrapping of the middle finger with the arm-*Tefillin* stimulates the 'Pericardium Channel' which 'calms the heart' and 'steadies the mind'. Interestingly, just as the head-*Tefillin* is interposed (donned) *between* the wrappings of the arm and hand, so are the 'point multipliers' on the hand added to advantage *after* stimulation of Shangxing DU-23 and Shenting DU-24.[2]

We have been exploring the contribution of *Tefillin* (phylacteries) to the Kabbalistic understanding of human consciousness by juxtaposing the former with the structural organization of the central and peripheral nervous systems. The following Talmudic discussion invokes an additional dimension to *Tefillin* that provides keen insight into human neuropsychology: Scripture lists excessive fear or disheartenment as one of the conditions which exempt Israelite men from going to battle for concern that it may demoralize and thereby weaken the troops.[338] The Talmud comments that the trepidation alluded to here is fear of sin that accrues specifically from speaking out between the donning of the arm and head *Tefillin*.[339] But why should this seemingly minor misdemeanor be singled out as the one which instils fear in the soldier? Surely there are more egregious transgressions that could come to mind.

Once again implying a relationship between *Tefillin* and the nervous system, the Talmud conflates arm-*Tefillin* with physical action (mediated by the peripheral nervous system) and head-*Tefillin* with thought and motivation (the purview of the brain). In the scenario we are considering, the Talmud construes talking aloud between his placing of the arm-*Tefillin* and head-*Tefillin* as an interruption or 'disconnect' between the actions required for the adept conduction of warfare and the belief system he carries with him into the campaign. Soldiers who lose faith in the righteousness of their cause may become psychologically compromised both on the battlefield and upon return to civilian life. The Torah deems it preferable that such individuals be relieved of military service lest the disillusionment spread like a contagion through the ranks.

In this chapter we garnered evidence implicating the ritual of *Tefillin* as the symbolic embodiment of neurological structure and function and wondered how construction of the former could have predated knowledge of basic neuroanatomy by so many years. We demonstrated multiple, fairly nuanced homologies between the design of head- and arm-*Tefillin* and the organization of various components of the brain, spinal cord and peripheral nerves including precise landmarks where both *Tefillin* straps and key nerve fiber tracts cross to the opposite sides. We observed that the contents of the box of the head-*Tefillin* (*Shel-Rosh*) allude to the *Sefirot*, *Chochmah-Binah-Da'at*, which in the corresponding human brain are the *Gimel Rishonim* (*G"R*) or *Mochin* harboring the immanent (*Ohr Pnimi*) phase of consciousness. The box of the head-*Tefillin* itself, in contrast, reflects the supernal *Sefirah* of *Keter* which mediates transcendent (*Ohr Makif*) aspects of consciousness responsible for transpersonal intuition and possibly extrasensory perception. In the next chapter we drill down to a discrete construct within *Keter* known as the *RADLA* which I believe is the critical nexus between quantum indeterminacy and classical reality and a key to understanding free will, prophecy and other riveting dimensions within consciousness.

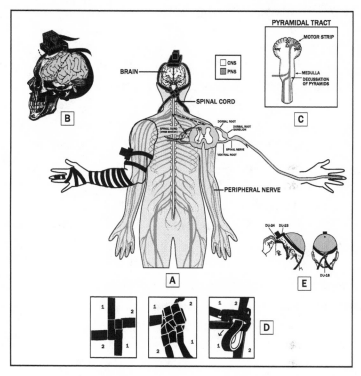

Figure 16. *Tefillin* and the human nervous system. A. Homologies between head-*Tefillin* (*Shel-Rosh*) and the central nervous system (CNS), and between arm-*Tefillin* (*Shel-Yad*) and the peripheral nervous system (PNS). **B.** Relationship of the head-*Tefillin* to skull and brain.

C. Decussation of the pyramids (corticospinal tracts) in the lower medulla oblongata. **D.** Variation in the knotting of the *Kesher Shel-Rosh*. Straps cross to opposite sides in square *end-Mem* (◘; left) and *Ari"ZL's* (middle) knots and remain uncrossed in the *Dalet* (ד) knot (right).

E. *Tefillin* and acupuncture points in Traditional Chinese Medicine, from [2] with permission.

Chapter 9

Consciousness and the *'Unknowable Head'*

It was suggested in Chapters 5 and 6 that human consciousness mirroring the panentheistic Mind of God both suffuses and transcends the confines of the material brain and that the *Sefirah Keter* is the vehicle mediating extra-corporeal awareness. More precisely the nexus between intrinsic or neural-based and transpersonal consciousness may be associated within a unique construct within *Keter* termed the *Raisha D'lo Ityadah* (acronym *RADLA*; רדל"א) or 'Unknowable Head'. The *RADLA* concept is described in the classical Kabbalistic texts (mainly the *Zohar* and *Etz Chaim*) and is elaborated further in the writings of the eighteenth century scholar, the *Ramchal*.[340-342] The *RADLA* consists of the first three *Sefirot* of the *Partzuf Atik Yomin*. Whereas the lower seven *Sefirot* (*Z"T*) of *Atik Yomin* are 'enclothed' (*Hitlabshut*; Section 4.3) within the 'subjacent' *Partzuf Arich Anpin*, the three *RADLA Sefirot* are 'naked' and stationed immediately 'outside' the frame of reference (World) under consideration (Fig. 7). This configuration renders the *RADLA* opaque to human understanding—"a head that is unknowable (*Ityadah*) and not merely unknown."[342]

We previously presented evidence that the workings of the *RADLA* are astonishingly consistent with Heisenberg's Uncertainty Principle and the Copenhagen interpretation of quantum mechanics.[3,12] In these publications, key statements concerning the nature of quantum uncertainty rendered by leading twentieth century physicists were juxtaposed with Kabbalistic descriptions of the *RADLA* (in original Hebrew and Aramaic with English translation) in order to convey their similarity of meaning. The gist of this extraordinary confluence of science and mysticism is captured in the following excerpts from our earlier work:

A. The Intrinsically Incomprehensible Universe—Quantum Physics:
- "Uncertainty is perhaps the central feature of quantum theory."[77]
- "It is safe to say that nobody understands quantum mechanics."[343]
- "We cannot know, as a matter of principle, the present in all its details."[73]
- "In more than forty years, physicists have not been able to provide a clear metaphysical model (of quantum reality)."[344]
- "The creation lies outside the scope of the known laws of physics."[345]

B. The Intrinsically Incomprehensible Universe—The Kabbalah:
- "(The *RADLA*) is the source; from it issues forth all uncertainty at the outset: שהיא הראשונה, שבה נולדים הספיקות בתחלה."
- "We cannot imagine or know anything (of the *RADLA*). This is the concept of 'unknowable' (by its very nature and not merely unknown): אינם מושגים ונודעים כלל, זהו עניין דלא אתידע."[341]

A. Worlds in Potentia—Quantum Physics:
- "In quantum mechanics, every possible outcome for an event exists in the unobserved state prior to collapse of the wave function."[346]

B. Worlds in Potentia—The Kabbalah:

- "Every combination... (of reality) that could possibly be found was, in fact, made: כל מיני החיבורים שהיה אפשר להמצא - באמת נעשו [342]

- "One moment it appears that (the outcome determined by the *RADLA*) is one thing, in another moment it looks like something else: כי פעם אחת נראה שיש בה כך, ופעם אחת יש בה כך.... ואם מסתכלים באותו העניין יותר נראה שאינו כך, אלא בדרך אחר מתחלף ממנו [341] [*An allusion, perhaps, to the seemingly random nature of wave function collapse—author.*]

- "These uncertainties (of the *RADLA*) are unlike the uncertainties of the (familiar) world. In the latter, we may be uncertain whether a thing exists or not; whereas, in truth, all things perceived as 'uncertain' are present in her (the *RADLA*): שאין הספיקות ההם כמו ספיקות דעלמא, שאנו בספק אם יש דבר אחד, או אם אינו, אלא האמת הוא, כל מה שאנו מזכירים בספיקות - כל אותם הדברים ישנם באמת בה."[341] [*This description of the inherent paradox of reality may be the most supportive Kabbalistic statement in favor of ontic as opposed to epistemic uncertainty. See Section 4.5—author.*]

A. Unicity on a Grand Scale—Quantum Physics:

- "Quantum physics reveals a basic oneness of the universe."[344]

- "The world acts more like a single indivisible unit, in which even the 'intrinsic' nature of each part (wave or particle) depends... on its relationship to its surroundings."[81]

- "The inseparable quantum interconnectedness of the whole universe is the fundamental reality, and (the) relatively independent behaving parts are merely particular and contingent forms within this whole."[87]

B. Unicity on a Grand Scale—The Kabbalah:

- "Everything is connected to it (the *RADLA*) and it is connected to all; it encompasses all: דהא כלא ביה מתדבקן וא[347] והוא מתדבק בכלא, הוא כלא."

- "All reality is governed by a single Light (force). The *RADLA* is in actuality a part of this encompassing Light: שכל ההנהגה היא אור אחד, והנה רדל"א הוא מין אור אחד."[341]

Before embarking on a discussion concerning the implications of the *RADLA* for consciousness *per se* it is worthwhile recapitulating from our earlier work[3,12] how juxtaposition of the *RADLA* construct with Heisenberg's Uncertainty Principle may impact epistemology in general and the current limitations of scientific knowledge. Figure 17 depicts the evolution and boundaries of human insight into the fabric and workings of the universe as a set of three nested cubes: a small Classical (Newtonian) box contained within an intermediate Quantum box which in turn is encompassed by a large Kabbalah box. The perimeters of the cubes indicate the theoretical limits of fundamental knowledge about the universe attainable by each discipline. In the classical (pre-quantum) era Newtonian physics sufficed to resolve with relative precision numerous queries concerning the mechanical operations of the universe (line 1). Deeper, more nuanced insights into the nature of reality could only be roughly approximated by (or were entirely opaque to) Newtonian thought and required the advent of quantum theory for their satisfactory resolution (line 2). The tenets of quantum mechanics dictate that it is impossible to predict future events with any degree of certainty because one can never attain full knowledge of the position and momentum of even a single particle. But this statement may be true only within the Quantum box which, restricted by the Uncertainty Principle and its *RADLA* homologue, establishes a barrier beyond which science cannot probe. By contrast, we are informed of named constructs situated *'above'* the *RADLA* of *Atzilut* in the Kabbalistic hierarchy such as *Adam Kadmon*. Although these Divine manifestations lie beyond the reach of modern science (bounded as it were by the Uncertainty Principle/*RADLA*), their registration within the Kabbalistic cascade implies the existence of, and may illuminate a roadmap to, realities beyond quantum uncertainty. Future expansion of human consciousness predicted by the Kabbalah as described in Chapter 13 may one day permit scientific exploration with far finer granularity (line 3) than anything we can imagine today.

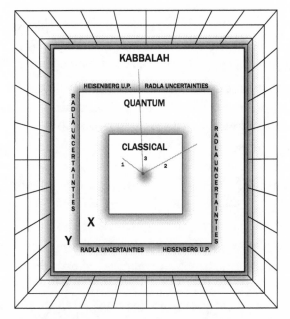

Figure 17. A model depicting boundaries of human insight into the fabric and workings of the universe imposed by Newtonian (classical) physics, quantum mechanics and the Kabbalah. Modified from [3] with permission.

According to the Ramchal[342] all possible outcomes devolving from a Schrödinger wave-like probability curve are rooted in the *RADLA*. As in Young's famous two-slit experiment,[75] only when assayed consciously (measured) do these possibilities 'collapse' into one or another classical realities. The 'chosen' outcome is relayed by the *RADLA* to *Arich Anpin*, progressively 'coarsens' in its trickle 'down' the entire Kabbalistic ladder (*Seder Hishtalshelut*; Chapter 4) and after a final transduction by the *Malchut* of *Malchut* of *Asiyah* materializes as a discrete physical entity within the familiar macro-world (Fig. 6 and 7).

The *RADLA* veil and the Uncertainty Principle set a limit on what can be known (ontic as opposed to epistemic uncertainty) and establish that the observed reality is 'selected' in a seemingly random manner. But this indeterminacy is only true from our perspective—the vital *Keter-Malchut* axis described in Chapter 6 ensures that the final products of Creation are in complete alignment with the Will of the Creator (*Ratzon Elyon*).[348] Let us take a simple example to illustrate this point: (i) God decrees that an object or event comprising the sequence A-B-C-D be brought into existence. (ii) The Willed outcome encoded by the *Ohr Ein-Sof* 'descends' to the level of the *RADLA* where from our vantage point it appears scrambled as a probability curve encompassing all combinations of A, B, C and D. (iii) Unable to permeate the *RADLA* barrier we cannot directly discern Divine Intent. What we encounter instead is a superposition of possible outcomes which upon observation collapses to the product A-B-C-D. The latter appears to us for all intents and purposes to have been selected entirely at random among numerous (in this case 24) possibilities. In actuality, the intended outcome A-B-C-D was preordained by God and guaranteed by the actions of the *Keter-Malchut* axis[281] in accord with the dictum סוף מעשה במחשבה תחילה "Last in deed, first conceived" (Sabbath liturgy).

The generation of apparent randomness from determinism *per se* is not the challenge here; this can be readily obtained on a benchtop Galton board where falling marbles upon colliding with the board's pegs (according to deterministic law) reproduce Gaussian distributions and Pascal's triangle (randomness) as they distribute among the vertical collection bins.[349] The novelty here is that in ways currently inscrutable by dint of the *RADLA*, the *Keter-Malchut* axis specifies in advance precisely which particular marble will end up in which bin. Perhaps a fitting analogy is the recent conjecture by Princeton physicist Ahmed Almheiri and colleagues that the seemingly random Hawking radiation emitted from a black hole (in apparent defiance of the quantum mechanical law of conservation of information) may actually contain subtly encrypted information we may one day be able to decipher.[350]

All of the above is not to say that we live in a rigidly deterministic universe. The Abrahamic faiths acknowledge that the Will of God is mutable and influenced by the actions, good deeds and prayers of humanity. Only once a Divine decision is taken the outcome is certain *a priori* notwithstanding its random and unpredictable appearance to anthropocentric eyes. Viewed from the unified perspective of *Oivi* (Section 4.4) the cosmos we know may be the finely-tuned end-product of a Divinely-collapsed 'universal wave function' selected from an infinitude of potential realities (a stark alternative to Wheeler's self-participatory universe discussed in Chapter 7). In support of this conjecture the *Ramchal* states that "the Omnipotent One observes the entirety of Creation as a unified whole: ועל הכללות הזה מביט הכל-יכול בכל יכילתו בכלל אחד."[351] From the vantage point of *Orech* (Section 4.4) there are nested within this grand collapsing field a vast hierarchy of *Ketarim* (plural of the *Sefirah Keter*) each containing a *RADLA* within its *Atik Yomin* aspect. Sealed off by these *RADLA* curtains, human consciousness encounters at each decision fork a smear of potential outcomes which, accruing from the act of observation, assumes a single trajectory in apparent stochastic fashion (but despite the unpredictability remains preordained). As noted previously,[3,12] little is known concerning the mechanism governing the translation of *RADLA*/ quantum phenomena into events of the experiential world. What can be said is that the seemingly random, uncaused fluctuations inherent to the former realm limit what can be predicted about all future events. Several implications of the *RADLA* construct for free will and prophecy follow.

9.1 On Prophecy and Free Will

From the above considerations we may conclude that the *RADLA* enables humankind to emulate God's Creativity (*Imitatio Dei*) on a microcosmic scale (by transmuting the potential to the real) while concomitantly blinding humanity to the Divine Blueprint informing the unfolding Creation in a manner that preserves our sense of free will (*B'chira Chofshit*).

We previously recounted the Biblical story of Balaam[177] as an exception that proves the rule:[3,12] The Moabite king Balak summons the prophet and master conjurer Balaam to curse the nation of Israel. When not the recipient of Divine prophecy (*Nevu'ah*) Balaam's consciousness is confined by the *RADLA* on par with the rest of humanity (point X in Fig. 17) and his prerogative to either curse or bless the Israelites is (seemingly, from the perspective of *Orech*) exercised as he desires. On the other hand Balaam is compelled to bestow blessing on Israel when receiving prophecy (as he himself admits) because permeation of the *RADLA* membrane necessary for prophetic instruction (point Y in Fig. 17; see also Fig. 20) interfaces and subjugates Balaam's will to the Divinely-inspired 'collapse of the universal wave function'[352,353]—a state incompatible with evil intent, autonomy and personal agendas.

Kabbalistic insight into the nature of prophecy has proved useful in resolving certain controversies in the Rabbinic literature. As a case in point, opinions differ as to whether Daniel was a full-fledged prophet or achieved an arguably lower level of spiritual awareness termed *Ruach Hakodesh* (Divine Inspiration).[354-357] To attain the stature of a prophet the practitioner's consciousness must be able to transcend the World of *Asiyah* in order to access information in the World of *Yetzirah* or higher. For example, in descending order of prophetic clarity Moses reached the upper levels of *Briah*; Isaiah the lower aspects of *Briah*; and Ezekiel the World of *Yetzirah*.[358,359] It is written that the lucidity of Daniel's visions extended to *Atik Yomin* of *Asiyah* which according to the aforementioned criteria fall short of the threshold for prophecy. Recall, however, that *Atik Yomin* can be legitimately reckoned as the top *Partzuf* of the lower World *or* the bottom aspect of the World immediately above (Section 4.2 and Figure 7). *Ergo*, those scholars who hold the view that *Atik Yomin* is top *Partzuf* of the lower World (*Asiyah*) limit Daniel's spiritual reach to *Ruach Hakodesh* whereas those of the latter persuasion accept Daniel as a *bona fide* prophet.[360] For further discussion of the *RADLA's* properties and their implications for cosmology, quantum physics, free will and prophecy, see our earlier publications on this topic.[3,12]

It is worthwhile at this juncture to contrast the Kabbalistic perspective on free will with the prevailing view of secular reductionism. As discussed in Chapters 1 and 2, with some notable exceptions[28,32,297,353] the majority of contemporary physicists, neuroscientists and philosophers surveyed subscribe to a 'closed' physical universe wherein all phenomena, be they material or psychological, are bound by natural law as it is currently understood. In its most orthodox iteration this *Weltanschauung* denies the possibility of top-down causation. It asserts that all conscious acts are the end-products of events strictly determined by a cascade that originates with quantum mechanics and 'ascends' by supervenience or emergence through classical physics, chemistry, biochemistry, molecular biology, neurobiology and psychology. Free will in this schema is an illusion—one belying the fact that the neurochemistry underpinning the conscious act is an inescapable consequence of a chain of prior (unconscious) physico-chemical reactions traceable in principle back to the Big Bang. So pervasive is this illusion of freedom that, ironically, even the staunchest reductionists still insist on erecting legal institutions to administer justice when by their logic perpetrators should never be held personally accountable for their crimes!

The Kabbalah expounds free will as both existent and nonexistent—yet another paradox (see Section 4.5). From the 'vertical' perspective of *Orech* where reality is intuited in bottom-up, hierarchical fashion (Section 4.4) free will remains fully engaged by every meaningful definition of the term and we are indeed held responsible for our actions. To think otherwise would render the Biblical exhortation החיים והמות נתתי לפניך הברכה והקללה ובחרת בחיים: "I have set before you life and death, a blessing and a curse; therefore choose life"[59] a complete *non sequitur*. In contradistinction to the assumptions of the reductionist community Kabbalistic panpsychism maintains that the universe is not physically 'closed' (see Chapters 4 and 5) and that the human spirit, fashioned in God's Image, may will matter to move. The latter choices are for all intents and purposes kept 'free' by operating within the confines of the *RADLA*—a construct within the *Atik Yomin* aspect of *Keter* absent which human consciousness would be thoroughly inundated and commandeered by Divine Intent (as transiently experienced during prophecy). Conceivably, by insulating our tiny 'bubbles' of consciousness from the Mind of God, the Heisenberg-like stochasticity inherent to the *RADLA* prevents the decoherence of superpositional states[361] and abrogation of all semblance of free agency which might otherwise accompany universal (Divinely-inspired) wave function collapse. In a sense this formulation parallels Bohmian mechanics wherein quantum behavior is essentially deterministic but hidden from observers.[84]

We also see conceptual overlap with the well-known quantum

thought experiment referred to as 'Wigner's friend paradox' (**Box 3A**) and the properties of Markov blankets (**Box 3B**). From God's vantage point and the holistic perspective of *Oivi* (Section 4.4) free will is more apparent than real; not for the reasons promulgated by the reductionists (above) but because the *Keter-Malchut* connection underpinning reality (Chapter 6) ensures that even the most palpably 'random' outcomes are at their most fundamental level supernally preordained.

Box 3A. The *RADLA* and Wigner's Friend. As described in Section 9.1 the *RADLA* component of the *Partzuf Atik Yomin* behaves as a veil that, barring rare instances of prophecy, shields human consciousness from the Mind of God. While the latter may collapse the 'universal wave function' to create a singular cosmos commensurate with Divine Intent,[351] the *RADLA* curtain preserves for humankind (prevents collapse of) the superposition of states dictated by the Schrödinger equation. Similarly, although Eugene Wigner's friend[362,363] inside the laboratory had already collapsed the wave function by observing whether Schrödinger's cat is alive or dead, before Wigner enters the lab to ascertain whether his assistant is happy (cat alive) or sad (cat dead) the entire contents of the lab, including the cat, remain *for Wigner* in superposition (Fig. 18). In this juxtaposition of paradoxical Kabbalistic and quantum affairs Wigner's friend connotes Divine knowledge, Wigner—human consciousness, and the wall occluding Wigner's awareness of the lab's interior—the *RADLA*.

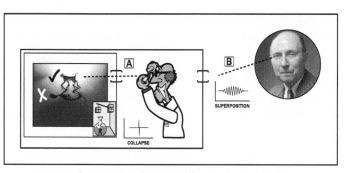

Figure 18. Wigner's friend paradox.

Box 3B. Markov blankets. Markov blankets are formal statistical objects which confer boundaries upon individual entities thereby distinguishing them from their surroundings (Figure 19; from [4] with permission). Markov blankets minimize the free energy and limit entropic decay of the enveloped entities permitting autonomous behavior far from the equilibrium of the embedding matrix. Influences between particulars and their environments are acknowledged as bidirectional.

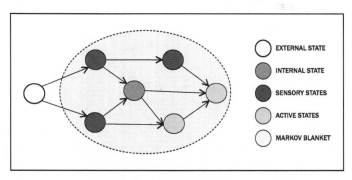

Figure 19. Markov blankets.

In **Box 3B** I introduced the Markov blanket, a mathematical construct with properties not unlike those attributable to the

Kabbalistic *RADLA*. Neurologist Karl Friston and others construe the scalar architecture of life beginning with cells and progressing to tissues, organs, organisms and societies as 'Markov blankets within Markov blankets'.[364,365] Inspired by Friston and Richard Conn Henry's "Mental Universe",[57] computer engineer and philosopher Bernardo Kastrup[4] advanced a theory based on idealism and the relational interpretation of quantum mechanics[366] which posits Universal Mind as the ontological primitive in which are lodged 'dissociated' bits of human (and other) consciousness. The latter remain distinct from, but indirectly interact with, each other and the Mental Ground via Markov blankets. The interactions collapse probabilistic wave functions (Kastrup's "thought waves") bounded by the Markov blankets thereby establishing realities which are uniquely perceived by each individual consciousness. Thus may the innumerable bubbles of immanent consciousness manifesting across all domains of the Creation depicted in Fig. 13 be distinguished from the surrounding Mental Ground (Mind of God) and from each other by the Markov-like attributes of their respective mini-*RADLA*s.

There are additional aspects of Kastrup's reasoning which to my mind dovetail nicely with Jewish mystical insight. I will first cite him *verbatim* and then render an interpretation of his words along Kabbalistic lines. Kastrup writes that Markov blankets are essential for independent existence because a

> hypothetical organism with perfect perception... would not have an upper bound on its own internal entropy... (and) would dissolve into an entropic soup.

In analogous fashion Markov-like features of the *RADLA* aspect of *Keter* (**Box 3B**) isolate human consciousness from the Mind of God thereby preserving for the former a semblance of free choice and unpredictability in the midst of Divinely-ordained universal wave function collapse (Fig. 20). Kastrup continues:

> To survive, organisms must... use their internal states to actively represent relevant states of the outside world in a *compressed, coded form* so to know as much as possible about their environment while remaining within entropic constraints compatible with maintaining their structural and dynamical integrity.

The *RADLA* similarly 'scrambles' knowledge of Divine Intent and conveys the encoded information to the lower *Partzufim* of the Tree of Life (Kabbalistic hierarchy). This ensures that for each

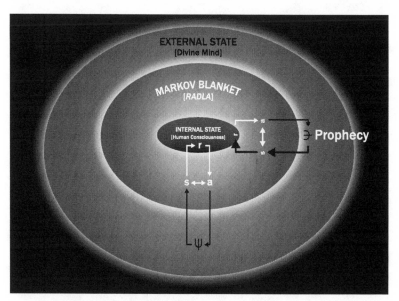

Figure 20. The *RADLA* as Markov blanket. 'r' denotes individual human consciousness; 'Ψ', universal consciousness (the 'Mind of God'); 'a', active state within Markov blanket allowing human consciousness to interact with Ψ. 's', sensory state within Markov blanket whereby Ψ impacts human consciousness. Thick arrows, permeation of the *RADLA* membrane (Markov blanket) during prophecy. Modified after [4] with permission.

individual, commensurate with his or her intellectual, moral and spiritual stature, a proper balance is struck between awareness of God ("And I will betroth you unto Me in faithfulness; and you shall know the Lord"[367] וארשתיך לי באמונה וידעת את ד') and the preservation of personal autonomy and free agency.

The aforementioned free will paradox can be reformulated drawing on concepts elaborated in Chapters 4-7 leading essentially to the same conclusions (inspired by Rabbi E. Goldstein[110]):

1) Every thing and event comprises a deca-*Sefirotic* $G''R$-$Z''T$ (mind-body) dipole.

2) Our world is a work-in-progress, a 'partnership' wherein God supplies the 'bodily' $Z''T$ components of the Creation and the willful actions of humankind 'bring down' the corresponding 'mental' $G''R$.

3) On Monday Alice is faced with an ethical dilemma. Before deciding on a course of action her baseline moral fiber is a $Z''T$ which integrates all the ethical decisions she made *in the past*. Her free-willed response to the *current* ethical challenge denotes the $G''R$ she now engages in order to bring her moral constitution to new deca-*Sefirotic* stability (for better or for worse).

4) When obliged to make another moral judgment (or any decision) on Tuesday, Monday's $G''R$ become incorporated into new, ground-level $Z''T$. This is metaphysically equivalent to the consolidation of a mineral's $G''R$ ('mind') within the $Z''T$ ('body') of a plant (Section 5.2).

5) Since all $Z''T$ are assigned by God, Alice's ethical (and other) decisions rendered on Monday, *now part of Tuesday's $Z''T$*, must in retrospect have been predetermined—a paradox! This

formulation is loosely consistent with a strand of compatibilism allowing for the coexistence of theological determinism and free will.[368,369] In the example given, only from the standpoint of *Orech* (Section 4.4) is it valid to say that Monday's free will *becomes*

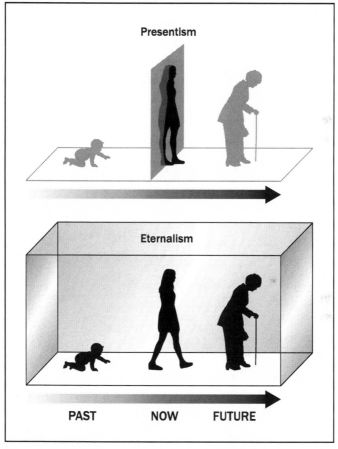

Figure 21. The Block Universe. Presentism (top) implies that only the present moment is real. The Block Universe or Eternalism (bottom) derives from Special Relativity and posits that all points in time and space are co-extant. The Block Universe is compatible with Kabbalistic notions of space-time as viewed from the holistic perspective of *Oivi*. Modified from https://www.resetera.com/threads/presentism-or-eternalism.107854.

Tuesday's predestination. Switching to an *Oivi* mode of consciousness (Section 4.4) we note that past, present and future Z"T we encounter sequentially are brought into being *'en bloc'* outside the space-time continuum by the Will of God (*Ratzon Elyon; Keter*). The Kabbalah specifies the *Sefirah Da'at* of *Partzuf Atik Yomin* concealed within a 'head' (known as the *Avirah*) of *Partzuf Arich Anpin* (see Section 4.2 and Fig. 7) as the nexus between holistic and linear time.[370] This Kabbalistic understanding of time is strikingly similar to the modern scientific idea of a 'Block Universe' otherwise known as 'Eternalism'. The latter is a logical consequence of Einstein's Special Relativity positing that space-time is not absolute and that the same event experienced by one being as happening 'now' already occurred in the timeline of another and has yet to materialize for a third[196,197] (Fig. 21). The modern conceptualization of a Block Universe breathes new life into the afore-cited commentary by *Rashi* to Genesis 29:3 that "All things currently in existence have always existed and will continue to exist in the future": שכל דבר ההוה תמיד כבר היה ועתיד להיות

The free will paradox is poignantly captured by Rabbi Mordechai Yosef Leiner, Rebbe of Izhbitze-Radzin (and relative of the author), who expanded on the famous Jewish dictum הכל בידי שמים חוץ מיראת שמים: "All is in the hands of heaven *except* for fear of heaven"[371] with the pithy refrain הכל בידי שמים אפילו יראת שמים: "All is in the hands of heaven *including* fear of heaven".[372,373] This theme was developed further by the Izhbitzer's student R' Tzadok Ha'Kohen of Lublin who concomitantly recognized human free will in the exoteric World of *Asiyah* while denying its existence in the timeless dimension of *Atzilut* where freedom is preempted by foreknowledge.[374,375] Even the term *'fore*knowledge' here is somewhat of a misnomer as elucidated by the sixteenth century sage, R' Shmuel ben-Yitzchak de Ozida: "For God is not bound by time—'before' and 'after' are not relevant terms to utilize concerning Him": כי הוא יתברך אינו תחת

הזמן ולא שייך ביה קדימה ואיחור.[375,376] Interested readers are referred to Moshe Idel's nuanced historical account of this intriguing 'atemporal-linear time' duality as conceived by the Abulafian school of Ecstatic Kabbalah and eighteenth century Chassidic masters.[377]

So ask a Kabbalist whether he is a libertarian who acknowledges free will in absolute terms or a compatibilist who reconciles human autonomy of choice with physical determinism and the short answer you're likely to hear is "yes". Personal decisions logically construed as rigidly predetermined in *Oivi*-consciousness are simultaneously experienced as indisputably real, at times agonizingly so, in *Orech*. As I attempted to show throughout this work, the Kabbalah is perfectly at ease with paradoxes of this kind which are adjudged as intrinsic characteristics of the warp and woof of Creation no less so than the wave-particle duality of light considered in Chapter 4. Under no circumstances would the Kabbalah permit dismissal of our mundane sense of agency, our qualia and our feelings as epiphenomenal or illusory as Daniel Dennett[36] and other material reductionists would have us do.

I suggest that the free will conundrum discussed above may be gainfully approached by analogy to how we cognitively assimilate our 'linear' existence within a Block Universe and the Kabbalah's treatment of time: Just as a deeper recognition of the atemporal nature of existence perceived through the lens of *Oivi* has little practical impact on our daily lives (after all, we still strive to learn from past mistakes and plan our future vacations) so too should we conduct our worldly affairs (e.g. rewarding good and punishing evil) assuming autonomous agency without concern for their preordination in more ethereal (supra-*RADLA*) realms.

How we intellectually navigate this *Orech-Oivi* divide is fundamental to an appreciation of the Kabbalah's ontology and so I ask that the reader ponder an additional (lighthearted) exemplification of the concept before leaving this chapter: From the everyday vantage point of *Orech* (or manifesting within Bohm's Explicate Order), each distillate of single malt Scotch expresses gustatory delights unique to its brand and vintage. At the same time, the Kabbalistic principle of Interinclusion (or Bohm's holographic Implicate Order) teaches that within each dram of whisky is enfolded the entire universe—including all manner of spirits. Thus, viewed from the holistic perspective of *Oivi*, all single malts are really hidden 'blends' which happen to reveal one or another of their charms to *Orech* consciousness. This dynamic, of course, holds true for all the particulars of Creation. A notable exception that highlights the rule is *Manna*—that miracle superfood we encountered in Section 5.2. The Oral Torah informs us that the gossamer nature of *Manna* was such that it left no digestive waste, could be consumed by angels and imparted any and all desired tastes.[378-380] This latter property, in line with the current thesis, may be interpreted as the unprecedented disclosure to the desert-faring Israelites of reality's concealed interinclusionary (holographic) substructure as perceived through *Oivi* consciousness. For the most part, however, just as mere *cognizance* of the underlying unity generally does not preclude the *experience* of some unique facet of that wholeness—a consequence of the Markov blanket-like *RADLA*—so is our profound sense of free choice (*B'chira Chofshit*) preserved in the face of recondite Divine determinacy. In rare instances of prophecy, permeabilization of the *RADLA* membrane to the transcendent *Ohr Ein-Sof* abolishes this sense of free agency as the prophet's consciousness is inundated by the immutable Will of God. In the following chapter, evidence is adduced that 'porosity' of the *RADLA* under pathological conditions may also be responsible for various perturbations of consciousness observed in the clinic.

Chapter 10

Clinical Models of Kabbalistic Panpsychism

A synthesis of key Kabbalistic concepts elaborated in this work may provide a novel framework with which to interpret a series of puzzling clinical observations related to altered states of consciousness and human brain physiology. As described in Chapter 1, a majority of contemporary neuroscientists, psychologists and philosophers adhere to the mainstream physicalist view that consciousness is an epiphenomenal by-product of brain physiology with no causal power *per se* and no representation outside of complex living organisms.

A major ongoing scientific endeavor aims to map out the salient 'neural correlates of consciousness (NCC)' — the specific brain loci and networks activated during various states of conscious experience — using an array of sensitive neuroimaging and electrophysiological techniques. A key premise undergirding this research is that increased brain activity (neurotransmitter release, generation of action potentials, altered gene expression profiles, etc.) subserving a given neurological or behavioral task is accompanied by a rapid enhancement of metabolic support to the active brain region. These metabolic changes can be measured as an increase in the delivery of blood, oxygen and glucose to the mobilized brain areas using sophisticated instrumentation such as functional magnetic resonance imaging (fMRI), magnetic resonance spectroscopy (MRS), single photon emission tomography (SPECT) and positron emission tomography (PET). These techniques have demonstrated that not only is there excellent correlation between the nature of the stimulus (e.g. images presented to the right visual field) and localization of the responding neural substrate (in this example, left occipital cortex), but the magnitude of the imaged response is often commensurate with the intensity of the stimulus.[381,382]

Although representing only 2% of the body by weight, the human brain accounts for about 20% of the body's total energy utilization. Moreover, approximately 80% of brain energy consumption is earmarked for neuronal signalling and other costly neurophysiological functions. Wolf Singer of the Max Planck Institute in Frankfurt/Main opined that "precise synchronization of oscillatory neuronal responses in the high frequency range (beta, gamma) plays an important role in gating the access of sensory signals to the workspace of consciousness",[383] a brain activity demanding a considerable expenditure of energy.[384] Subscribing to the position that consciousness is a mere 'secretion' of neural activity, most materialists anticipated that biomarkers of metabolic activation would correlate closely with the intensity of subjective experience in their experimental subjects. In his book *The Idea of the World* Bernardo Kastrup reviewed diverse experimental data indicating, quite unexpectedly, that this may not be the case at all.[385]

Bernardo surveyed published literature reporting on subjects experiencing self-transcendence or an expansion of consciousness as a consequence of cerebral hypoxia,[386] G-force acceleration,[387] near-death experiences,[388] transcranial magnetic stimulation,[389] trance-induced psychography (transcendent transcribing[390]), brain trauma (frontal or parietal lobe injury[391]) or exposure to psychedelic substances (psilocybin, lysergic acid diethylamide[392,393]). Surprisingly, indices of brain metabolism were significantly *suppressed* in most of these individuals while they concurrently reported vivid self-transcendence, mystical experiences and expanded consciousness. Brain metabolism rather than being augmented appeared to correlate *inversely* with the 'richness' or 'informational density' of the conscious experience.[385] Kastrup presented a cogent argument why the expanded consciousness in these subjects was not likely due to selective suppression of inhibitory brain connections by, or dissipation of, the provocative stimuli. His important message was that the disparity between the metabolic signature and the subjective experience ran contrary to hypothesis thereby airing a challenge to the materialist view of consciousness. For if the expansion of consciousness under these circumstances is not linked to neural metabolism (enhanced activity within the NCCs), either some underlying physical property unknown to science is responsible for the phenomenon or the latter is a manifestation of a non-material process.

Kastrup maintains that a strictly physicalist understanding of consciousness only admits scenarios where reduced neurometabolic activity results in diminished cognition and constricted consciousness, never self-transcendence and cognitive enrichment. On the other hand, he posits that the tenets of idealism and panpsychism allow for conditions where *either* impoverishment or enhancement of consciousness is the experiential correlate of neurometabolic suppression. How might this come about?

In the previous chapter we learned that according to Kastrup's idealism Markov blankets act to 'cordon off' dissociated pockets of consciousness (which he calls 'alters') from the embedding 'mind-at-large' thereby preserving for the former some degree of structural and functional autonomy. He hypothesizes that certain neuropsychiatric states such as those elicited by hypoxia or psychedelic drugs impair both the physical substrate of the brain (the nerve cells and their connections) as well as the delimiting Markov blanket. Damage or dysfunction of the neural tissue *per se* would account for curtailment of the brain's metabolic activity as ascertained by fMRI or PET. However, concomitant disruption ('increased porosity') of the Markov blanket would flood the alter with conscious experience of unprecedented intensity emanating from the 'mind-at-large'. These experiences may manifest as transpersonal perception, frenetic anxiety, hallucinosis, paranoia, bliss, vivid dreaming or mystical union—all the while registering *suppression* of neurometabolic activity in the laboratory. Alternatively, conditions which interfere with brain physiology while sparing Markov blanket integrity would again reveal hypoactivity on scanning but this would now be associated with cognitive or emotional impoverishment and a shrinking of consciousness.[385] Alzheimer dementia, structural and metabolic causes of coma and general anesthesia may be emblematic of this category.[394-396]

The conceptual landscape of Kabbalistic panpsychism exhibits significant nodes of overlap with Kastrup's idealist philosophy as it applies to altered clinical states of consciousness. The Kabbalah obviously employs a very different lexicon, adheres to the doctrine of panentheism and offers additional nuances of interpretation specific to its unique ontology. I have argued in Chapter 9 that the Kabbalistic construct known as the *RADLA* behaves as a Markov blanket which insulates 'bubbles' of human (and other) consciousness (Kastrup's alters) from the Mind of God. In what follows, the Mind of God is in some, but not all, ways homologous with Kastrup's 'mind-at-large'. One glaring difference is the status of Omniscience ascribed to God whereas Kastrup denies this attribute to 'mind-at-large':

> *External state psi (ψ) is a model of what it is like to be mind-at-large in the process of entertaining conflicting alternatives concurrently in its imagination. As such, the wave function of ψ does represent epistemic uncertainty;* **but—crucially—the epistemic uncertainty of mind-at-large itself, not of the alter observing it** *(original emphasis).*[397]

This of course is hardly a criticism of Kastrup as he elected to describe an internally consistent idealist ontology in purely secular terms independently of what his religious inclinations toward the subject matter may be.

In Chapter 9, I posited that information originating with the

Ein-Sof becomes 'scrambled' as a probabilistic wave function (ostensibly the spiritual underpinning of the Schrödinger equation) within the *RADLA* aspect of the *Partzuf Atik Yomin*. It is this 'distorted' message encompassing a range of possible outcomes that presents to human consciousness (Kastrup's alter). Upon observation, the wave of possibilities 'collapses' according to the Copenhagen interpretation of quantum mechanics yielding a single, seemingly random outcome as dictated by Heisenberg's Uncertainty Principle. The intimate relationship between the *Sefirah Keter* (the Will of God) and the *Sefirah Malchut* (the final transducer within each deca-*Sefirotic* system) establishes a pivotal *Keter-Malchut* axis assuring that despite the apparent stochasticity the final product (thing or event) conforms perfectly to God's original Intent. This mechanism, as described above at length, preserves for us a sense of agency and free will in the face of Divine determinacy (Chapters 6 and 9).

We saw that on rare occasions the *RADLA* curtain can be pierced by prophetic experience enabling glimpses of Divine Intent at the cost of personal autonomy as exemplified by the story of Balaam (Section 9.1). In some instances prophetic instruction 'leaks through' the *RADLA* membrane in the form of phantasmagorical sensations and surrealistic perceptions as in the case of Isaiah's Vision[398] and Ezekiel's Chariot.[399] Were such prophets to undergo functional neuroimaging in the midst of the prophetic experience what would their metabolic profiles look like? Would they show enhanced, unchanged or attenuated metabolic activity? One might suspect the latter for the following reason:

Recall from Chapter 5 that the Torah acknowledges a hierarchy of consciousness ascending from the lowly inanimate (*Domem*) to plant life (*Tzomeach*), animal sentience (*Chaye*) and human self-awareness (*M'daber*). We also noted that human consciousness is destined to 'evolve' to a sublime state of cosmic consciousness beginning in the Seventh (Messianic) Millennium. Axiomatic to the Kabbalah and establishing its panpsychist ontology is the idea that all entities and events comprise ten *Sefirot*, with the first three or *Gimel Rishonim* (*G"R*) *viz. Keter-Chochmah-Binah* or *Chochmah-Binah-Da'at* serving as the 'consciousness' (*Mochin*) for the bottom seven 'bodily' *Sefirot*. Also — and this is key — the Kabbalistic hierarchy of consciousness is patently relativistic. By this I mean that the consciousness-rendering *G"R* of one domain, say that of an isolated mineral, become 'absorbed' (Bohm might say 'enfold' or 'become implicate') within the unconscious *Z"T* of a plant as the latter acquires (reveals latent or renders explicit) 'higher-level' *G"R* mediating growth and reproduction (Chapter 5). This relativistic nature of the *G"R-Z"T* relationship is bidirectional and remains in flux with movement up and down the consciousness hierarchy. Thus, when a plant (*Tzomeach* domain) dies its *G"R* promoting growth and propagation no longer manifest and there is *de novo* expression of the lower-level *G"R* latent within the plant's organic and mineral constituents (*Domem* domain).

In humans (*M'daber* domain) the *Chaya* component of Soul mediating rationality may be suppressed or made implicate as a consequence of delirium, psychosis or coma at which time lower, *Neshama*-level consciousness (*Chaye* sentience) may predominate. With further disease progression, as in the case of certain neurovegetative states or brain death, the *Chaye* sentience may be superceded by *Ruach*-consciousness characteristic of *Tzomeach* (plant kingdom) which may still permit rudimentary physiological functions such as hypothalamic-pituitary regulation of salt and water balance[400] and epithelial cell division (hair and nail growth[401]). The *Nefesh* manifestation of Soul is essential for conferring existence to the inanimate (*Domem*) realm and thus remains with a corpse after all biological activity ceases.

I submit that under 'normal' circumstances (no prophecy,

intoxication or disease) human consciousness is predominantly an Immanent Light (*Ohr Pnimi*) inhering to brain matter and displaying direct correlations with metabolic profiles on neuroimaging. During prophecy, as the RADLA becomes 'permeable', human consciousness is transiently inundated with the surrounding Light of the *Ohr Ein-Sof* (Mind of God), an *Ohr Makif* which impinges on the recipient's mind in all manner of self-transcendence and expanded awareness. This may be mechanistically analogous to being granted sudden and precocious access to the kind of cosmic consciousness destined for humanity in and beyond the Seventh Millennium (see Chapter 13). The critical observation here based on the paradigm of relativistic consciousness is this: *When the Markov-like properties of the RADLA are compromised, influx of the surrounding Ohr Makif forces the recipients' baseline consciousness (an immanent Ohr Pnimi) to amalgamate with their unconscious bodily Z"T. Attenuation of the brain's endogenous consciousness (the Ohr Pnimi) in turn effects suppression of the corresponding neurometabolic activity.*

This model assumes that while *Ohr Pnimi* (Immanent Consciousness) operating *within* the brain co-registers with indices of tissue metabolism, the transcendent *Ohr Makif* like other instantiations of the *Sefirah Keter* manifests predominantly 'outside the system' — the brain in this case — and is therefore silent on neurometabolic imaging. The greater the effulgence of *Ohr Makif* (Transcendent Light), the less conscious is the baseline *Ohr Pnimi* (Immanent Light) and the lower would be the latter's associated neurometabolic fingerprint. This formulation is consistent with and may be deduced from the central Kabbalistic teaching that all things and phenomena are composed of ten *Sefirot* which generally omit or de-emphasize the 'interior' Light of the *Sefirah Da'at* when the 'exterior' Light of *Keter* is included and *vice versa* (see Fig. 4). Thus, in order to preserve deca-*Sefirotic* equilibrium we see reciprocal 'suppression' of the *Da'at* (intrinsic) aspect of *Mochin* ('brains') and its associated neurometabolic signature as the influence of the 'surrounding' Light of *Keter* (transpersonal consciousness) becomes increasingly salient.

One may ask: If the *Ohr* (Light) entering through the permeable *RADLA* transcends the *Keli* (brain), how does the recipient come to recognize the accruing subjective experience as enhanced? Queries of this nature assume that the transcendent *Ohr* of *Keter*, being as it were a 'crown *on*, but not *in*, the head' (Chapter 5), has no discernible influence on the recipient's consciousness. But this is incorrect. The Kabbalah indicates unequivocally that whereas an immanent *Ohr Pnimi* 'fills' and actualizes the potential of its Vessel (*Keli*), the transcendent *Ohr Makif* purifies the Vessel from the 'outside',[402] may impart to it novel qualities[403] and more closely aligns the Vessel with the Will of its Creator. The pivotal *Keter-Malchut* axis established by the latter process and its implications were discussed at length in Chapter 6 and need not be repeated here. But the following metaphors, which vary in degrees of abstraction, help place the 'incoming' *Ohr* of *Keter* in its proper context: (i) The waters of a Jewish ritual bath (Heb., *Mikvah*) are a quintessential *Ohr Makif* (surrounding Light) capable of spiritually 'cleansing' body and mind:[404] that the water molecules remain extracorporeal does not preclude the transfer of heat to, and the evocation of feelings in, the bather. (ii) A student may fail to absorb the lessons of her master (the *Ohr* remains a *Makif*) but may nonetheless experience rousing inspiration and awe in the mentor's presence. (iii) While the statement referring to *Keter as a* 'crown *on*, but not *in*, the head' is technically true (Chapter 5), how profoundly the thoughts and emotions of kings and queens must change at the moment of their coronation.

The model developed here would predict that mind-expanding exercises (e.g. ecstatic prayer or meditation), neuropsychiatric diseases (schizophrenia, bipolar psychosis, temporal lobe epilepsy) or chemical exposures (lysergic acid diethylamide, psilocybin, dimethyltryptamine, ayahuasca, ketamine) which enhance the 'porosity' of the *RADLA* would magnify the intensity of subjective experience while simultaneously reducing brain blood flow, oxygenation and glucose consumption. The latter may therefore accrue as a result of two distinct mechanisms: (i) noxious impact of the disease process or drug on brain metabolism as evinced by Kastrup[385] and (ii) relativistic suppression of the subject's intrinsic consciousness (*Mochin*) and its associated neurometabolic signature upon 'irradiation' with the transpersonal Light of *Keter*. Although these mechanisms need not be mutually exclusive, it may be feasible to design psychophysical experiments to differentiate between them, e.g. confirmation of neurometabolic inhibition or lack thereof in states of expanded awareness unrelated to tissue injury or intoxication.

Regardless of which mechanism is at play, it is reasonable to assume that the expansion of consciousness and neurometabolic suppression are graded phenomena which may vary in magnitude as a function of disease stage, dose of hallucinogenic drug, environs of the meditator or depth of prophetic instruction (see Section 9.1). However, we first learned in Section 4.2 and observed throughout this volume that *Ohr* (Light) is everywhere undifferentiated (*Pashut*) and only takes on 'color', 'texture' or 'shape' upon interacting with specific *Kelim* (Vessels). As such, whether the transcending Light surging through the permeable *RADLA* veil is experienced as rational or incoherent, exhilarating or demoralizing, a 'good trip' or a 'bad trip' is very much influenced by the neurological and psychosocial makeup of the recipient (*Keli*). This I believe may hold the key to a more universal and profound message concerning the health and welfare of individuals and society at large:

Whether by way of intuition, education or trial-and-error Kabbalistic teachings advocate that we should consciously strive to achieve optimal 'pairings' of our Lights and Vessels. A capable Vessel starved for Light will see fulfillment of its innate potential squandered. Just as inadequate activation of the *Reshimu* by an insufficient *Kav* would have preempted the Creation of the world we know (see Section 4.2) so might depriving a naturally intelligent youth (*Keli*) of proper parental upbringing, education and community life (*Ohr*) impose substantial limitations regarding future opportunities, accomplishments and sense of well-being. At the other extreme is the equally damaging outcome that results when the *Keli* (Vessel) is too weak to sustain its share of *Ohr* (Light). In Lurianic Kabbalah this is precisely what occurred in the primordial World of *Atzilut* when the initial Lights of the seven bottom *Sefirot* overcame and shattered their 'defective' Vessels (*Shvirat Hakelim*; Section 4.2) thereby giving rise to the 'lower' Worlds of *Briah*, *Yetzirah* and *Asiyah*.[106,112,134] As a 'world-in-miniature' (*Olam Katan*) reflecting the dynamics of the cosmos at large, we should appraise our aptitudes and qualifications as honestly and accurately as possible lest we take on more than we can chew and risk physical, mental or social decompensation (shattering of *our* Vessels). One size does not fit all—the same physical stressors, psychological challenges and social commitments that stimulate growth in Alice may prove egregiously burdensome and even crippling to Bob.

The religions of the world all have their 'formulae' for achieving a proper balance in the lives of their adherents. In the case of Judaism the prescription comes in the shape of 613 *Mitzvot* (commandments/actions) designed to sculpt the human psyche into *Kelim* appropriate for the optimal containment and implementation of Torah *Ohr*. This principle, captured by the simple verse נר מצוה ותורה אור ('*Mitzvot* are candles and Torah is Light'),[405] is the 'prime directive' of Jewish observance and a lifelong summons to refine.

Chapter 11

Kabbalah and Process Philosophy

An effective method for conveying subtle Kabbalistic insights to the uninitiated is to adduce compelling analogies with contemporary secular thought. Alignment of Interinclusion (*Hitkallelut*) with Bohm's Holographic Universe (Section 3.2) and the *RADLA* construct with Heisenberg's Uncertainty Principle (Chapter 9) exemplified this approach. In like fashion several Kabbalistic concepts discussed herein resonate strongly with twentieth century process philosophy championed by Alfred North Whitehead (1861-1947) and others.[406] The following is a juxtaposition of process philosophy with Kabbalistic thought and its implications for the mystery of consciousness:

1) Just as the deca-*Sefirotic* infrastructure applies to any defined entity — be it a 'thing', event or thought — so in process philosophy are changing experiences or 'actual occasions' more the stuff of reality than finite objects.[352,407,408] A similar theme was taken up by physicist Lee Smolin at the Perimeter Institute for Theoretical Physics in Waterloo, Ontario who, influenced by Leibniz's *Monadology*, regards 'events' rather than objects as the fundamental building blocks of nature.[409] According to Smolin it is the interpenetration (see Section 4.3) of 'like' events throughout the universe which gives rise to the mainstream quantum mechanical principle of 'entanglement' (*ibid.*). Physicist Menas Kafatos at Chapman University (California) construes the emergence of the material universe as originating in an unbroken field of consciousness along analogous process lines.[410]

2) A major Kabbalistic position germane to the evolution of consciousness is the emergence of something from nothing (*Yesh*

M'ayin) and the ongoing relationship of the finite (Gvul) to the infinite (Bilti-Gvul). By the same token "the core issue for both Whiteheadian Process and Quantum Process is the emergence of the discrete from the continuous."[411]

3) Akin to the Kabbalah, process philosophy is monist and panpsychist in so far as all 'occasions' are regarded to be experiential, self-determining and internally related to each other (i.e. manifesting interactions not mediated by external forces).[412] The two systems conceive of each event and entity as bearing both a bodily and mental dimension[413] thereby solving Chalmers' 'hard' mind-body problem[414] and permitting downward causation.[415,416]

4) Although process philosophy and panpsychism per se do not demand theism[417] and although there are important, even irreconcilable, differences in the conceptualization of God's relationship to the Creation between process thought and the Kabbalah (a topic beyond the scope of this monograph), both the Kabbalah (Chapter 5) and the Whitehead-Hartshorne school of process theology are decidedly panentheistic.[418]

5) The Kabbalistic vision of hierarchical and relativistic consciousness (Chapter 5) is mirrored in process philosophy by experiential 'molecule-occasions' and 'cell-occasions' combining to form a 'regnant' or dominant society of occasions and reaching peak expression in the self-aware human mind.[412]

6) In the example cited in Section 9.1 the baseline constitution Alice brings to each new moral decision was construed as a Z"T (seven lower or 'bodily' Sefirot) amalgamating the sum total of all her previous experiences pertaining to ethics. Process philosophy invokes the term 'prehension' to advance a similar notion whereby "every actual occasion receives data from every

other actual occasion in its past."[412] Whitehead refers to the process of combining current indeterminate data (reminiscent of the Kabbalistic $G''R$ or three top 'conscious' *Sefirot*) with determinate past data (the $Z''T$) as "concrescence". Concrescence distils the entire past universe of the individual into a single moment of particular experience not unlike the integration of $G''R$ and $Z''T$ for completion of a new deca-*Sefirotic* dyad. Once relegated to the past the latter is 'compressed' as a fully determinate $Z''T$ ('body') ready to interact with a newly presenting $G''R$ ('mind'; Chapter 9). Similarly, concrescence generates "an objectively immortal datum for all future occasions."[412,419] The dynamics of process concrescence and $G''R$-$Z''T$ compactification are further embodied in Bohm's ontology alluded to in Chapter 3 wherein "each mental side (of every physical-mental dipole) becomes a physical side as we move in the direction of greater subtlety."[231]

Chapter 12

Consciousness and Conscience

Roundly resisted by contemporary science and reductive materialism, Kabbalistic metaphysics envisions a seamless interpenetration of cosmology with ethics, of consciousness with morality. Whereas animal consciousness (*Chaye*) aims for as its highest goal the preservation of the self and the species, human consciousness (*M'daber*) incorporates and transcends animal consciousness exercising altruism and self-denial in order to achieve a greater, future good for humanity and the world. Sourced 'above' *Briah/Binah* (Section 5.2), according to the Kabbalah *M'daber* is the sole creation endowed with a semblance of free will (*B'chira Chofshit*; Section 9.1). When one actively engages the path of evil, consciousness contracts to the level of *Chaye* and the *Nefesh Ha'bahamit* (Animal Soul) reigns supreme.[232,233] The Torah maintains that mankind only lapses into Sin when overtaken by a 'spirit of folly' (*Ruach Shtut*)[420] — a 'moral encephalopathy' which obviates awareness of the Higher Good rooted in the *Ohr Ein-Sof*.[421] When one embarks on the path of righteousness *Chaye* consciousness is transcended, the Divine Will (*Ratzon Elyon*) is actualized and the proclivities of the *Nefesh Ha'bahamit* are harnessed or sublimated by the *Nefesh Ha'Elokit* (Godly Soul). The Kabbalah makes the radical claim that the full blossoming of human consciousness may align more with moral clarity and ethical behavior than with sheer intellectual prowess or brute perceptual awareness.

Contemporary physics has made great strides in the last century unifying four of five fundamental 'axes' described by the ten *Sefirot*: the *Chochmah-Binah* axis denoting time and the three axes of space, *Chesed-Gevurah*, *Netzach-Hod* and *Tiferet-Yesod*[422,423] (Fig. 4A and 22). According to the Kabbalah, a complete understanding of nature or 'Theory of Everything' will not be achievable until the fifth axis, *Keter-Malchut* referring to the Will of God or Holiness and its ethical imperatives, is brought into the equation (R' E. Goldstein, *personal communication*). As *Keter* is a Transcendent Light (*Ohr Makif*) that resides 'outside' whatever frame of reference we are dealing with, it often assumes the mathematical value of infinity. *Ergo*, there exists an inexhaustible number of 'infinities' corresponding to all the mini-*Keters* disseminated in fractal fashion throughout the Kabbalistic universe (see Chapter 5). It was not until the late nineteenth century that Georg Cantor, father of set theory, laid out mathematical proofs implying the existence of a 'hierarchy of infinities' ... and he designated the infinite cardinals (number of elements that a set has) using the first Hebrew letter *Aleph* ($\aleph_0, \aleph_1, \aleph_2$...).[424]

It is commonplace for the exoteric (revealed) Torah to employ the number 'eight' to convey a sense of transcendence akin to that connoted by *Keter*. Thus do Jews circumcise their sons on the eighth day,[425] a supra-rational act Willed by God which transcends the 'natural' order of the seven-day week (days of Creation). Another instantiation is the miracle of Chanukah where a cruse of olive oil sufficient for one day burned 'unnaturally' for eight consecutive days.[426] Hinting further at this '*Keter*-eight' duality is the fact that a) the numerical diminutive (*Mispar Katan*; see Section 4.4) of the Hebrew word *Keter* כתר amounts to eight (20 + 400 + 200 → 2 + 4 + 2 = 8), b) the mathematical symbol for infinity (∞) is an eight lying on its side, c) musical scales recognized by the Kabbalah for their transcendent qualities[427] are defined by octaves, and d) the Hebrew words for 'eight' שמנה and 'oil' שמן share common roots, with 'eight' transcending frames of reference much as oil separates out above water. R' Pinchas of Koretz extends this simile further teaching that שמן (oil) and השכינה (the Divine Presence) have the same *Gematria* (numerical value) of 345. The

Koretzer thereby conflates the indelible stain left by oil on cloth and the perpetuity conferred to objects touched by Holiness such as the Western Wall of the Temple in Jerusalem:השכינה נקראת שמן...וכמו שמן שנופל על הבגד נשאר רשימו לעולם, כך כל דבר שבקדושה עושה רושם לעולם...כמו כותל המערבי.[428]

Although beloved by mathematicians, 'infinities' as the following quote indicates are often a major headache for physicists when they appear in their equations:

Infinities are unruly quantities that tend to blow up any theory they appear in. They delayed by decades the unified electroweak theory that explains most things above the level of the atomic nucleus. Now in the form of black holes and other incalculable singularities like the Big Bang, they stand in the way of a unified quantum theory of gravity. Trouble is, no one's worked out how to do the maths without it (infinity).[429]

Perhaps we will one day succeed in factoring into our unified field equations the operations of this fifth, *Keter-Malchut* axis and the role of Divine Will or Holiness. Maybe then will those annoying 'infinities' that keep cropping up in the mathematics of physics and cosmology find their true place or disappear altogether.

The moral grounding of consciousness and the physical cosmos, although foreign to mainstream secular thinking, is not unique to Judaism and figures prominently in definitions of 'enlightenment' espoused by Zoroastrianism, Buddhism, Hinduism and other Eastern mystical traditions.[430] So what shape does the Kabbalah predict the metaphysic of human consciousness will assume once this 'fifth axis' is universally acknowledged and incorporated into our equations? This we explore in the following chapter.

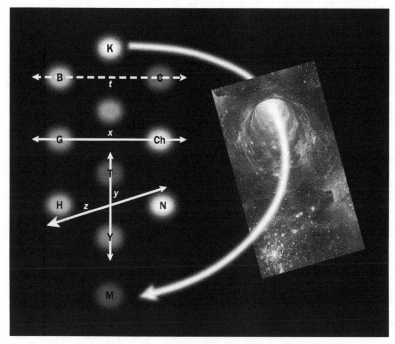

Figure 22. Fundamental axes of reality. Science currently acknowledges three revealed dimensions of space (x, y, z) and one of time (t) described by eight (four pairs) of the ten *Sefirot*. The Kabbalah insists that a 'Theory of Everything' will remain elusive pending incorporation of *Keter-Malchut* ($K{\rightarrow}M$), a fifth axis of *Kedushah* (Holiness) originating beyond the physical universe.

Chapter 13

The Future of Human Consciousness

In the 600th year of the Sixth Millennium (1840 CE) the upper gates of wisdom (Kabbalah) will be opened and also the wellsprings of wisdom below (secular knowledge). This will prepare the world for the Seventh millennium like a person prepares himself on Friday for Shabbat, as the sun begins to wane.
— The Zohar[431]

ובשית מאה שנין שתיתאה יתפתחון תרעי דחכמתא לעילא ומבועי לתתא,
ויתתקן עלמא לאעלא בשביעאה. כבר נש דמתתקן ביומא שתיתאה כי ערב
שמשא לאעלא בשבתא

A major emphasis of this volume is the frustratingly enigmatic nature of consciousness as viewed through the prism of contemporary physics, neuroscience and philosophy. Many have argued, indeed accept as axiomatic, that there is nothing more obvious to our minds than the brute fact that we are conscious, have feelings and experience qualia. Yet, we remain utterly stymied by Chalmers' 'Hard Problem' — how and why is the electrochemical activity in our neural circuitry transduced to subjectively palpable percepts, thoughts, memories and emotions? How can the physical laws that govern the workings of our material universe possibly account for first-person experience? In this volume, I laid out a framework which strives to make sense of these elusive matters based on remarkable congruencies which have come to light (and continue to emerge) between the ancient tenets of Kabbalistic panpsychism and several of the most counterintuitive aspects of modern physics. Further questions one may raise at this juncture are: 'What does the Kabbalah tell us about the epistemology of consciousness?

Will mainstream science and philosophy ever arrive at a meaningful understanding of the phenomenon? When, if ever, will the "Hard Problem" soften?'

Readers may be surprised to learn that the Kabbalah addresses these queries with considerable precision. The Kabbalah teaches that the entire Creation is ultimately founded upon the Tetragrammaton—the 4-letter Name of God י-ק-ו-ק transliterated as *Y-K-V-K*. In this configuration the *Y-K* part of the Tetragrammaton represents the *G"R* (*Mochin* or 'brains') for everything created within the Primordial Void (*Makom Panoi*; see Section 4.2). The latter two letters, the *V-K*, are dual to the *Z"T* (*Keli* or 'body') and to the general *Partzufim Zeir Anpin* and *Nukvah* of the Creation. We currently (and for the last 5780 years according to the Hebrew calendar) inhabit a universe overtly governed by the influences of the Worlds, *ABY"A* which 'dress' the *Netzach-Hod-Yesod* (lower *Sefirot*) and constitute the *Zeir Anpin* and *Nukvah* of the supernal World of *Adam Kadmon*. *ABY"A* do not 'cloth' the higher aspects of *Adam Kadmon* (i.e. *Chesed-Gevurah-Tiferet*) which comprise the *Partzufim Abba* and *Imma*. Consciousness represented by the *Y-K* aspect of God's Name thus 'resides' in *Adam Kadmon above* the point of its overlap with *ABY"A*. Because consciousness is transmitted from *Adam Kadmon* to the lower Worlds of *ABY"A* only *indirectly* via *the* former's *Netzach-Hod-Yesod*, consciousness is 'felt' (qualia are experienced) in the physical world but remains impenetrable to us intellectually. This, according to Kabbalistic reasoning, is what renders Chalmers' consciousness problem 'hard'. Jewish mystical tradition teaches, however, that beginning in the year 6000 (the Seventh or Sabbatical Millennium), the hitherto concealed influence of *Partzuf Imma* in *Adam Kadmon* ('above' the latter's *Netzach-Hod-Yesod*) will be revealed (*Gilui*) at which point consciousness as a fundamental force of nature will prove as accessible to human understanding as space-time, matter and energy are today.

What is the metaphysical underpinning of this transition to Seventh Millennium consciousness? To get some inkling as to how this phenomenon may unfold several basic principles of mainstream Kabbalah outlined in Chapter 4 must be revisited, combined and applied. The first such principle is Interinclusion— the notion that the entire universe is recapitulated, like a Mandelbrot set, within each of its parts. The miniature 'burning bush' contained within each stone hewn from Mount Sinai[148,149] and the information required to 'program' a whole person latent within the DNA of each cell[1] were examples of this. The second principle we need to consider here is Interpenetration—that intimate spiritual and non-local physical bonds exist between every particular and its doppelgängers distributed throughout the entire fractal infrastructure of the Creation. To illustrate the concept I cited R' Moshe Schatz's example of the fullest expression of an organism's right eye requiring a synthesis of the right orbit *per se* with attributes of "right-eyeness" permeating all of the creature's myriad parts.[168] The third principle concerns the *Orech-Oivi* divide—a paradigm shift of perspective between the multipartite 'vertical' hierarchy of the Creation as commonly experienced by humankind (*Orech*) and the 'horizontal' vantage point of reality's deeper underlying unity (*Oivi*) as God would see it.

We noted in Chapter 4 that as the relationship between Alice and Bob matures, they progressively and reciprocally identify the presence of (Interinclusion) and bond with (Interpenetration) mini-personas of themselves which lay latent within one another. The interaction effects a spiritual 'exchange' (*Chiluf*) of Alice's mini-Bob for Bob's mini-Alice thereby promoting the unification of both parties.[110] We noted in Chapter 8 in our discussion of *Tefillin* (phylacteries) how 'exchanges' or 'crossings' of this kind promote a 'strengthening' of the spirit and by extension to their physical correlates within the brain, putative optimization of neurological and psychological functioning. Next, imagine Alice and Bob repeating this 'entanglement' with their innumerable mini-counterparts distributed in fractal fashion throughout the vast expanse of the Creation. Picture this Interpenetration sweeping across large swaths of humanity. Now extrapolate the Interpenetration process to *all* interincluded facets of the cosmic hologram—be they galaxies, life forms, elements or quarks—and thence to the latter's fundamental deca-*Sefirotic* substructures (see Fig. 12). Complete this exercise by mentally conjuring a seamless 'lattice' of *G"Rs* (*Mochin* or 'brains') accruing from the enormous assemblage of Interpenetrated *Sefirot* and the utopian vision of a 'cosmic consciousness' begins to take shape.

Bear in mind that Seventh Millennium consciousness only unfolds as a gradual, linear process when viewed from the mundane, temporal perspective of *Orech*. From the holistic, supra-temporal standpoint of *Oivi*, absolute consciousness is ever-omnipresent throughout the cosmos in so far as "regarding the Creator, no change occurred from before the Creation to after": שלגבי הבורא לא חל שום שינוי בין קודם הבריאה ואחריה.[178] The Kabbalah here is expounding the proverb אין כל חדש תחת השמש "There is nothing new under the Sun"[432] in its most profound sense. What we experience in *Orech*-consciousness as the historical unraveling of reality and incremental enlightenment is but the piecemeal *revelation* of an all-pervasive and immutable Consciousness—the *Ohr Ein-Sof*. I submit that the holomovement of Bohmian mechanics (Section 3.2) and Kastrup's mind-at-large (Section 9.1) are scientific and philosophical expressions of panpsychism that are theologically non-committal but operationally isomorphic with the *Ohr Ein-Sof*. (Although Bohm enjoyed intense and protracted intellectual discourse with the Indian philosopher Jiddu Krishnamurti (1895-1986), he was generally coy about his personal religious beliefs. In an interview conducted by Harvard professor Renée Weber in 1986 Bohm was reminded of a statement he made affirming the existence of a "super-intelligence that is benevolent and compassionate, not neutral". Asked how his Implicate Order differs from what the great mystics have been saying all along Bohm admitted: "I don't know that there's necessarily any difference".[433])

From the above considerations, and true to its panpsychist ontology, revelations of heightened consciousness in the Messianic era are anticipated to impact the whole of Creation and not be limited to humankind. Hinting at the broader implications of this transformation the prophet Isaiah informs us that "the wolf shall dwell with the lamb and the leopard shall lie down with the kid... and a little child shall lead them: וגר זאב עם כבש, ונמר עם גדי ירבץ...ונער קטן נהג בם[434] That the global enhancement of awareness will be felt across all domains of existence is similarly expressed in the closing prayers of the Yom Kippur (Day of Atonement) liturgy: תן פחדך...על כל מעשיך ...ויעשו כלם אגדה אחת לעשות רצונך בלבב שלם "Instill Your awe... upon all Your works... Let them all become a single society to do Your Will wholeheartedly".

A full discussion regarding the extent of change anticipated to accompany the advent of the Messianic era is beyond the scope of this work. This is a sharply debated topic in ancient and medieval sources. Some authorities, Nachmanides for example, anticipate fairly radical perturbations in physical law, human nature, the status of free will and sin, etc. Others, notably Maimonides, predict a less dramatic transition from the current natural order.[435] All would agree, however, that what we will witness is nothing short of, as Thomas Nagel aptly framed it, a "universe gradually waking up and becoming aware of itself".[436]

The Kabbalah forecasts that between the Seventh and Tenth Millennium (the end of linear time and the complete 'retraction' of Orech into Oivi—see Fig. 9C), every thousand years will mark a significant milestone in the expansion of human consciousness that ultimately culminates in the revelation of the Yechida component of Soul.[437,438] The Yechida is a Transcendent Light (Ohr Makif) that, unlike the 'personal' surrounding Light of the Chaya aspect of Soul, encompasses the whole of Creation—a final universal consciousness (see Chapter 5 and Table 3) where the boundaries between self and non-self are erased.[439] The French paleontologist and Jesuit priest Pierre Teilhard de Chardin (1881-1955) envisioned a similar, albeit far more distant, future where life evolves a consciousness that saturates the entire cosmos before converging in a singularity ('*Omega point*') of unimaginable intelligence and complexity.[440] A number of accomplished scientists and philosophers (e.g. Andrei Linde, David Deutsch) have espoused similar views, with some (Raymond Kurzweil, Frank Tipler) predicting that technology and artificial intelligence are likely to propel the universe to the Omega point long after humanity's exit from the cosmic stage.[23]

Although veiled in mystery, there may be more we can deduce from Kabbalistic teachings concerning the ultimate fate of human consciousness. Fittingly, homologues (*Kinuim*) of the *Yechida* dimension of Soul are the *Sefirah Keter*, the *Partzufim Arich Anpin* and *Atik Yomin* and the World of *Adam Kadmon* (Section 5.2). These dualities signify (i) the nothingness (*Ayin*) that 'preceded' and gave birth to the *Chochmah Nekudah* (singularity);[441] (ii) a profound shift from divisibility (*Pirud*) to unicity (*Shlaymut*); and (iii) 'reabsorption' of the finite (*Gvul*) back into the infinite (*Bilti-Gvul*). So refined (*Birur*) will the Vessel (*Keli*) eventually become as to render it indistinguishable from the Light (*Ohr*). The surrounding *Ohr Ein-Sof* will be entirely assimilated as an interiorized *Ohr Pnimi* within the future Void (*Makom Panoi* or primordial *Keli*). The *Leshem* alludes to this eventuality with the words: לעתיד יתייחד כל אור מקיף באור פנימי "In the future, all transcendent Light will become unified with the immanent Light".[442] This is analogous to a student enlightened by *all* the wisdom of her master (Chapter 8) in consummation of the verse: כי תמלא הארץ לדעת את כבוד ד' כמים יכסו על ים "knowledge of God will fill the Earth like the sea fills the ocean bed."[443] Given such circumstances one may wonder what will be the ultimate fate of *individual* human consciousness when the *Yechida* aspect of Soul predominates. If no remnants of discrete consciousness survive this Great Merger of Being, what 'added value' will have accrued from Creation (and humankind in particular) in the first place? The answer to this question is not known and may never be known; some argue that the query may not even be legitimately posed.[444]

The sixth of Thirteen Principles of Torah Exegesis elaborated by R' Yishmael, interpreted allegorically, may provide a hint in support of the Creation's paramount significance long after dissipation of its component particulars. The Sixth Principle states: כלל ופרט וכלל, אי אתה דן אלא כעין הפרט.[445] This translates literally as "General and specific and general—no rulings are made (on the general category) except in light of the specifics." It is a hermeneutical instrument which refocuses the application and scope of Torah law *vis-à-vis* a general category repeated in Scripture based on the intervening citation of one or more specific examples drawn from that general category. Inasmuch as the Torah is conceived as the 'blueprint' of Creation—הסתכל באורייתא וברא עלמא "(God) looked into the Torah and created the World"[167]—R' Yishmael's principle may be understood as follows: ...כלל—unicity preceding the Creation (prior to *Tzimtzum*)...; ...ופרט—the current state of affairs (separateness/ *Pirud*)...; ...וכלל—return in End-Times to conditions of absolute wholeness (*Shlaymut*)[446]...אי אתה דן אלא כעין הפרט—the final wholeness is impacted (in some ineffable way only understood by God) by the interim Creation. If true, the profundity of human consciousness at the pinnacle of Creation would be monumental— the furthest cry imaginable from the epiphenomenal status ascribed to it by mainstream psychology and neuroscience.

Chapter 14

Conspectus

For reasons of religion, language, demographics and politics, until the period known as the *Haskalah* (Jewish Emancipation; c. 1770-1880) the popular world and Jewish literatures were in large measure self-contained and non-intersecting. Notwithstanding the widespread acquaintance with early Biblical literature, the West (including many secular Jews) to this day remains unaware of a deep reservoir of metaphysical and philosophical thought contained within large compendia of (mainly Hebrew and Aramaic) extra-Biblical Jewish manuscripts. In this book I attempted to crystallize a conceptualization of consciousness based on the teachings of Judaism's mystical tradition, the Kabbalah. Evidence from the writings of leading Kabbalistic and Chassidic authorities, buttressed by Scripture, the Talmud and other mainstream Jewish sources, support a formulation of consciousness that is panpsychist in nature and informed by the tenets of panentheism. According to the Kabbalah the mental pole of reality transcends and pervades the entirety of Creation while remaining absolutely unified at its source. The Kabbalah understands consciousness to be hierarchically and holographically organized, relativistic and capable of downward causation. Metaphysical constructs unique to humankind (in the spirit of *imago Dei*) augment intrinsic neural consciousness manifesting as self-awareness, enhanced intuition and subjective moral autonomy.

I endeavored in this volume to provide a vivid conceptualization of consciousness based on the tenets of Kabbalistic panpsychism in the context of contemporary psychology, quantum mechanics and neuroscience. Nowhere did I make claims to the testability or veracity of the notions expounded or their exclusivity to the Jewish mystical tradition. In so far as the latter ultimately rests on matters of faith—such as belief in the existence of an omniscient Deity—after all applications of the intellect are exhausted, efforts to 'validate' the positions elaborated here are unlikely to succeed using scientific or other objective methodologies.

But is scientific ratification the only hallmark of truth? Many leading scientists including Einstein were confident about the correctness of their theories *a priori*, not for any definitive experimental proof (for there was often precious little of that initially) but because they held them to be majestic or beautiful![447] Others deny such linkage or view it as potentially counter-productive. For example, Stony Brook biologist Douglas Futuyma cautioned that recent efforts invoking epigenetic modifications (the so-called Extended Evolutionary Synthesis) as a mitigating force against the role of genetic hard-wiring in human evolution may be motivated more by the theory's emotional or esthetic appeal (people 'preferring' not to be enslaved to their genomes) than by any commitment to scientific objectivity.[448]

On which side of this dialectic does Judaism weigh in? That truth is somehow predicated on beauty is supported by the prophet Micah's proclamation "Grant truth to Jacob":[449] תתן אמת ליעקב. Why specifically Jacob? Why not Abraham or Isaac? The Kabbalah associates the Patriarchs Abraham, Isaac and Jacob respectively with the *Sefirot Chesed* (Lovingkindness), *Gevurah* (Strength) and *Tiferet* (Beauty). "Granting truth to Jacob" thereby sets up an 'equation' directly linking truth with beauty (*Tiferet*). Kabbalistic panpsychism displays high internal consistency, elegant parsimony, a broad explanatory reach and remarkable convergence with ideas at the cutting edge of science and philosophy. As such, it is the author's deep conviction that notwithstanding its inaccessibility to scientific scrutiny Kabbalistic panpsychism is ripe for further investigation into the elusive nature of consciousness. Before dyed-in-the-wool materialists balk at this suggestion they should remind themselves how utterly opaque the consciousness phenomenon is to current reductionist thinking and how equally refractory are a number of popular scientific formulations of reality—such as the Multiverse[79] and Superstring theories[450]—to any modicum of formal verification. Indeed, if the *sine qua non* of the scientific method is a theory's potential falsifiability[451] one may question whether concepts such as the Multiverse qualify as science altogether! Kabbalistic and other revelation-based formulations of reality are, of course, also non-falsifiable. But theological truths need not meet criteria for falsifiability inasmuch as they make no claims to having been derived scientifically. For this reason I find reference to the 'science of Kabbalah'[452,453] oxymoronic.

Some thinkers acknowledge the value of scientific modeling to capture computational features of mind but nonetheless cast doubt whether certain phenomena of consciousness will ever prove amenable to scientific analysis. In this vein, cognitive neuroscientist and philosopher Jerry Fodor opined that "the problem of creativity, imagination and emotion... [are] aspects of the world [for] which scientific theory construction may not be the appropriate approach;... if you want to know about emotion, read Henry James."[454]

Kabbalistic panpsychism may go further than many other traditions, scientific or otherwise, to capture the physical, psychological and spiritual dimensions of the human condition in a highly integrated and comprehensive manner. Salient contributions of the Kabbalah to the understanding of human and other consciousness presented in this work may be summarized as follows:

1) Rather than contradicting Kabbalistic doctrine, current scientific knowledge unavailable to earlier generations, such as

Heisenberg's Uncertainty Principle and Bohm's Implicate Order (Chapter 3), has clarified with uncanny precision Jewish mystical perspectives on the workings of the human mind and the nature of consciousness.

2) As a panpsychist discipline promulgating the ubiquity of proto-conscious *Sefirot* in every facet and at all scales of Creation, the Kabbalah effectively does away with Chalmers' Hard Problem of consciousness (Chapters 1 and 2). Furthermore, in its assertion that the primordial three upper *Sefirot* (*Mochin*; 'brains') remained intact as the lower seven 'bodily' *Sefirot* 'shattered' (*Shvirat Hakelim*) in the course of Creation, Lurianic Kabbalah explains why consciousness regardless of form or complexity always manifests as a unified whole (Chapter 4).

3) In its sweeping insistence on the unicity of nature at its core, the Kabbalah rejects any hard distinctions between 'things' and 'events', a view echoed in recent times by proponents of process philosophy and Bohmian mechanics (Chapters 3 and 11).

4) A major criticism leveled against general panpsychism is the so-called 'Combinational Problem' — how mediators of simple consciousness characteristic of 'lesser' creatures synergize within 'higher' organisms to yield more complex psychic phenomena. In common with aspects of idealism and cosmopsychism, the Kabbalah neutralizes this challenge by emphasizing the existence of a Universal Mind, specifically the Mind-of-God, which in top-down, panentheistic fashion progressively reveals itself within the Creation hierarchy. Mechanistically, this revelation is realized in the relativistic and contextual unfolding of the $G''R$ (conscious) and $Z''T$ (unconscious) components of all deca-*Sefirotic* dipoles. As described in Chapter 5, $G''R$ endowing consciousness to objects occupying lower strata of Creation (e.g. minerals in the *Domem*

domain) are compactified within the unconscious $Z"T$ of higher-order objects (e.g. trees in the *Tzomeach* domain) as the latter complete their deca-*Sefirotic* dipoles with novel, more complex $G"R$ (growth and reproduction in the case of plants).

5) Mainstream neuroscience construes consciousness as a 'secretion' and prisoner of the brain. The Kabbalah begs to differ. It intimates that trans-corporeal (non-local) properties of human consciousness, mediated by the *RADLA* aspect of *Partzuf Atik Yomin*, represented by the box of the head phylacteries (*Bayit* of *Tefillin Shel-Rosh*) and mirroring or 'entangled' with transcendent aspects of Divinity (*Ohr Makif*), may account for extrasensory perception, prophecy, the near-death experience and other 'paranormal' phenomena documented in virtually every culture (Chapters 5, 6 and 8).

6) For millennia the Kabbalah has endorsed the intriguing albeit counterintuitive notion of ontologic paradox—paradox that is intrinsic to the Creation and not contingent upon limitations of human knowledge. This position was anathema to the business of scientific inquiry until the early twentieth century when physicists were compelled to reappraise their grasp on reality after embracing the wave-particle duality of light. In its description of the *RADLA* and the complementary *Orech/Oivi* modes of awareness the Kabbalah paints a picture of human consciousness which paradoxically permits free choice and the exercise of morality in a universe preordained by God (Chapters 4, 7, 9 and 12).

7) Combining insights adduced from the relativistic nature of consciousness (Chapter 5), the Markov-like properties of the *RADLA* (Chapter 9) and a series of clinical observations, a model is proposed whereby mind-expanding exercises, certain neuropsychiatric diseases or psychotropic drug exposures

would markedly enhance the intensity of subjective experience while concomitantly and paradoxically reducing brain metabolism (Chapter 13). The inverse relationship between the brain's metabolic signature and the vividness of subjective experience constitutes a challenge to the materialist view of consciousness.

8) Extrapolating from its analysis of the Golem (Section 5.3), the Kabbalah might predict that artificial intelligence irrespective of its level of complexity or sophistication will never achieve the status of human (*M'daber*) consciousness and therefore will not require protection by legislation equivalent to human rights. On the other hand, the Torah does ascribe to the Golem animal-like (*Chaye*) sentience and, by extension, it is conceivable that future robotics may be similarly endowed with *Chaye*-level consciousness. Should this prove to be the case, Jewish law (*Halachah*) currently in place to minimize animal suffering may be applicable to advanced AI.

9) While Bible scholarship across the board would concur that the Tower of Babel incident was a watershed moment in human history, a Kabbalistic understanding of the event may have far-ranging implications well beyond the diversification of language. Although the human domain *M'daber* technically means 'speaker', the Kabbalah attributes to humankind *Chaya*-level consciousness which in addition to language confers aspects of self-awareness and intuition not accessible by lower strata (Section 5.1). We argue here that God's response to the challenge posed by the Tower of Babel was to 'demote' *Chaya* consciousness in a broad sense whereby individuals lost the ability to not only comprehend their neighbors' spoken language but to 'read' the impact of shared experiences on their qualia, mindset and motives (Section 5.5). The latter would conceivably instill suspicion, fear, and hostility which in turn may sow the seeds of

racism, xenophobia and genocide.

10) Kabbalistic predictions regarding a future epistemology of consciousness is decidedly optimistic. In Chapter 9 we encountered a barrier to scientific inquiry delimited by the Uncertainty Principle of quantum mechanics and its Kabbalistic equivalent, the *RADLA*. Extrapolating from the fact that there are named entities beyond the *RADLA* of *Atzilut* in the Kabbalistic 'Tree of Life' (e.g. *Adam Kadmon*), it is conceivable that science may eventually discover the means to probe the fundamentals of the Creation at 'resolutions' currently prohibited by Heisenberg's principle. In so doing the Kabbalah anticipates that a missing fifth epistemic pillar of reality — the *Keter-Malchut* axis — denoting the ingredient of *Kedushah* (Holiness) and linked to conscience and morality will combine with the four axes of space-time to complete a Theory of Everything (Chapter 12). Germane to the topic of consciousness the Kabbalah specifically alludes to the advent of the Seventh (Messianic) Millennium as a phase transition (i) when revelation of the hitherto subliminal influences of *Partzuf Imma* in the World *Adam Kadmon* will render tractable an appreciation of consciousness as a fundamental force of nature and (ii) inaugurating humankind's ultimate journey towards revelation of the *Yechida* aspect of Soul and a state of cosmic consciousness (Chapter 13).

Epilogue

My motivation for compiling this work was multifaceted. Foremost was an attempt to provide fresh and compelling insight into human (and other) consciousness, a phenomenon fiendishly resistant to scientific and philosophical analysis, based on authentic Kabbalistic doctrine. I believe the timing of this effort was propitious in so far as (i) interest in the study of consciousness has spiked over the last decade or so, (ii) there are signs of spreading disillusionment with the materialist model of reality, in large part fueled by the non-locality implications of contemporary quantum physics and (iii) humanity may in light of the above considerations be at the cusp of a more unified worldview that favors the meaningful integration of our immense storehouse of scientific knowledge with the vastness of subjective experience.

An equally strong incentive for this writing was to elucidate a stunning convergence of ancient Jewish mystical thought, largely inspired by revelation and classical Torah scholarship, with contemporary scientific theory informed by mathematics and experimentation. I find it ironic that the same scientific enterprise which over the millennia lured countless Jews and Christians away from their faith with its proclamations of Aristotelian eternity, Newtonian determinacy and Darwinian evolution may now, in light of Big Bang cosmogony, quantum entanglement and the purported statistical untenability of biological complexification by random mutation,[455] be re-positioning itself as a wellspring of support for Western monotheism.

In a psychological sense, science may now be repaying an underrecognized 'debt' I believe it owes monotheism for the longest time: In a polytheistic universe, there can be no a priori assumption that nature is whole at its core in so far as the 'gods' of biology, chemistry and physics would be free to elaborate their own independent, even logically contradictory, sets of physical laws. The West has made astonishing progress in science and our understanding of physical reality precisely because it strives, consciously or subliminally, for a unification of nature across all scales and modes of interrogation—an approach which belief in or cultural acclimatization to a single Creator renders virtually axiomatic. And so it is that the drive to amalgamate General Relativity (gravity) and the Standard Model of particle physics—with increasing calls for consciousness to be thrown into the mix—surges confidently ahead.

To the extent that panpsychism, process philosophy, quantum/Bohmian mechanics and the Kabbalah share common ground in their understanding of consciousness, ongoing exchange among these disciplines could prove mutually reinforcing moving forward. The extraordinary advances in quantum physics, cosmology and neuroscience we are witnessing today, in fulfillment of the *Zohar*'s prophecy,[431] may arm ancient mystical traditions such as the Kabbalah with powerful analogies and vocabulary to open the fountainhead of the latter's (hitherto arcane) wisdom to modern audiences. As a *quid pro quo* the splendidly imaginative Kabbalistic tradition may demarcate novel and potentially disruptive avenues of scientific inquiry and enlighten the enterprise of consciousness study.

Bibliography

1. Schipper HM. Kabbalah and the physics of David Bohm. In: Amoroso RL, Kauffman LH, Rowlands P, Albertini G, editors. *Unified Field Mechanics II: Preliminary Formulations and Empirical Tests.* London: World Scientific; 2018. pp. 354-68.

2. Schram S. Tefillin: An ancient acupuncture point prescription for mental clarity. *Journal of Chinese Medicine.* 2002;70:5-8.

3. Afilalo R, Schipper HM. The Kabbalistic Radla and quantum physics: Analogies and differences. *Torah u-Madda Journal.* 2012-2013;16:134-52.

4. Kastrup B. Making sense of the mental universe. *Philosophy and Cosmology.* 2017;19:33-49.

5. Aviezer N. Kabbalah, Science and the Creation of the Universe. *Jewish Action.* FALL 2004/5765.

6. Matt D. *God and the Big Bang: Discovering Harmony between Science and Spirituality.* Woodstock, VT: Jewish Lights Publishing; 1996.

7. McLean A. Kabbalistic Cosmology and its Parallels to the Big Bang of Modern Physics. *Hermetic Jour.* 1988;39:11.

8. Primack JR. Quantum Cosmology and Kabbalah. *Tikkun.* 1995:66-73.

9. Schreiber AM. *Quantum Physics, Jewish Law, & Kabbalah: Astonishing Parallels.* New York: J Levine/Millenium; 2009.

10. Schroeder G. *Genesis and the Big Bang: The Discovery Of Harmony Between Modern Science And The Bible.* New York: Bantam; 1991.

11. Smith H. *Let There Be Light: Modern Cosmology and Kabbalah: A New Conversation Between Science and Religion.* Novato, CA: New World Library; 2006.

12. Schipper HM, Afilalo R. Did the Kabbalah anticipate Heisenberg's uncertainty principle? In: Amoroso RL,

Kauffman LH, Rowlands P, Albertini G, editors. *Unified Field Mechanics II: Preliminary Formulations and Empirical Tests*. London: World Scientific; 2018. pp. 344-53.

13. Schipper HM. Kabbalah and the physics of David Bohm [HEBREW]. *DAAT: Journal of Jewish Philosophy & Kabbalah*. 2019;87:383-409.

14. *Plotinus Ennead V*. Harvard, MA: Harvard University Press; 1984. p. 336.

15. Aquinas T. *Summa Theologica*. Claremont, CA: Coyote Canyon Press; 2018. p. 1116.

16. Capra F. *The Tao of Physics: An Exploration of the Parallels Between Modern Physics and Eastern Mysticism*. Boulder, CO: Shambhala Publications; 1975.

17. Krishnamurti J, Bohm D. *The Ending of Time: Where Philosophy and Physics Meet*. San Francisco, CA: HarperOne; 2014.

18. Koch C. *Consciousness: Confessions of a Romantic Reductionist*. Cambridge, MA: MIT Press; 2012.

19. Nagel T. *Mind & Cosmos: Why the materialist neo-Darwinian conception of nature is almost certainly false*. New York: Oxford University Press; 2012.

20. Ells P. *Panpsychism: The Philosophy of the Sensuous Cosmos*. Winchester, UK: John Hunt Publishing Ltd.; 2011. p. 213.

21. Stapp HP. *Mindful Universe*. 2nd ed. Heidelberg: Springer; 2011. p. 212.

22. Rosenberg G. *A Place for Consciousness: Probing the Deep Structure of the Natural World*. Oxford, UK: Oxford University Press; 2004. p. 344.

23. Nelson AD. *Origins of Consciousness*. Nottingham, UK: Metarising Books; 2015. p. 210.

24. Kastrup B. *The Idea of the World*. Winchester, UK: John Hunt Publishing Ltd.; 2019. p. 297.

25. Chalmers D. *The Conscious Mind*. Oxford, UK: Oxford University Press; 2003. p. xi.

26. Oxford Dictionary. Available from: https://en.oxford

dictionaries.com/definition.

27. Walling PT, Hicks KN. *Consciousness: Anatomy of the Soul.* Bloomington, IN: AuthorHouse; 2009. p. 1.

28. Chalmers DJ. *The Conscious Mind.* Oxford: Oxford University Press; 1996. p. 4.

29. Ells P. *Panpsychism: The Philosophy of the Sensuous Cosmos.* Winchester, UK: John Hunt Publishing Ltd.; 2011. p. 67.

30. Ball P. Neuroscience Readies for a Showdown over Consciousness. *Quanta Magazine* [Internet]. 2019. Available from: https://www.quantamagazine.org/neuroscience-readies-for-a-showdown-over-consciousness-ideas-20190306/.

31. Seager W. History of Philosophical Theories of Consciousness. In: Banks WP, editor. *Encyclopedia of Consciousness.* 1. Amsterdam: Elsevier; 2009. pp. 1-12.

32. Koch C. *Consciousness: Confessions of a Romantic Reductionist.* Cambridge, MA: MIT Press; 2012. p. 2.

33. Chalmers DJ. Facing up to the problem of consciousness. *Journal of Consciousness Studies.* 1995;2:200-19.

34. Nelson AD. *Origins of Consciousness.* Nottingham, UK: Metarising Books; 2015. p. 5.

35. Li O. Panentheism, Panpsychism and Neuroscience: In Search of an Alternative Metaphysical Framework in Relation to Neuroscience, Consciousness, Free Will, and Theistic Beliefs. Uppsala: Acta Universitatis Upsaliensis; 2018.

36. Dennett DC. *Consciousness Explained.* New York: Little, Brown and Company; 1991. p. 511.

37. Robinson H. Dualism. In: Zalta EN, editor. *The Stanford Encyclopedia of Philosophy.* Stanford, CA: Stanford University; FALL 2017.

38. Seager WE. Consciousness, information and panpsychism. *Journal of Consciousness Studies.* 1995;2:272-88.

39. Pinker S. *How the Mind Works.* New York: W. W. Norton & Co.; 2009. p. 562.

40. Griffin DR. *Reenchantment without Supernaturalism.* New York: Cornell University Press; 2000. pp. 95-6.

41. Leidenhag J. The Revival of Panpsychism and its Relevance for the Science-Religion Dialogue Theology and Science [Internet]. 2018. Available from: https://www.tandfonline.com/doi/abs/10.1080/14746700.2018.1525228?journalCode=rtas20.

42. Skirbina D. *Panpsychism in the West.* Cambridge: MIT Press; 2005. p. 314.

43. Brüntrup G. Alter Wein in neuen Schläuchen. In: Müller T, Watzka H, editors. *Ein Universum voller Geiststaub? Der Panpsychis mus in der Geist-Gehirn-Debatte.* Paderborn: Mentis Verlag; 2011. pp. 23-59.

44. Kouider S. Neurobiological Theories of Consciousness. In: Banks WP, editor. *Encyclopedia of Consciousness.* 1. Amsterdam: Elsevier; 2009. pp. 87-100.

45. Tononi G. Consciousness: Philosophy. In: Squire LR, editor. *Encyclopedia of Neuroscience.* 4th ed. Cambridge: Academic Press; 2009. pp. 117-23.

46. Tononi G. Integrated information theory of consciousness: An updated account. *Arch Ital Biol.* 2012;150:56-90.

47. Zeman A. Consciousness. *Brain.* 2001;124(Pt 7):1263-89.

48. Roelofs L. *Combining Minds: How to Think about Composite Subjectivity.* Oxford, UK: Oxford University Press; 2019. p. 360.

49. Hameroff S, Penrose R. Orchestrated reduction of quantum coherence in brain microtubules: a model for consciousness. *J Conscious Stud.* 1996;3:36-53.

50. Ouellette J. A new spin on the quantum brain. *Quanta Magazine* [Internet]. 2016. Available from: https://www.quantamagazine org/a-new-spin-on-the-quantum-brain-2 0161102.

51. Sarfatti J, Shimansky A. Solution to David Chalmers's "Hard Problem". *Cosmos and History: J Natural Soc Philosophy.*

2018;14(1).

52. Skopec R. Coding by quantum entanglement entropy. *NeuroQuantology*. 2017;15(2):200-7.

53. Engel GS, Calhoun TR, Read EL, Ahn TK, Mancal T, Cheng YC, et al. Evidence for wavelike energy transfer through quantum coherence in photosynthetic systems. *Nature*. 2007;446(7137):782-6.

54. Ghosh S, Sahu S, Bandyopadhyay A. Evidence of massive global synchronization and the consciousness. Comment on "Consciousness in the universe: A review of the 'Orch OR' theory" by Hameroff and Penrose. *Physics of life reviews*. 2014;11:83-4.

55. Nelson AD. *Origins of Consciousness*. Nottingham, UK: Metarising Books; 2015. p. 37.

56. Bohm D. A new theory of the relationship of mind and matter. *Philosophical Psychology*. 1990;3(2-3):271-86.

57. Henry RC. The mental Universe. *Nature*. 2005;436(7047):29.

58. Kastrup B. The quest to solve problems that don't exist: Thought artifacts in contemporary ontology. *Studia Humana*. 2017;6:45-51.

59. Deuteronomy 30:19.

60. Deuteronomy 4:39.

61. Tauber Y. *Inside Time: A Chassidic Perspective on the Jewish Calendar*. 1. New York: Meaningful Life Center; 2015. pp. 89-94.

62. Genesis 1:27.

63. Clayton P. *God and Contemporary Science*. Grand Rapids: Eerdmans Publishing Co.; 1997.

64. Peacocke A. *Theology for a Scientific Age*. Minneapolis: Fortress Press; 1993.

65. Li O. Panentheism, Panpsychism and Neuroscience: In Search of an Alternative Metaphysical Framework in Relation to Neuroscience, Consciousness, Free Will, and Theistic Beliefs, pp. 26-29, 229. Uppsala: Acta Universitatis

Upsaliensis; 2018.

66. Crick F. *The Astonishing Hypothesis*. New York: Charles Scribner's Sons; 1994. p. 336.

67. Sullivan JWN. Interviews with Great Scientists. *The Observer*. 25 January 1931.

68. Wigner EP. Remarks on the Mind-Body Question. In: Wheeler JA, Zurek WH, editors. *Quantum Theory and Measurement*. Princeton, NJ: Princeton University Press; [1961] 1984. p. 169.

69. Ells P. *Panpsychism: The Philosophy of the Sensuous Cosmos*. Winchester, UK: John Hunt Publishing Ltd.; 2011. p. 129.

70. Aspect A, Grangier P, Roger G. Experimental realization of Einstein-Podolsky-Rosen-Bohm Gedankenexperiment: A new violation of Bell's inequalities. *Phys Rev Lett*. 1982;49:91-4.

71. d'Espagnat B. *On Physics and Philosophy*. Princeton, NJ: Princeton University Press; 2013. pp. 51-88.

72. Albert DZ. *Quantum Mechanics and Experience*. Cambridge: Harvard University Press; 1992.

73. Heisenberg W. Über den anschaulichen Inhalt der quantentheoretischen Kinematik und Mechanik. *Zeitschrift für Physik*. 1927:172-98.

74. Weinberg S. *Dreams of a Final Theory*. New York: Pantheon Books; 1992.

75. Young T. The Bakerian lecture: On the theory of light and colours. *Philosophical Transactions of the Royal Society of London*. 1802;92:12-48.

76. Chalmers D. Consciousness and the collapse of the wave function. YouTube; 2014.

77. Gribbin J. *In Search of Schrödinger's Cat*. Toronto: Bantam Books; 1984. pp. 154-7.

78. Seife C. *Decoding the Universe*. London: Penguin Books; 2006. p. 296.

79. Everett H. Relative state formulation of quantum mechanics.

Rev Mod Phys. 1957:454-62.

80. Nelson AD. *Origins of Consciousness.* Nottingham, UK: Metarising Books; 2015. p. 53.

81. Peat FD. *Infinite Potential: The Life and Times of David Bohm.* New York: Basic Books; 1997. p. 353.

82. Falk D. New support for alternative quantum view. *Quanta Magazine.* May 16, 2016.

83. Talbot M. *The Holographic Universe.* 2nd ed. New York: HarperCollins; 2011. pp. 38-40.

84. Bohm D. *Wholeness and the Implicate Order.* London: Routledge; 1980. p. 284.

85. Nichol L. *The Essential David Bohm.* London: Routledge; 2003. p. 349.

86. Peat FD. *Infinite Potential: The Life and Times of David Bohm.* New York: Basic Books; 1997. p. 106.

87. Bohm D. On the Intuitive Understanding of Nonlocality as Implied by Quantum Theory. *Foundations of Physics.* 1975;5:93-109.

88. Peat FD. *Infinite Potential: The Life and Times of David Bohm.* New York: Basic Books; 1997. p. 260.

89. Marcer PJ, Schempp W. Model of the neuron working by quantum holography. *Informatica.* 1997;21:519-34.

90. Marcer PJ, Schempp W. The brain as a conscious system. *International Journal of General Systems.* 1998 27:131-248.

91. Mitchell E. Nature's Mind: The Quantum Hologram. 2014. Available from: http://www.cosmicdreaming.com/pdf2011/Nature's%20Mind%20the%20Quantum%20Hologram%20by%20Edgar%20Mitchell,%20Ph_D.pdf.

92. Penrose R. *The Emperor's New Mind.* Oxford: Oxford University Press; 1999.

93. Bekenstein JD. Information in the holographic universe. *Scientific American.* 2003;289(2):58-65.

94. De Valois KK, De Valois RL, Yund EW. Responses of striate cortex cells to grating and checkerboard patterns. *The*

Journal of Physiology. 1979;291:483-505.

95. Jibu M, Hagan S, Hameroff SR, Pribram KH, Yasue K. Quantum optical coherence in cytoskeletal microtubules: implications for brain function. *Bio Systems.* 1994;32(3):195-209.

96. Pribram KH. Ch. 13. Localization and Distribution of Function in the Brain. In: Orbach J, editor. *Neuropsychology after Lashley: Fifty Years since the Publication of* Brain Mechanisms and Intelligence. New York: Lawrence Erlbaum; 1982. p. 450.

97. Amoroso RL. An introduction to noetic field theory: The quantization of mind. *The Noetic Journal.* 1999;2:28-37.

98. Di Biase F. Quantum-holographic informational consciousness. *NeuroQuantology.* 2009;7(4):657-64.

99. Hameroff S, Penrose R. Conscious events as orchestrated space-time selections. *NeuroQuantology.* 2003;1:10-35.

100. Jibu M, Yasue K. *Quantum Brain Dynamics and Consciousness.* Amsterdam: John Benjamins; 1995.

101. Globus G. Toward a quantum psychiatry: Hallucination, thought insertion and DSM. *NeuroQuantology.* 2010;8(1):1-12.

102. Pylkkänen P. Implications of Bohmian quantum ontology for psychopathology. *NeuroQuantology.* 2010;8(1):37-48.

103. Woolf NJ, Craddock TJA, Friesen DE, Tuszynski JA. Neuropsychiatric illness: A case for impaired neuroplasticity and possible quantum processing derailment in microtubules. *NeuroQuantology.* 2010;8(1):13-28.

104. Yisraeli O. Jewish medieval traditions concerning the origins of the Kabbalah. *The Jewish Quarterly Review.* 2016;106:21-41.

105. Hillel YM. *Petach Sha'ar HaShamaim.* Jerusalem: Ahavat Shalom; 2008. pp. 79-114.

106. Ullman S. *Da'at Elokim.* Jerusalem: Hamesorah; 1996. p. 207.

107. Goldstein E. *Da'at Elokim.* 2007. Available from: https://

www.kolhalashon.com/New/Shiurim.aspx?Path=English I
EMusar I R7096 I R7099 I R7099-1&English=True&Order=
New2Old.

108. Luzzatto MC. *Klach Pitchei Chochmah*. Friedlander C, editor. Bnei Brak: Sifriati; [1785] 1992.

109. Luzzatto MC. *138 Openings of Wisdom*. Jerusalem: Azamra Institute; 2005.

110. Goldstein E. *Etz Chaim*. 2006. Available from: http://www. kolhalashon.com/New/Ravs.aspx?Path=English%7CEMusa r%7CR7052-3%7CR7052-3-1&English=True).

111. Eliashiv S. *Leshem Shevo V'achlamah—Chelek Habiurim*. Tel-Aviv: Aharon Barazani & Son; [1935] 2011. p. 696.

112. Eliashiv S. *Leshem Shevo V'achlamah—Drushei Olam Hatohu*. Tel-Aviv: Aharon Barazani & Son; [1912] 2006. p. 735.

113. Sharabi S. *Nahar Shalom* [River of Peace]. Salonica [Jerusalem]: Yeshivat Hamekubalim; 1806.

114. De la Rosa C. *Torat Chacham*. Jerusalem: Raphael de la Rosa; [1848] 2005. p. 266.

115. Schneersohn SD. *B'Shaa Shehikdimu*. New York: Kehot Publishing; [1911] 2011. p. 635.

116. Abulafia A. *Chaye Ha'Olam Ha'Ba—Life in the World to Come*. In: del Tin F, editor. Trieste, Italy: Euniversity Pub; [1280] 2008. p. 260.

117. Idel M. *Abraham Abulafia: An Ecstatic Kabbalist*. Essex, UK: Labyrinthos; 2002. p. 573.

118. Ruelle D, Takens F. On the nature of turbulence. *Communications in Mathematical Physics*. 1971;20:167-92.

119. Peitgen H, Jurgens H, Saupe D. *Chaos and Fractals: New Frontiers of Science*. Heidelberg: Springer-Verlag; 2004.

120. Csikszentmihalyi M. *Creativity: Flow and the Psychology of Discovery and Invention*. New York: Harper Perennial; 2013. p. 480.

121. *Bamidbar Rabbah* 13:15.

122. Yitzchaki [Rashi] S. Commentary to *Genesis* 32:25.

123. Afterman A. *Kabbalah and Consciousness.* Riverdale-on-Hudson, NY: The Sheep Meadow Press; 1992. p. 25.

124. Notarikon. Encyclopediacom: CENGAGE; 2019.

125. Babylonian Talmud *Bava Kamma* 83b.

126. Exodus 21:24.

127. Shimshon-ben-Pesach-Ostropola. *Nitzotzei Shimshon.* Jerusalem: Bombach, Avraham Yaakov; [ca. 1640] 1981. pp. 79-80.

128. O'Toole G. Everything Should Be Made as Simple as Possible, But Not Simpler. 2011. Available from: http://quoteinvestigator.com/2011/05/13/einstein-simple/.

129. Afilalo R. *Kabbalah Concepts.* Montreal: Kabbalah Editions; 2006.

130. Ginsburgh Y. *What You Need to Know about Kabbalah.* Jerusalem: Gal Einai Institute; 2006. p. 200.

131. Shpilman YM. *Tal Orot* I:2. [Lviv] Jerusalem: Y. Boker; [1875-1883] 2015. p. 419.

132. Shyfrin E. *From Infinity to Man: The Fundamental Ideas of Kabbalah within the Framework of Information Theory and Quantum Physics.* Nova Scotia, Canada: White Raven Press; 2019. p. 117.

133. Psalms 36:10.

134. Vital C. *Etz Chaim.* Bnei Brak: Videbsky, TM; [1782] 1998.

135. Luzzatto MC. Portal 17. In: Friedlander C, editor. *Klach Pitchei Chochmah.* Bnei Brak: Sifriati; [1785] 1992. p. 50.

136. Afterman A. *Kabbalah and Consciousness.* Riverdale-on-Hudson, NY: The Sheep Meadow Press; 1992. p. 19.

137. Isaiah 43:7.

138. *Sefer Yetzirah* 1:4.

139. *Zohar.* In: Margoliot R, editor. Jerusalem: Mossad Harav Kook; 1999.

140. Kastrup B. *The Idea of the World.* Winchester, UK: John Hunt Publishing Ltd.; 2019. p. 30.

141. Ashlag Y, cited by Leitman, Michael. Hakdamah L'Talmud

Eser Sefirot, Item 144. Mada HaLev World Press; 2012. Available from: https://madahalev.wordpress.com/2012/10/08/chotem-venechtam/.

142. Eliashiv S. *Leshem Shevo V'achlamah—Hakdamot V'Shearim*. Tel-Aviv: Aharon Barazani & Son; [1908] 2006. p. 17.

143. Eliashiv S. *Leshem Shevo V'achlamah—Chelek Haklalim* II: 182. Tel-Aviv: Aharon Barazani and Son; [1935] 2011.

144. Luzzatto MC. Portal 87. In: Friedlander C, editor. *Klach Pitchei Chochma*. Bnei Brak: Sifriati; [1785] 1992. pp. 272-3.

145. Vazza F, Feletti A. The Strange Similarity of Neuron and Galaxy Networks. Nautilus [Internet]. 2017. Available from: http://nautil.us/issue/50/emergence/the-strange-similarity-of-neuron-and-galaxy-networks.

146. Love AC. Functional homology and homology of function: biological concepts and philosophical consequences. *Biology & Philosophy*. 2007;22:691-708.

147. Greslehner GP. What do molecular biologists mean when they say 'structure determines function'? 2018:[pp. 1-21]. Available from: http://philsci-archive.pitt.edu/15189/1/PSA_2018_Greslehner_What_do_molecular_biologists_mean.pdf.

148. ben Moses (Efodi) I. Commentary to Maimonides' Guide for the Perplexed. c. 1400.

149. Eibeschutz S. *Parshat Sh'mot*. Arvei Nachal; 1871.

150. Genesis 29:3.

151. Blake W. Auguries of Innocence. In: Erdman DV, editor. *The Complete Poetry and Prose of William Blake*. New York: Anchor Books; [1803] 1988. p. 490.

152. Babylonian Talmud *Sanhedrin* 111a.

153. Babylonian Talmud *Shabbat* 59.

154. *Shulchan Aruch*: 344.

155. Babylonian Talmud *Sanhedrin* 102a.

156. Yitzchaki [Rashi] S. Commentary to *Exodus* 32:34.

157. Babylonian Talmud *Sanhedrin* 27b.

158. Babylonian Talmud *Shavuot* 39a.

159. Babylonian Talmud *Sotah* 37a.

160. Babylonian Talmud *Sanhedrin* 37a.

161. Bohm D. *On Creativity*. London: Routledge Classics; 2004. p. 153.

162. Shyfrin E. *From Infinity to Man: The Fundamental Ideas of Kabbalah within the Framework of Information Theory and Quantum Physics*. Nova Scotia, Canada: White Raven Press; 2019. p. 65.

163. Shyfrin E. *From Infinity to Man: The Fundamental Ideas of Kabbalah within the Framework of Information Theory and Quantum Physics*. Nova Scotia, Canada: White Raven Press; 2019. p. 74.

164. Psalms 145.

165. Anonymous. *Sefer Me'orot Eliyahu*. Tel-Aviv: Aharon Barazani & Son; 2017. p. 73.

166. Yitzchaki [Rashi] S. Commentary to *Exodus* 14:21.

167. *Zohar Terumah* 161B.

168. Schatz M. *Sparks of the Hidden Light*. Jerusalem: Ateret Tiferet Institute; 1996.

169. *Genesis Rabba* 53:8.

170. Talbott S. What do organisms mean? *The New Atlantis*. 2011;Winter:24-49.

171. Nelson AD. *Origins of Consciousness*. Nottingham, UK: Metarising Books; 2015. p. 108.

172. Zechariah 14:9.

173. Hendler M. *Baruch U'mevorach*. Brooklyn: Bet Knesset Ha'Arizal; 2011. pp. 211-5.

174. Vital C. *Pri Etz Chaim*. Bnei Brak: Videbsky, TM; [1782] 1998. p. 72 (Ha'gaa).

175. Leiner J, as cited by Boshnack R. *Pathways to the Heart: Opening the Teachings of the House of Izhbitz*. New York: Kodesh Press; 2020. pp. 112-3.

176. *Mechilta* commentary to Exodus 20:1.

177. Numbers 22:2-25:25.

178. Shneur-Zalman-of-Liadi. *Likkutei Torah: Balak* 73. New York: Kehot Publication Society; [1848] 1999. p. 1010.

179. Malachi 3:6.

180. Leiner MY. *Mei HaShiloach*, Parshat Shoftim 1. 1860.

181. Edwards BP. *Living Waters: Mei Hashiloach Parshat Shoftim.* Northvale, NJ: Jason Aronson Inc.; 2001. p. 365.

182. Riek C, Seletskiy DV, Moskalenko AS, Schmidt JF, Krauspe P, Eckart S, et al. Direct sampling of electric-field vacuum fluctuations. *Science*. 2015;350(6259):420-3.

183. *Sefer Yetzirah* 1:2.

184. Imhausen A. *Mathematics in Ancient Egypt: A Contextual History*. Princeton, NJ: Princeton University Press; 2016. p. 248.

185. Wolchover N. Cosmic Triangles Open a Window to the Origin of Time. *Quanta Magazine* [Internet]. 2019. Available from: https://www.quantamagazine.org/the-origin-of-time -bootstrapped-from-fundamental-symmetries-20191029/.

186. Amoroso RL. A comparative study of 10(11) D superstring theory and the 10(11) Sefirot in the Tree of Life metaphor of the Hebrew Kabbalah. *Noetic Journal*. 1999;2:333-6.

187. *Sefer Yetzirah* 1:3.

188. Schneersohn SD. *B'Shaa Shehikdimu*. 1. New York: Kehot Publishing Society; [1911] 2011. p. 219.

189. Afilalo R. *The Kabbalah of the Ari Z'al according to the Ramhal (Klalot Ha'Ilan HaKadosh)*. Montreal: Kabbalah Editions; 2005. p. 288.

190. How Is the Sun Completely Blocked in an Eclipse? NASA; 2019. Available from: https://spaceplace.nasa.gov/total-solar-eclipse/en/.

191. Shpilman YM. *Tal Orot* I:1. [Lviv] Jerusalem: Y. Boker; [1875-1883] 2015. p. 419.

192. Schneider SY. *Kabbalistic Writings on the Nature of Masculine & Feminine*. Devora Publishing; 2010. Available from: http://

www.devorapublishing.com/.

193. Afterman A. *Kabbalah and Consciousness*. Riverdale-on-Hudson, NY: The Sheep Meadow Press; 1992. p. 71.

194. Nagel T. *Origins of Consciousness*. Nottingham, UK: Metarising Books; 2015. p. 164.

195. Moreva E, Brida G, Gramegna M, Giovannetti V, Maccone L, Genovese M. Time from quantum entanglement: an experimental illustration. 2013. Available from: https://arxiv.org/pdf/1310.4691.pdf.

196. Rauscher EA, Hurtak JJ, Hurtak DE. What is Time? What Time is it? In: Amoroso RL, Kauffman LH, Rowlands P, Albertini G, editors. *Unified Field Mechanics II: Preliminary Formulations and Empirical Tests*. London: World Scientific; 2018. pp. 412-27.

197. Vaccaro JA. The quantum theory of time, the block universe, and human experience. *Philos Trans A Math Phys Eng Sci*. 2018;376(2123).

198. First M. What Is the Meaning of the Word 'Olam'? *Jewish Link of New Jersey*. 2018. Available from: https://www.jewishlinknj.com/features/22659-what-is-the-meaning-of-the-word-olam.

199. Shani I. Cosmopsychism: A holistic approach to the metaphysics of experience. *Philosophical Papers*. 2015;44:389-437.

200. Vital C. *Etz Chaim* 39:3. Bnei Brak: Videbsky, TM; [1782] 1998.

201. Kauffman S. Cosmic Mind? *Theology and Science*. 2016;14:36-47.

202. Rubin E, Abugov M. Do Chabad Teachings Say Anything About the Mind-Body Problem? 2016. Available from: chabad.org/library/article_cdo/aid/3432275/jewish/Do-Chabad-Teachings-Say-Anything-About-the-Mind-Body-Problem.htm.

203. Moltmann J. *Gott in der Schöpfung*. Munich: Kaiser Verlag;

1985.

204. Chaim-ben-Yitzchak-of-Volozhin. *Nefesh Ha'Chaim*: Gate 2, Section 17. Volozhin; 1780-1820.

205. Schneersohn SD. *B'Shaa Shehikdimu*. 1. New York: Kehot Publishing; [1911] 2011. p. 401.

206. Eliashiv S. *Leshem Shevo V'achlamah—Chelek Habiurim* II:70. Tel-Aviv: Aharon Barazani & Son; [1935] 2011.

207. Luzzatto MC. Portal 104. In: Friedlander C, editor. *Klach Pitchei Chochmah*. Bnei Brak: Sifriati; [1785] 1992. pp. 306-7.

208. Nelson AD. *Origins of Consciousness*. Nottingham, UK: Metarising Books; 2015. p. 125.

209. Numbers 19:2.

210. Exodus 20:13.

211. Deuteronomy 5:17.

212. Exodus 24:7.

213. *Pirkei Avot* 4:2.

214. Birnbaum D. *God and Evil: A Unified Theodicy/Theology/Philosophy*. Brooklyn, NY: Ktav; 1989. p. 266.

215. Babylonian Talmud *Ta'anit* 21a.

216. Babylonian Talmud *Pesachim* 50a.

217. Einstein A. Zur Elektrodynamik bewegter Körper. *Annalen der Physik*. 1905;17:891.

218. Poltorak A. Relativity of Manna. *Quantum Torah* [Internet]. 2016. Available from: https://www.quantumtorah.com/relativity-of-manna/.

219. Yitzchaki [Rashi] S. Commentary to Exodus 12:18.

220. Schneersohn SD. *B'Shaa Shehikdimu*. 1. New York: Kehot Publishing; [1911] 2011. p. 418.

221. Shpilman YM. *Tal Orot* II:15. [Lviv] Jerusalem: Y. Boker; [1875-1883] 2015. p. 419.

222. Hendler M. *Baruch U'mevorach*. Brooklyn: Bet Knesset Ha'Arizal; 2011. pp. 208-11.

223. Butterfield J. On dualities and equivalences between physical theories. 2018. Available from: https://arxiv.org/

abs/1806.01505.

224. Castellani E, De Haro S. Duality, Fundamentality, and Emergence. 2018. Available from: https://arxiv.org/abs/1803.09443.

225. Wolchover N. A physicist's physicist ponders the nature of reality. *Quanta Magazine* [Internet]. 2017. Available from: https://www.quantamagazine.org/edward-witten-ponders-the-nature-of-reality-20171128.

226. Dijkgraaf R. There Are No Laws of Physics. There's Only the Landscape. *Quanta Magazine* [Internet]. 2018. Available from: https://www.quantamagazine.org/there-are-no-laws-of-physics-theres-only-the-landscape-20180604/.

227. Eliashiv S. *Leshem Shevo V'achlamah—Chelek Habiurim* II:221. Tel-Aviv: Aharon Barazani & Son; [1935] 2011.

228. Eliashiv S. *Leshem Shevo V'achlamah—Hakdamot V'Shearim.* Tel-Aviv: Aharon Barazani & Son; [1908] 2006. p. 20.

229. Leiner MY. *Mei HaShiloach*, Parshat Bereshit 1. 1860.

230. Edwards BP. *Living Waters: Mei Hashiloach Parshat Bereshit.* Northvale, NJ: Jason Aronson Inc.; 2001. p. 19.

231. Bohm D. A new theory of the relationship of mind and matter. *Philosophical Psychology.* 1990;3(2-3):271-86.

232. Shneur-Zalman-of-Liadi. *Likkutei Amarim* [Tanya]: Ch. 9. New York: Kehot Publication Society; [1797] 1993.

233. Wiederblank N. *Illuminating Jewish Thought: Explorations of Free Will, the Afterlife, and the Messianic Era.* Jerusalem: Koren Publishers; 2018. pp. 392-5.

234. *Zohar* 2:83a. In: Margoliot R, editor. Jerusalem: Mossad Harav Kook; 1999.

235. Eliashiv S. *Leshem Shevo V'achlamah—Hakdamot V'Shearim.* Tel-Aviv: Aharon Barazani & Son; [1908] 2006. p. 19.

236. Eliashiv S. *Leshem Shevo V'achlamah—Chelek Habiurim* II:156. Tel-Aviv: Aharon Barazani & Son; [1935] 2011.

237. Deleniv S. The 'me' illusion: How your brain conjures up your sense of self. *New Scientist* [Internet]. 2018. Available

from: https://www.newscientist.com/article/mg23931940-100-the-me-illusion-how-your-brain-conjures-up-your-sense-of-self/.

238. Raatz J. Wigner's Friend's Quantum Mind. 2011. Available from: https://www.youtube.com/watch?v=crzgOuUtvrg.

239. Frosh S. Freud, psychoanalysis and anti-Semitism. *The Psychoanalytic Review.* 2004;91:309-30.

240. Afterman A. *Kabbalah and Consciousness.* Riverdale-on-Hudson, NY: The Sheep Meadow Press; 1992. pp. 11-2.

241. Luzzatto MC. Portal 29. In: Friedlander C, editor. *Klach Pitche Chochmah.* Bnei Brak: Sifriati; [1785] 1992. pp. 83-9.

242. Horowitz I. *Shnei Luchot HaBrit.* I. Jerusalem: Bet Yisrael; [1648] 1975. p. 7d.

243. Shpilman YM. *Tal Orot* II:16. [Lviv] Jerusalem: Y. Boker; [1875-1883] 2015. p. 419.

244. Leoni E. Rabbi Pinchas of Koretz. 2015. Available from: https://www.jewishgen.org/yizkor/Korets/kor031.html#f31-8r.

245. Psalms 139:16.

246. Kaplan A. *Sefer Yetzirah: The Book of Creation.* San Francisco: Weiser Books; 1997. pp. 38-40.

247. Triballeau C. Japan roboticists predict rise of the machines. 2019. Available from: https://news.abs-cbn.com/spotlight /09/23/19/japan-roboticists-predict-rise-of-the-machines.

248. Hinchliffe T. AI and Spirituality: Toward the recreation of the mythical, soulless Golem. *The Sociable* [Internet]. 2017. Available from: https://sociable.co/technology/ai-spiritua lity-soulless-golem/.

249. Babylonian Talmud *Sanhedrin* 65b.

250. Job 14:1.

251. Job 15:14.

252. Shelley M. *Frankenstein; or, The Modern Prometheus.* UK: Lackington, Hughes, Harding, Mavor & Jones; 1818. p. 280.

253. Marcus G. Am I Human? Researchers need new ways to

distinguish artificial intelligence from the natural kind. *Scientific American.* 2017;316:58-63.

254. *Responsum* Chacham Tzvi 93.

255. *Divrei Rabeinu Meshulam* 10.

256. Sheilot Yaavetz 2:82.

257. Azulai A. *Chesed L'Avraham* 4:30.

258. Cordovero M. *Pardes Rimonim* 24:10.

259. Genesis 9:4.

260. Babylonian Talmud *Bava Metzia* 32b.

261. Deuteronomy 22:6-7.

262. Deuteronomy 22:10.

263. Cepelwicz J. An Ethical Future for Brain Organoids Takes Shape. *Quanta Magazine* [Internet]. 2020. Available from: https://www.quantamagazine.org/an-ethical-future-for-brain-organoids-takes-shape-20200123/.

264. Genesis 6:9-9:17.

265. Genesis 11:1-9.

266. Bible Hub Genesis 11:1 2014-2019. Available from: https://biblehub.com/genesis/11-1.htm.

267. *The Torah with Ramban's Commentary*: Genesis Part I. New York: Mesorah Publications Ltd.; 2004. p. 597.

268. Premack D, Woodruff G. Does the chimpanzee have a theory of mind? *Behavioral and Brain Sciences.* 1978;1:515-26.

269. *Sefer Yetzirah* 1:5.

270. Scholem G. *On the Kabbalah and its Symbolism.* New York: Schocken; 1996. p. 240.

271. Scholem G. *Major Trends in Jewish Mysticism.* New York: Schocken; 1995. p. 496.

272. Kaplan A, Sutton A. *Inner Space: Introduction to Kabbalah, Meditation and Prophecy*, 2nd ed. New York: Moznaim Publishing Corporation; 1990. p. 254.

273. Idel M. *Kabbalah: New Perspectives.* New Haven: Yale University Press; 1990. p. 464.

274. Idel M. *The Privileged Status of the Divine Feminine in*

Theosophical-theurgical Kabbalah: Examining Keter Malkhut.
Boston: De Gruyter; 2018. p. 262.

275. Matt DC. *The Essential Kabbalah: The Heart of Jewish Mysticism.*
San Francisco: HarperOne; 2009. p. 240.

276. Matt DC. *Zohar Collector's Edition* (Zohar: The Pritzker
Editions). Stanford: Stanford University Press; 2018. p.
7792.

277. Garb J. *Yearnings of the Soul: Psychological Thought in Modern
Kabbalah.* Chicago: The University of Chicago Press; 2015.

278. Dan J. *The Ancient Jewish Mysticism.* Jerusalem: Gefen
Publishing House; 1990. p. 227.

279. Riggio RE. Women's intuition: Myth or reality? *Psychology
Today* [Internet]. 2011. Available from: https://www.
psychologytoday.com/us/blog/cutting-edge-
leadership/201107/women-s-intuition-myth-or-reality.

280. Kinsley CH, Lambert KG. The maternal brain. *Scientific
American.* 2006;294:72-9.

281. Shpilman YM. *Tal Orot* I:14. [Lviv] Jerusalem: Y. Boker;
[1875-1883] 2015. p. 419.

282. *Sefer Yetzirah* 1:7.

283. Genesis 21:12.

284. Genesis 3:16.

285. Eliashiv S. *Leshem Shevo V'achlamah—Chelek Habiurim* II:169-
171. Tel-Aviv: Aharon Barazani & Son; [1935] 2011.

286. *Shulchan Aruch* 17:2.

287. Nelson AD. *Origins of Consciousness.* Nottingham, UK:
Metarising Books; 2015. p. 148.

288. Ullman S. *Da'at Elokim.* Jerusalem: Hamesorah; 1996. p. 96.

289. Eliashiv S. *Leshem Shevo V'achlamah—Chelek Habiurim* II:83-
87. Tel-Aviv: Aharon Barazani & Son; [1935] 2011.

290. Eliashiv S. *Leshem Shevo V'achlamah—Chelek Habiurim* II:208-
210. Tel-Aviv: Aharon Barazani and Son; [1935] 2011.

291. Seager W. Reduction and emergence in philosophy and
science. *Analysis.* 2018;78(3):552-7.

292. Eliashiv S. *Leshem Shevo V'achlamah—Chelek Habiurim* II:132-135. Tel-Aviv: Aharon Barazani & Son; [1935] 2011.

293. Luzzatto MC. Portal 4. In: Friedlander C, editor. *Klach Pitchei Chochma*. Bnei Brak: Sifriati; [1785] 1992. p. 14.

294. Yitzchaki [Rashi] S. Commentary to Genesis 2:5.

295. Ellis GFR, Noble D, O'Connor T. Top-down causation: an integrating theme within and across the sciences? *Interface Focus*. 2012. pp. 1-3.

296. Wolchover N. A theory of reality as more than the sum of its parts. *Quanta Magazine* [Internet]. 2017. Available from:https://www.quantamagazine.org/a-theory-of-reality-as-more-than-the-sum-of-its-parts-20170601/.

297. Schwartz JM, Stapp HP, Beauregard M. Quantum physics in neuroscience and psychology: a neurophysical model of mind-brain interaction. *Philos Trans R Soc Lond B Biol Sci*. 2005;360(1458):1309-27.

298. Sas P. The Self-Observing Universe: Wheeler & Absolute Idealism 2.0. 2016. Available from: http://critique-of-pure-interest.blogspot.com/2016/07/the-self-observing-universe-wheeler_96.html.

299. Wheeler JA. Genesis and Observership. *Foundational Problems in the Special Sciences*. 1977;10:3-33.

300. Rees M. The anthropic universe. *New Scientist*. 1986;115:44-7.

301. *Otzar HaMidrashim, Olam Katan* 406.

302. Genesis 37:1-50:26.

303. Genesis 41:45, 50-52.

304. Genesis 50:20.

305. The Book of Esther.

306. Senor D, Singer S. *Start-Up Nation: The Story of Israel's Economic Miracle*. New York: Twelve–Hachette Book Group; 2011.

307. Babylonian Talmud *Bava Batra* 137b.

308. Babylonian Talmud *Megillah 8b* [*Rashi*].

309. Luria RM. Cited in Schneider, SY. *A Still Small Voice*. 2018. Available from: https://astillsmallvoice.org/zot-chanuk-ka-2018.

310. Crivellato E, Ribatti D. Soul, mind, brain: Greek philosophy and the birth of neuroscience. *Brain Research Bulletin*. 2007;71(4):327-36.

311. Engelhardt E. Cerebral localization of the mind and higher functions: The beginnings. *Dement Neuropsychol* [Internet]. 2018; 12(3). Available from: http://dx.doi.org/10.1590/1980-57642018dn12-030014.

312. Lokhorst G-J. Descartes and the Pineal Gland. In: *The Stanford Encyclopedia of Philosophy* (Winter 2018 Edition) [Internet]. Available from: https://plato.stanford.edu/archives/win2018/entries/pineal-gland.

313. Laureys S, Tononi G, editors. *The Neurology of Consciousness: Cognitive Neuroscience and Neuropathology*. Cambridge, MA: Academic Press; 2008. p. 440.

314. Fox MD, Geerling JC, et al. A human brain network derived from coma-causing brainstem lesions. *Neurology*. 2016;87(23):2427-34.

315. Tononi G, Koch C. The neural correlates of consciousness. *Annals of the New York Academy of Sciences*. 2008;1124(1):239-61.

316. *Tikkunei HaZohar* 21:67.

317. Job 19:26.

318. Exodus 13:9.

319. Exodus 13:16.

320. Deuteronomy 6:8.

321. Deuteronomy 11:18.

322. The Talmud on Tefillin. *Chabad.org*. 2018. Available from: https://www.chabad.org/library/article_cdo/aid/313832/jewish/The-Talmud-on-Tefillin.htm.

323. Deuteronomy 6:4.

324. Turliuc D, Costea CF, Dumitrescu GF, Cucu A, Turliuc Ş,

Salamastrakis I, et al. Origins of neurosurgery and neuroanatomy. Part 1: Ancient period. *Revista Română de Anatomie funcțională și clinică, macro- și microscopică și de Antropologie.* 2015;14(1):100-5.

325. Finding the Tefilin boundary on a balding head. *Mi Yodea.* 2011. Available from: https://judaism.stackexchange.com/questions/5948/finding-the-tefilin-boundary-on-a-balding-head.

326. Sperling AY. *Ta'amei Haminhagim U'mekorei Hadinim.* Jerusalem: Eshkol; [1890] 1982. pp. 11-9, 613-26.

327. Rubik B. The biofield: Bridge between mind and body. *Cosmos and History: The Journal of Natural and Social Philosophy.* 2015;11(2): 83-96.

328. *Shulchan Aruch Orach Chaim* 33:1.

329. Pinson D. The Kabbalah of Tefillin. *IYYUN.* 2010. Available from: http://iyyun.com/teachings/the-kabbalah-of-tefillin.

330. Nelson AD. *Origins of Consciousness.* Nottingham, UK: Metarising Books; 2015. pp. 58-120.

331. Waldenberg EY. Tzitz Eliezer-Milchemet Kesher Shel Rosh 9:9. Jerusalem; 1985.

332. Mistichelli D. Researches on the intimate structure of the brain, human and comparative. First Series. On the structure of the medulla oblongata. *Philos Trans R Soc Lond B Biol Sci.* 1709;148:231-59.

333. Capozzoli NJ. Why are vertebrate nervous systems crossed? *Medical Hypotheses.* 1995;45(5):471-5.

334. Shinbrot T, Young W. Why decussate? Topological constraints on 3D wiring. *Anatomical Record.* 2008;291(10):1278-92.

335. Frisch D. *Matok Midvash—Commentary on the Zohar.* 5. Jerusalem: Machon Daat Yosef; 2011. p. 280.

336. Exodus 6: 26-27.

337. Genesis 48:13-16.

338. Deuteronomy 20:8.

339. Babylonian Talmud *Sotah* 44b.

340. *Zohar* 3:288b, *Idra Zuta*. In: Margoliot R, editor. Jerusalem: Mossad Harav Kook; 1999.

341. Luzzatto MC. Portal 86. In: Friedlander C, editor. *Klach Pitchei Chochma*. Bnei Brak: Sifriati; [1785] 1992. pp. 268-71.

342. Luzzatto MC. Portal 85. In: Friedlander C, editor. *Klach Pitchei Chochma*. Bnei Brak: Sifriati; [1785] 1992. pp. 267-8.

343. Feynman R. *The Character of Physical Law*. Cambridge, MA: MIT Press; 1965.

344. Schrödinger E, cited in Capra Fritjof. *The Tao of Physics: An Exploration of the Parallels Between Modern Physics and Eastern Mysticism*. Boulder, CO: Shambhala Publications; 1975.

345. Hawking SW. *The Large Scale Structure of Space-Time*. Cambridge University Press; 2003. p. 364.

346. Gribbin J. *In Search of Schrödinger's Cat*. Toronto: Bantam Books; 1984. p. 302.

347. *Zohar* 3:288a, *Idra Zuta*. In: Margoliot R, editor. Jerusalem: Mossad Harav Kook; 1999.

348. Luzzatto MC. Portal 14. In: Friedlander C, editor. *Klach Pitchei Chochmah*. Bnei Brak: Sifriati; [1785] 1992. p. 43.

349. Mutalik P. Solution: 'Randomness From Determinism'. *Quanta Magazine* [Internet]. 2019. Available from: https://www.quantamagazine.org/solution-randomness-from-determinism-20191122/.

350. Wood C. Hologram within a Hologram Hints at Fate of Black Holes. *Quanta Magazine* [Internet]. 2019. Available from: https://www.quantamagazine.org/hologram-within-a-hologram-hints-at-solution-to-black-hole-information-paradox-20191119/.

351. Luzzatto MC. Portal 27. In: Friedlander C, editor. *Klach Pitchei Chochmah*. Bnei Brak: Sifriati; [1785] 1992. p. 80.

352. Larson CS. Process philosophy, optimalism and free will in quantum theory. *Cosmos and History: The Journal of Natural and Social Philosophy*. 2018;14(2):116-28.

353. Stapp HP. *Quantum Theory and Free Will*. New York City: Springer International Publishing; 2017.

354. Halachot Gedolot Ch. 76.

355. Seder Olam Habbah Ch. 20.

356. Maimonides M. *The Guide for the Perplexed* 2:45.

357. Shurpin Y. Why isn't the Book of Daniel part of the Prophets? The difference between divine inspiration and prophecy. 2012. Available from: https://www.chabad.org/library/article_cdo/aid/1735365/jewish/Why-Isnt-the-Book-of-Daniel-Part-of-the-Prophets.htm.

358. Dubov ND. The Four Worlds. 2006. Available from: https://www.chabad.org/library/article_cdo/aid/361902/jewish/The-Four-Worlds.htm.

359. Hillel YM. *Faith and Folly: The Occult in Torah Perspective*. Jerusalem: Feldheim Publishers; 1990. p. 119.

360. Eliashiv S. *Leshem Shevo V'achlamah—Chelek Haklalim* II:12-13. Tel-Aviv: Aharon Barazani & Son; [1935] 2011.

361. Schlosshauer MA. *Decoherence and the Quantum-To-Classical Transition*. Berlin: Springer-Verlag; 2007.

362. Ananthaswamy A. New quantum paradox clarifies where our views of reality go wrong. *Quanta Magazine* [Internet]. 2018. Available from: https://www.quantamagazine.org/frauchiger-renner-paradox-clarifies-where-our-views-of-reality-go-wrong-20181203/.

363. Wigner EP. Remarks on the mind-body question. In: Good IJ, editor. *The Scientist Speculates*. London: Heinemann; 1961.

364. Kirchhoff M, Parr T, Palacios E, Friston K, Kiverstein J. The Markov blankets of life: autonomy, active inference and the free energy principle. *Journal of the Royal Society, Interface*. 2018;15(138).

365. Ramstead MJD, Badcock PB, Friston KJ. Answering Schrödinger's question: A free-energy formulation. *Physics of Life Reviews*. 2018;24:1-16.

366. Rovelli C. Relational Quantum Mechanics. arXiv:quant-ph/96090022v2 [Internet]. 2008.

367. Hosea 2:22.

368. Timpe K. *Free Will in Philosophical Theology*. London: Bloomsbury Academic; 2013. p. 9.

369. van Inwagen P. How to think about the problem of free will. *The Journal of Ethics*. 2008;12(3-4):327-41.

370. Luzzatto MC. Portal 99. In: Friedlander C, editor. *Klach Pitchei Chochma*. Bnei Brak: Sifriati; [1785] 1992. pp. 297-8.

371. Babylonian Talmud *Brachot* 33b.

372. Leiner MY. *Mei HaShiloach*, Parshat Korach 1. 1860.

373. Edwards BP. *Living Waters: Mei Hashiloach Parshat Korach*. Northvale, NJ: Jason Aronson Inc.; 2001. p. 294.

374. Rabinowitz-Tzadok-HaKohen. *Tzidkat Ha'Tzadik* 40. 1902.

375. Wiederblank N. *Illuminating Jewish Thought: Explorations of Free Will, the Afterlife, and the Messianic Era*. Jerusalem: Koren Publishers; 2018. pp. 67-176.

376. Shmuel-de-Uzida. *Midrash Shmuel Avot* 3:21. Venice; 1579.

377. Idel M. "Higher than Time": Observations on Some Concepts of Time in Kabbalah and Hasidism. In: Ogren B, editor. *Time and Eternity in Jewish Mysticism*. Leiden: Brill; 2015. pp. 179-210.

378. Yitzchaki [Rashi] S. Commentary to Numbers 21:5.

379. Nachmanides. Commentary to Exodus 16:1-36.

380. Babylonian Talmud *Yoma* 75a.

381. Laureys S, Boly M, Tononi G. Functional Neuroimaging. In: Laureys S, Tononi G, editors. *The Neurology of Consciousness*. Amsterdam: Academic Press; 2009. pp. 31-42.

382. Polonsky A, Blake R, Braun J, Heeger DJ. Neuronal activity in human primary visual cortex correlates with perception during binocular rivalry. *Nature neuroscience*. 2000;3(11):1153-9.

383. Singer W. Consciousness and Neuronal Synchronization. In: Laureys S, Tononi G, editors. *The Neurology of*

Consciousness. Amsterdam: Academic Press; 2009. pp. 43-52.

384. Lord LD, Expert P, Huckins JF, Turkheimer FE. Cerebral energy metabolism and the brain's functional network architecture: an integrative review. *Journal of Cerebral Blood Flow and Metabolism*: official journal of the International Society of Cerebral Blood Flow and Metabolism. 2013;33(9):1347-54.

385. Kastrup B. *The Idea of the World*. Winchester, UK: John Hunt Publishing Ltd.; 2019. pp. 171-97.

386. Taylor K. *The Breathwork Experience: Exploration and Healing in Nonordinary States of Consciousness*. Santa Cruz, CA: Hanford Mead Publishers, Inc.; 1994. p. 192.

387. Whinnery JE, Whinnery AM. Acceleration-induced loss of consciousness: A review of 500 episodes. *Archives of Neurology*. 1990;47(7):764-76.

388. van Lommel P, van Wees R, Meyers V, Elfferich I. Near-death experience in survivors of cardiac arrest: a prospective study in the Netherlands. *Lancet*. 2001;358(9298):2039-45.

389. Blanke O, Ortigue S, Landis T, Seeck M. Stimulating illusory own-body perceptions. *Nature*. 2002;419(6904):269-70.

390. Peres JF, Moreira-Almeida A, Caixeta L, Leao F, Newberg A. Neuroimaging during trance state: a contribution to the study of dissociation. *PloS One*. 2012;7(11):e49360.

391. Urgesi C, Aglioti SM, Skrap M, Fabbro F. The spiritual brain: selective cortical lesions modulate human self-transcendence. *Neuron*. 2010;65(3):309-19.

392. Carhart-Harris RL, Muthukumaraswamy S, Roseman L, Kaelen M, Droog W, Murphy K, et al. Neural correlates of the LSD experience revealed by multimodal neuroimaging. *Proceedings of the National Academy of Sciences of the United States of America*. 2016;113(17):4853-8.

393. Lewis CR, Preller KH, Kraehenmann R, Michels L, Staempfli P, Vollenweider FX. Two dose investigation of the 5-HT-agonist psilocybin on relative and global cerebral blood

flow. *NeuroImage*. 2017;159:70-8.

394. Schipper HM. Brain iron deposition and the free radical-mitochondrial theory of ageing. *Ageing Research Reviews*. 2004;3(3):265-301.

395. Pietrini P, Salmon E, Nichelli P. Consciousness and Dementia: How the Brain Loses Its Self. In: Laureys S, Tononi G, editors. *The Neurology of Consciousness*. Amsterdam: Academic Press; 2009. pp. 204-16.

396. Tononi G, Laureys S. The Neurology of Consciousness: An Overview. In: Laureys S, Tononi G, editors. *The Neurology of Consciousness*. Amsterdam: Academic Press; 2009. pp. 375-412.

397. Kastrup B. *The Idea of the World*. Winchester, UK: John Hunt Publishing Ltd.; 2019. p. 115.

398. Isaiah 6:1-13.

399. Ezekiel 1:1-28.

400. Nair-Collins M, Northrup J, Olcese J. Hypothalamic-pituitary function in brain death: A review. *Journal of Intensive Care Medicine* [Internet]. 2014. Available from: https://diginole.lib.fsu.edu/islandora/object/fsu:208114/datastream/PDF/view.

401. Pallis C. ABC of brain stem death: Reappraising death. *British Medical Journal*. 1982;285:1409-12.

402. Steinsaltz A. *Understanding the Tanya*, Vol. III. San Francisco, CA: John Wiley & Sons; 2007. p. 310.

403. Schneersohn SD. *B'Shaa Shehikdimu*. New York: Kehot Publishing; [1911] 2011. p. 447.

404. de Vidas E. *Reishis Chochmah*, Shaar HaAhavah, Ch. 11. ca. 1550.

405. Proverbs 6:23.

406. Li O. Panentheism, Panpsychism and Neuroscience: In Search of an Alternative Metaphysical Framework in Relation to Neuroscience, Consciousness, Free Will, and Theistic Beliefs, pp. 110-113. Uppsala: Acta Universitatis

Upsaliensis; 2018.

407. Boundas CV. The Promise of Process Philosophy. *Columbia Companion to Twentieth-Century Philosophies*. New York: Columbia University Press; 2009. Cited in: Cynthia Sue Larson. Process Philosophy, Optimalism and Free Will in Quantum Theory. *Cosmos and History: The Journal of Natural and Social Philosophy*. Vol. 14, no. 2, 2018, pp. 116-128. Available from: www.cosmosandhistory.org/index.php/journal/issue/view/35.

408. Rescher N. The Promise of Process Philosophy. *Columbia Companion to Twentieth-Century Philosophies.* New York: Columbia University Press; 2007. pp. 143-55.

409. Gefter A. How to Understand the Universe When You're Stuck Inside of It. *Quanta Magazine* [Internet]. 2019. Available from: https://www.quantamagazine.org/were-stuck-inside-the-universe-lee-smolin-has-an-idea-for-how-to-study-it-anyway-20190627/.

410. Kafatos M, Tanzi RE, Chopra D. How consciousness becomes the physical universe. *Journal of Cosmology*. 2011;14:1119-29.

411. Stapp HP, editor. Whitehead, James, and Quantum Theory: Whitehead's Process Ontology as a Framework for a Heisenberg/James/von Neumann Conception of Nature and of Human Nature. Mind and Matter Research: Frontiers and Directions; 2006; Wildbad Kreuth, Germany.

412. Hustwit JR. Process Philosophy. In: *Internet Encyclopedia of Philosophy*. ISSN 2161-0002 [Internet]. Available from: https://www.iep.utm.edu/processp/.

413. Griffin DR. Reenchantment without Supernaturalism. New York: Cornell University Press; 2000. p. 109.

414. Griffin DR. *Unsnarling the World-Knot: Consciousness, Freedom, and the Mind-Body Problem*. Berkeley: University of California Press; 1998. pp. 77-116.

415. Barbour IG. *Nature, Human Nature and God*. Minneapolis:

Fortress Press; 2002. p. 32.

416. Li O. Panentheism, Panpsychism and Neuroscience: In Search of an Alternative Metaphysical Framework in Relation to Neuroscience, Consciousness, Free Will, and Theistic Beliefs, p. 116. Uppsala: Acta Universitatis Upsaliensis; 2018.

417. Li O. Panentheism, Panpsychism and Neuroscience: In Search of an Alternative Metaphysical Framework in Relation to Neuroscience, Consciousness, Free Will, and Theistic Beliefs, p. 179. Uppsala: Acta Universitatis Upsaliensis; 2018.

418. Li O. Panentheism, Panpsychism and Neuroscience: In Search of an Alternative Metaphysical Framework in Relation to Neuroscience, Consciousness, Free Will, and Theistic Beliefs, pp. 180-183. Uppsala: Acta Universitatis Upsaliensis; 2018.

419. Stapp HP, editor. Retrocausation in quantum mechanics and the effects of minds on the creation of physical reality. AIP Conference; 2017; San Diego: AIP Publishing.

420. Babylonian Talmud *Sotah* 3a.

421. Shneur-Zalman-of-Liadi. *Likkutei Amarim* [Tanya]: Ch. 24. New York: Kehot Publication Society; [1797] 1993.

422. Eliashiv S. *Leshem Shevo V'achlamah—Chelek Haklalim* II: 80. Tel-Aviv: Aharon Barazani & Son; [1935] 2011.

423. Afterman A. *Kabbalah and Consciousness*. Riverdale-on-Hudson, NY: The Sheep Meadow Press; 1992. pp. 63-4.

424. Visos BG, Mosquera DA. Georg Cantor, the Man Who Discovered Different Infinities. *OpenMind BBVA* [Internet]. 2019. Available from: https://www.bbvaopenmind.com/en/science/mathematics/georg-cantor-the-man-who-discovered-different-infinities/.

425. Genesis 17:11-12.

426. Babylonian Talmud *Shabbat* 21b.

427. Glazerson M. *Music and Kabbalah*. New York: Jason Aronson

Publishers; 1988. p. 109.

428. Shapira P. *Imrei Pinchas*: Chanukah 61. ca. 1750.

429. Webb R. Five things physicists hate about physics. *New Scientist* [Internet]. 2017. Available from: https://www.newscientist.com/article/2140261-five-things-physicists-hate-about-physics/.

430. Daffern TC, editor. ENLIGHTENMENTS: Towards a Comparative Analysis of the Philosophies of Enlightenment in Buddhist, Eastern and Western Thought and the Search for a Holistic Enlightenment Suitable for the Contemporary World. SOAS Buddhist Conference for Dongguk University on Global Ecological problems and the Buddhist Perspective; 2005; Seoul.

431. *Zohar* 1:117a.

432. Ecclesiastes 1:9.

433. Nichol L. *The Essential David Bohm*. London: Routledge; 2003. pp. 139-57.

434. Isaiah 11:6.

435. Wiederblank N. *Illuminating Jewish Thought: Explorations of Free Will, the Afterlife, and the Messianic Era*. Jerusalem: Koren Publishers; 2018. pp. 521-46.

436. Nagel T. *Mind & Cosmos: Why the materialist neo-Darwinian conception of nature is almost certainly false*. New York: Oxford University Press; 2012. p. 66.

437. Luzzatto MC. Portal 98 (Editor note). In: Friedlander C, editor. *Klach Pitchei Chochma*. Bnei Brak: Sifriati; [1785] 1992. pp. 292-7.

438. Ullman S. *Da'at Elokim*. Jerusalem: Hamesorah; 1996. pp. 33-4.

439. Shneur-Zalman-of-Liadi. *Likkutei Amarim* [Tanya]: Ch. 36-37. New York: Kehot Publication Society; [1797] 1993.

440. de Chardin PT. *The Future of Man*. New York: Penguin Random House; 2004. p. 336.

441. Schneersohn SD. *B'Shaa Shehikdimu*. 1. New York: Kehot

Publishing; [1911] 2011. p. 404.

442. Eliashiv S. *Leshem Shevo V'achlamah—Hakdamot V'Shearim.* Tel-Aviv: Aharon Barazani & Son; [1908] 2006. pp. 68-9.

443. Habbakuk 2:14.

444. Babylonian Talmud *Chagigah* 13a.

445. *Sifra:* Braita d'Rabbi Yishmael—Parashah 1.

446. Luzzatto MC. Portal 16. In: Friedlander C, editor. *Klach Pitchei Chochma.* Bnei Brak: Sifriati; [1785] 1992. p. 47.

447. Weinberg S. Beautiful Theories. *Dreams of a Final Theory.* New York: Pantheon Books; 1992. pp. 81-107.

448. Zimmer C. Scientists Seek to Update Evolution. *Quanta Magazine* [Internet]. 2016. Available from: https://www.quantamagazine.org/scientists-seek-to-update-evolution-20161122/.

449. Micah 7:20.

450. Greene B. *The Elegant Universe: Superstrings Hidden Dimensions and the Quest for the Ultimate Theory.* New York: W. W. Norton; 2010. p. 464.

451. Thornton S. Karl Popper. In: *The Stanford Encyclopedia of Philosophy* (Fall 2018 Edition) [Internet]. Available from: https://plato.stanford.edu/archives/fall2018/entries/popper/.

452. Laitman M. *The Science of Kabbalah (Pticha).* Brooklyn, NY: Kabbalah Books; 2015. p. 612.

453. Michaelson Y. *The Science of Kabbalah.* Amazon Digital Services LLC; 2018.

454. Fodor J. Jerry Fodor Interview on Philosophy of Mind. YouTube; 2015.

455. Hoover Institution. Mathematical Challenges to Darwin's Theory of Evolution. YouTube; 2019.

Index

Aaron, 114-5
Abba (*Partzuf*), 33, 39-41, 70, 76, 99, 109, 157
Abraham (-ic; see Patriarch), 31, 94, 126, 164
Abulafia, Abraham, 28, 137
ABY"A (*Atzilut, Briah, Yetzirah, Asiyah*; Worlds), 39, 92, 95, 157
Adam, 26, 77, 101
Adam Kadmon (Primordial Man; World), 33, 39-40, 43, 70, 92, 95, 124, 157, 161, 169
Afilalo, Raphael, xv, 108
Afterman, Allen, 59, 78
Almheiri, Ahmed, 126
alphabet, 32, 36, 105
Alzheimer dementia, 142
Amoroso, Richard, xv
analogia relationis, 64
Ancient Rome, 89
Angel of Esau, 31
animal (-istic), 23,72,75-8, 81, 82-6, 88, 91, 143, 152, 168
Anthropic Principle, 17, 104, 106
Aquinas, Thomas, 1
Aramaic, 30, 32, 120, 163
Arich Anpin (*A"A, Partzuf*), 39, 41, 99, 120, 125, 136, 161
Aristotelian, 170

artificial intelligence (AI), 84, 161, 168
Asenath (*Osnat*), 105
Ashkenazi, 27, 113, 117
Asiyah (World of Action), 33, 39, 41-3, 50, 71, 76, 125, 128, 136, 148
Aspect, Alain, 14, 16
atheism (-ist), 8
Atik Yomin (*A"Y, Partzuf*), 33, 39, 41-2, 99, 120, 126, 128-130, 136, 143, 161, 167
Atzilut (World of Emanation), 33, 39, 43, 54, 75-7, 79, 81, 109, 124, 136, 148, 169
autism, 88

Balaam, 127, 143
Bar-Yochai, Shimon, 26
beauty (-iful), 37, 164
behavior (-al), 6, 17, 22, 30, 49-50, 76, 85, 91, 104, 129, 131
Bekenstein, Jacob, 22
Bell's inequality, 16
Ben-Azzai, 68
Berkelyan (see idealism), 64
Bible (-ical), 27, 30, 51, 89, 104, 110, 127, 129, 163, 168
Big Bang, 16, 60, 129, 154, 170
bioenergy, 111
biology (neuro-, -ical, -ist), 3, 7,

9-10, 22, 29, 47, 51-2, 75, 86-7, 90, 104, 114-5, 128, 144, 164, 170-1

black hole, 22, 126, 154

blackbody radiation, 14

Blake, William, 48

blessing, 48, 96-7, 105, 115, 127, 129

block universe, 107, 135-7

blood, 89-90, 109, 139, 147

Bohm, David (see Bohmian mechanics), 1, 18-24, 46, 49, 51-2, 59, 75, 78-9, 82, 115, 138, 144, 149, 151, 159-160, 166

Bohmian mechanics (see Bohm, David), 2, 13-5, 17, 19, 21, 23-4, 29, 46, 48, 129, 159, 166, 171

Bohr, Niels, 14, 16-8

Book of Creation (*Sefer Yetzirah*), 44, 58, 84, 86

brain, 1, 6-7, 10-11, 22-3, 40-1, 43, 46-7, 51-2, 63-5, 67, 70, 72, 80, 83-4, 87-8, 101-3, 106, 108-14, 116, 118-120, 139-42, 144-7, 157-9, 166-8

Brawer, Yaakov, xv

Briah (World of Creation), 33, 39, 42-3, 50, 54, 76-7, 109, 128, 148, 152

Buddhism, 154

Cantor, Georg, 153

cell (-ular), 10, 23, 29, 46, 51-2,

74, 87, 132, 141, 144, 15, 158

cell-occasions, 150

central nervous system (CNS), 23, 109-10, 115

cerebral, 47, 87-8, 109, 140

Chalmers, David, 5, 7-9, 16, 97, 108, 150, 156-7, 166

Chanukah, 106, 153

Chassidic, 2, 18, 28, 76, 79, 84, 113, 117, 137, 163

chemistry (bio- ,-cal, electro- ,neuro- , physico- ,), 1, 6-7, 52, 108-9, 128-9, 146, 156, 171

Christian, 89, 170

clairvoyance, 23

clinic (-al), 2, 92, 102, 138-9, 142, 167

coma, 142, 144

combination (-al) problem, 9-10, 166

compatibilism (-ist), 135, 137

concrescence, 151

consciousness, 1-3, 5-11, 13-9, 23, 25, 27, 43-4, 46-9, 53-4, 56, 59-68, 70-79, 81-92, 97-8, 100-104, 106-113, 116-21, 123-4, 126-30, 132-3, 136-47, 149-50, 152, 154, 156-63, 165-71

Contraction (*Tzimtzum*), 35, 39-40, 56-7, 79, 95, 99, 162

Copenhagen (interpretation), 14-8, 63

corpus callosum, 109

corpus symbolicum, 30

cosmic consciousness, 27, 53, 72-3, 82, 110, 143-145, 159, 169

cosmic web, 47

cosmology (-gony), 14, 57-8, 77, 103, 128, 152, 154, 171

cosmopsychism, 63, 166

cosmos (-ic), 2, 5, 11, 19, 21, 24, 33, 47, 49, 51, 53, 55, 58-9, 91, 97-9, 103, 106-8, 126, 130, 148, 154, 1579, 161, 169

Creation, 11, 13, 24-5, 33, 39-40, 42-5, 49, 51, 54-6, 59-61, 65, 67, 70, 72, 75-6, 82, 84, 89-91, 94-6, 98, 102, 106, 108, 112, 121, 125-7, 132, 134, 137-8, 148, 150, 153, 157-163, 166-7, 169

Creator, 11, 13, 17, 29, 55-6, 60, 65, 67, 99-100, 106, 125, 146, 159, 171

Crick, Francis, 11

Dan, Joseph, 92

Daniel, 127-8

Darwinian, 8, 170

de Chardin, Pierre Teilhard, 161

De la Rosa, Chaim, 28

de Sitter space (geometry), 57, 74

decussation, 113, 115, 119

deism, 11, 64

Deity, 64, 100, 164

delayed choice paradigm, 103

Dennett, Daniel, 137

Deutsch, David, 161

disunity (*Pirud*), 24, 43, 45, 54-5

DNA, 51-52, 158

dualism, 8, 64

duality (-ies; *Kinuim*), 61, 73, 103, 137, 153, 161, 167

Eastern, 1, 18, 64, 154

Ecstatic Kabbalah, 28, 137

eight, 153, 155

Ein-Sof (also *Ohr Ein-Sof*; see Godhead), 24, 36-7, 39-40, 45, 54, 56-7, 65, 70, 79-80, 95, 98, 111, 125, 138, 143, 145, 152, 159, 161

Einstein, Albert, 14, 16-8, 32, 62, 68, 81, 136, 164

Einstein-Podolsky-Rosen (EPR) paradox, 16

Eliyashiv, Shlomo (*Leshem*), 2, 22, 44, 77, 98-9, 161

Ells, Peter, 2, 5, 13, 63-4

emergence, 8, 10, 20, 49, 75, 102, 104, 128, 149-50

empathy, 91, 93

energy, 9, 14, 42, 48, 51, 61, 97, 105, 131, 140, 157

enfoldment (see Bohm, David), 19-21, 24

enlightenment, 154, 159

Ensheathment (*Hitlabshut*), 19, 23-4, 44-6, 51, 53

entropy (-ic), 131-3
Ephraim, 115
epiphenomena (-l), 1, 5, 63, 137, 139, 162
epistemic (-ology), 2, 30, 62, 122-3, 125, 142, 156, 169
eternalism, 135-6
ethic (-al, bio-), 2, 28, 67, 87-8, 134, 150, 152-3
Etz Chaim, 2, 28, 34, 44, 56, 120
Everett, Hugh (Many-Worlds interpretation), 17
evil, 54, 77, 105, 127, 137, 152
ex nihilo, 65, 77
Expansion, 57, 95, 98-101, 106
explicate order (see Bohm, David), 19-20, 22, 24, 59, 138
extendable telescope metaphor (see also Ensheathment), 45, 54-5
Extended Evolutionary Synthesis, 164
extracorporeal, 109, 146
eye-for-an-eye, 32
Ezekiel, 128, 143
Ezra of Gerona, 26

Feletti, Alberto, 47
female intuition, 2, 92-3, 96
Feminine (Divine, *Nukva*), 35, 37, 41, 59, 93-7, 99, 115, 157
Feynman, Richard, 14
Fodor, Jerry, 165
foreknowledge, 136

fractal, 25, 33, 40, 43, 46, 49-50, 53, 59, 79, 95, 99-100, 153, 158-9
Frankenstein's monster, 86
free will, 1-2, 23, 54, 76, 92, 102, 107, 119, 127-30, 134-7, 143, 152, 160
Freud, Sigmund, 78
Friston, Karl, 132
Futuyma, Douglas, 164

Ganzfeld sensory deprivation, 53
Garb, Jonathan, 92
Gell-Mann, Murray, 14
Gematriya, 31, 34, 36, 55
Genesis, 11, 26, 29, 40, 89, 99, 101, 136
Genovese, Marco, 61
Gimel Rishonim (*G"R*, 3 top 'conscious' *Sefirot*; see also *Mochin*), 34, 66-7, 72-6, 79-82, 98-102, 106-7, 111, 115, 118, 134, 144, 151, 157, 159, 166-7
God (-head, -ly), 10-11, 24, 26, 29, 30-1, 37, 39-40, 45, 48, 51, 54-6, 58-60, 62, 65, 67-9, 71, 73, 76-7, 84, 86, 89, 90, 93-5, 99-101, 105-7, 110, 112, 114, 116, 120, 125-7, 129-30, 132-4, 136, 138, 142-3, 145, 150, 152-3, 157-8, 161-2, 166-8
Goldilocks universe, 104
Goldstein, Ephraim, xv, 28,

134, 153

Golem, 83-8, 168

Governing Vessel (see Traditional Chinese Medicine), 116

Great Merger of Being, 162

Halacha (-ic; law), 30, 34, 86, 96, 168

Hameroff, Stuart, 10

Hawking radiation, 126

head, 71, 83, 88, 110-13, 115-20, 136, 146, 167

Hebrew, 24, 26-32, 36, 45-6, 49, 55, 62, 68, 73, 84-5, 105, 113, 120, 153, 157, 163

Heisenberg, Werner (see Uncertainty Principle), 1, 15, 120, 123, 129, 143, 149, 166, 169

Henry, Richard Conn, 132

hermeneutical, 31-2, 162

hidden variables (see Bohm, David), 18-9

hierarchy (Kabbalistic; consciousness), 24, 32, 38, 41-2, 44, 49, 54, 64, 67, 70-1, 73, 75, 77, 82, 89, 94, 96, 99, 124, 126, 133, 143-4, 158, 166

hieroglyphics, 57

Hillel, Yaakov Moshe, 28

Hinduism, 154

Hoel, Erik, 102

holiness, 32, 39, 80, 109, 111, 153-5, 169

holographic universe (see Bohm, David), 21-2, 25, 46, 149

holomovement (see Bohm, David), 19-20, 24, 49, 75, 79, 159

holonomic brain theory, 23

human (-ity, -kind, -oid), 8, 9, 11, 19, 23, 33, 39, 44, 47-8, 51-2, 54-5, 55-8, 63-4, 66-8, 71-2, 75-8, 80, 81-91, 94, 97, 99-101, 103-4 106-20, 123-4, 126-7, 129-30, 132-4, 136-7, 139-40, 142-5, 148, 150, 152, 154, 156-170

idealism, 2, 64, 132, 141, 166

Idel, Moshe, 92, 94, 137

imaging (neuro-), 102, 139, 143, 145

imago Dei, 163

Imma (Partzuf), 34, 39-41, 70,, 99, 1079, 157, 169

immanent, 11, 63-4, 7-73, 77-8, 83, 93-4, 96, 110, 112, 118, 132, 145-6, 161

implicate order (see Bohm, David), 18-20, 22, 24, 46, 49, 59, 75, 138, 160, 166

inanimate, 8, 51, 54, 63, 72, 74-6, 82-3, 85, 90, 108, 143

infinity (-ite, -tude), 17, 19, 33, 40, 48, 77, 79, 95, 126, 150,

153-24, 161
inflationary cosmology, 57
Information theory, 7, 17
injury, 140, 147
interconnectedness, 18, 21, 122
Interinclusion (*Hitkallelut*), 23,
    25, 44, 46, 48-9, 51, 53, 66, 75,
    79, 82, 99, 106, 115, 138, 149,
    158
Interpenetration (*Hitkashrut*),
    10, 23-5, 44, 49-53, 55, 59, 149,
    152, 158-9
intoxication, 145, 147
Isaac (see Patriarch), 31, 164
Isaiah, 39, 128, 143, 160
Israel (-ites), 26, 31, 48, 68, 89,
    105, 114, 117, 127, 138
Izhbitze-Radziner Rebbe (see
    also Leiner, Mordechai
    Yosef), 57, 74, 136

Jacob, 31, 104, 115, 164
James, Henry, 165
Jewish Emancipation
    (*Haskalah*), 163
Jewish mysticism, 1-2, 26
Job, 110, 116
Joseph, 104-5, 115
Judaism, 11, 30, 33, 59, 62, 67,
    148, 154, 163-4
Judeo-Christian, 91, 100, 104
Julia set, 30

Kabbalah (see also Kabbalistic,

Lurianic Kabbalah), 1, 2, 11,
    13, 18, 24-33, 37, 39, 42-4,
    49-51, 53, 56-7, 60, 62, 62, 65,
    70-72, 75, 83, 85, 88-9, 91, 93-
    4, 97-9, 102, 104-6, 108-9, 121-
    24, 129, 136-7, 142, 144, 146,
    148-50, 152-60, 163-9, 171
Kabbalistic, 1-2, 10, 12-5, 17-9,
    23-33, 38, 40, 44-6, 49, 51, 53-
    4, 57-66, 71, 73-4, 77, 79, 81,
    83-4, 87-8, 92, 94-6, 99-100,
    102, 104, 106-8, 110, 114-7,
    120, 122, 124-5, 127-30, 132-3,
    135-6, 138-9, 142, 144-5, 147,
    149-53, 156-8, 161, 163-5, 168-
    71
Kafatos, Menas, 149
Kaplan, Aryeh, 92
Kastrup, Bernardo, 2, 132-3,
    140-43, 147, 159
Katz, Levi, xv
Keter-Malchut axis, 32, 66, 93-4,
    96-7, 100, 125-46, 130, 143,
    146, 153-5, 169
Koch, Christof, 2, 7-8
Krishnamurti, Jiddu, 18, 159
Kurzweil, Raymond, 97, 161
language, 30, 32, 76, 89-90, 109,
    163, 168
Leibniz's *Monadology*, 149
Leiner, Mordechai Yosef
    (see also Izhbitze-Radziner
    Rebbe), 136
Leviathan gas field, 105

Light (*Ohr*), 11, 26, 29, 33, 35-7, 39-40, 37-8, 43-5, 52, 56, 60, 67, 70-1, 77-80, 83, 93-6, 98-100, 109-11, 114, 123, 145-8, 153, 160-61
Linde, Andrei, 161
liver, 51-2, 83, 108-9
Loew, Yehuda, 85
Lt. Commander Data, 84-5
Lubavitch (-er), 11, 28, 79
Lurianic Kabbalah, xv, 28, 43, 56, 70, 93, 98, 148, 166
Luzzatto, Moshe Chaim (*Ramchal*), xv, 2, 28, 44, 50, 79-80, 120, 5

Maimonides, 160
Manasseh, 115
Mandelbrot set, 46, 9 158
Manna, 68-9, 138
Markov blanket, 107, 130-3, 138, 141-3, 145, 167
Masculine (Divine), 37, 41, 59, 94-7, 115
materialism (see materialist), 2, 5, 8, 64, 152
materialist (see materialism), 8, 140-1, 165, 168, 170
mathematic (-al, -ally, -ian), 7, 16, 19, 22, 29-30, 41-3, 46, 55, 62, 74, 102, 131, 153-4, 170
Matriarch, 31, 52
medulla oblongata, 113, 119
memory, 20, 23, 109, 116

mental (-ly), 7, 49, 53, 74-5, 102, 112, 117, 132, 134, 148, 150-1, 159, 163
metabolism (-ic), 139-43, 145, 147, 168
metaphysic (-al), 1-2, 10, 23, 29, 32, 48, 53, 60, 70, 90, 93-4, 99, 107, 121, 134, 152, 154, 158, 163
microcephaly, 88
Midrashic, 34, 52, 55, 84
mind (-ful, -set, theory-of-), 5, 8-9, 22, 40, 43-4, 48, 62, 64-6, 73, 77-9, 90-1, 93, 97, 102-3, 108, 112, 117, 134, 141, 145-6, 150-1, 156, 165-8
Mind of God, 11, 73, 112, 120, 129-30, 132-3, 142, 145, 166
mind-at-large, 141-2, 159
mind-body problem, 150
mineral, 74-5, 81, 83, 134, 144, 166
miracle (-ulous), 68, 105, 138, 153
Mistichelli, Domenico, 113
Mitchell, Edgar, 23
Mitzvah (-*ot*), 34, 48, 54, 56, 67-8, 102, 148
Mochin ('brains', consciousness; see also *Gimel Rishonim*), 34, 40-3, 45, 63, 65-7, 70, 72, 74, 76, 79-80, 98, 101, 111, 113, 118, 144-5, 147, 157, 159, 166

molecule-occasions, 150
monism (-ist), 8-9, 150
monotheism, 170
moon, 58-9, 97
Moses, 26, 29, 48, 114-5, 128
Mount Sinai, 26, 30, 48, 158
multiverse, 17, 165
murder, 86
musical, 153

Nachmanides, 26, 160
Nagel, Thomas, 2, 8, 160
Nazi Germany, 89
near-death experience, 112, 140
Nelson, Adrian, 2, 7, 17, 53, 60, 97
Neo-Realism, 17
nerve, 23, 110, 116, 118, 141
nervous system, 10, 23, 58, 83, 107, 110-1, 114, 117-9
neural correlates of consciousness (NCC), 139, 141
neural, 2, 6-8, 10, 23, 47, 63, 87, 114-6, 120, 139-41, 156, 163
neuropsychiatric, 23, 112, 116, 141, 146, 167
neuroscience, 12, 18, 22, 27, 29, 102, 156, 162-3, 167, 171
Newtonian, 13, 123-4, 170
Notarikon, 31
numerical diminutive, 56, 153

observer, 1, 5, 15, 61-2, 64, 68,
70, 81, 104, 129
oil, 153-4
Oivi ('horizontality'), 11, 24, 45, 54-6, 58-62, 75, 79, 100, 107, 126, 130, 135-8, 158-60, 167
Omega point, 161
Omer, 48, 68-9
oneness, 13, 78, 122
Oral Law (Tradition), 26, 28, 110
Orech ('verticality'), 11, 24, 45, 54-6, 58-62, 75, 79, 82, 100, 107-8, 126-7, 129, 135, 137-8, 158-60, 167
organoid, 87-8

panentheism (-istic), 2, 9, 10-11, 63-4, 70, 108, 112, 120, 142, 150, 163, 166
panpsychism (see panpsychist), 1-2, 8-10, 23, 60, 63-4, 81, 83, 92, 98-100, 108, 129, 139, 141-2, 150, 156, 159, 163-6, 171
panpsychist (see panpsychism), 9-10, 53, 63, 85, 88, 98, 106, 144, 150, 160, 163, 166
pantheism, 11, 64
paradox (-ical), 14, 16, 60-2, 64, 77, 79, 102, 107, 122, 129-31, 134, 136-7, 167-8
paranormal, 23, 67, 112, 167
participatory universe (see

Wheeler, Archibald), 102-3, 106, 126
particle, 14-7, 20-1, 48, 50, 57, 61, 63-4, 66, 74, 103-4, 122, 124, 137, 167, 171
Partzuf (-im), 35-42, 45-6, 54, 65-6, 70, 73, 75, 92-3, 95, 98-9, 109, 111, 115, 120, 128, 130, 133, 136, 143, 157, 161, 167, 169
Passover (Pesach), 48
Patriarch, 31, 164
Penrose, Roger, 10
Perelmuter, Nosson, xiii, 31
peripheral nervous system (PNS), 110, 116, 119
photon, 61-2, 69, 103, 112, 139
physiology (-ical), 1, 46, 51, 76, 92, 110, 139, 144
Pinker, Steven, 8
Planck, Max, 13-4
plant, 10, 72, 74-6, 81-85, 90, 134, 143-4, 167
Plotinus, 1
Poltorak, Alexander, 68
polytheistic, 17
prayer, 58, 101, 110, 126, 146, 160
precognition, 112
prehension, 150
preordain (-ination), 107, 125, 127, 130, 137, 167
Pribram, Karl, 23
priest, 114, 161

process philosophy, 2, 23, 92, 149-50, 166, 171
process theology, 150
proof, 29, 153, 1624
prophecy, 2, 31, 77, 92, 112, 119, 127-30, 133, 138, 144-5, 167, 171
Prophets (The), 29
proto-consciousness, 9, 81, 100
Providence (-tial), 31, 104-6
Psalms, 37, 84
psi, 7, 53, 67, 112, 142
psychedelic, 140-1
psychosis, 116-7, 144, 146,
Purim, 105-6
pyramidal tract, 113

qualia, 1, 5, 9, 87, 90, 108, 137, 156-75, 168
quantum entanglement, 10, 17, 50, 170
quantum indeterminacy, 102, 119
quantum mechanics, 13-8, 52, 57, 61, 613, 120-1, 123-4, 128, 132, 143, 163, 169
quantum physics, 1, 14-5, 17, 23, 121, 122-8, 170-2

Rabbi Yishmael, 162
Rabbinic, 85, 88, 104
Radin, Dean, 112
random (-ness), 57, 105, 112, 122, 125-7, 130, 143, 170

Rashi, 31, 48, 68, 101, 136
Ray (Divine, *Kav*), 40, 56, 79-80,
    95, 98
reality, 1, 10-1, 13, 16-7, 19, 21,
    24, 33, 41-2, 45, 53-4, 57, 60,
    62-3, 68, 77-8, 100-1, 104, 106,
    119, 121-23, 125, 129-30, 138,
    149, 155, 158-9, 163, 165, 167,
    169-71
reductionist, 1-2, 7, 52, 98, 102-
    3, 129-31, 137, 165
Rees, Martin, 104
relativity (-istic), 13, 44, 46,
    62-3, 68-71, 74-5, 79-84, 135-
    6, 144-5, 147, 150, 163, 166-7,
    171
religion (-ous), 3, 18-9, 142,
    148, 159, 163
Responsa (The), 30
retro-causal (-ity), 106
revelation, 1, 24, 30, 37, 45, 49,
    53, 58, 66, 72-3, 75, 83, 100,
    108, 110, 159-60, 165-6, 169-70
rights, 85-6, 88-9, 168
ritual bath, 146
robot, 85
Roelofs, Luke, 9
Rosenberg, Gregg, 2
Rubinstein, Rachel, xv, 97
Rutherford, Ernest, 14

Sabbath (-tical), 48, 66, 73, 94,
    125, 157
Sarah (see Matriarch), 31, 52,
    94
Schatz, Moshe, xv, 52, 158
schizophrenia, 23, 88, 112, 146
Schneersohn, Menachem
    Mendel, 11
Schneersohn, Sholom DovBer,
    28
Schneider, Sarah Yehudit, 94
Scholem, Gershom, 92
Schrödinger equation, 61, 125,
    130, 143
Schrödinger, Erwin, 14
Schwartz, Jeffrey, 102
Scripture (-al), 11, 28, 30, 48,
    89, 110, 117, 162-3
Seager, William, 7
seal-upon-seal (*Chotem
    V'nechtom*; see also 'signet-
    ring' metaphor), 42, 57
self-awareness, 54, 77-8, 81, 85,
    90, 103, 109, 143, 163, 168
sense, 19, 67, 78, 87, 93, 110,
    117, 127, 137-8, 143, 148
Sephardi, 27, 113, 117
Seventh (Messianic)
    Millennium, 26, 53, 73, 91, 95,
    97, 100, 109-10, 144-5, 156-9,
    169
Shamir, Yitzchak, 89
Shapira, Pinchas (of Koretz),
    84, 153-4
Sharabi, Shalom (*Rashash*), 2,
    28, 44, 51, 54
Shattering of the Vessels

(*Shvirat Hakelim*), 42-4, 59, 75, 79, 96, 148, 166

Shimshon of Ostropol, 32

Shmuel ben-Yitzchak de Ozida, 136

signet-ring metaphor (see also seal-upon-seal), 42-4

sin, 48, 117, 152, 160

Singer, Wolf, 140

singularity, 16, 96, 161

Sixth Principle (of Torah exegesis), 162

Smolin, Lee, 149

social (-iety, psycho-), 53, 86, 90-1, 132, 147-8, 150, 160

Soul, 64, 73, 76-7, 80, 82-3, 86, 90-2, 109-10, 144, 152, 160-2, 169

space-time (see also time), 22-3, 42, 50, 62, 68, 77, 81-2, 135-6, 157, 169

speaker, 11, 72, 85, 90, 168

speed of light, 68-9, 81

spinal cord, 110, 113, 115-6, 118

Spinozan (see pantheism), 64

spirit (-uality), 3, 8, 24, 28-9, 31-2, 39-42, 45, 50, 53, 55-8, 60-1, 63, 65, 93-4, 105-6, 110, 112, 114, 117, 128-9, 134, 138, 143, 146, 152, 158, 163, 165

spirit of folly, 152

Standard Model (see particle, quantum physics), 171

Stapp, Henry, 2, 102

subjective experience, 3, 5, 89-91, 140-1, 146-7, 168, 170

sun, 58-9, 97, 156, 159

superposition, 16, 63, 125, 129-30

superstring theory, 57, 165

supervenience, 32, 98-100, 108, 128

Talmud (-ic), 30, 32, 85-6, 110, 117-8, 163

Tauber, Yanki, 11

Tefillin (phylacteries), 58, 107, 110-9, 158, 167

telekinesis, 23

telepathy, 23, 53, 112

Temurah, 31-2

Ten Commandments, 56

Tenth Millennium, 160

Tetragrammaton, 114, 157

Thirteen Principles (of Torah exegesis), 162

time (see also space-time), 11, 14, 20, 22, 26, 29, 54, 61-2, 68, 70, 77, 80-2, 96-7, 105-7, 135-7, 152, 155, 160, 162

Tipler, Frank, 161

tomography, 139

top-down causation, 1, 5, 32, 98, 100, 106, 108, 110, 128

Torah, 11, 14, 26-7, 29-32, 43, 48, 51, 56, 58-9, 67-8, 76, 83, 86-7, 90, 101, 109-11, 118, 138, 143, 148, 151-3, 162, 168, 170

Tower of Babel, 88-91, 168

Traditional Chinese Medicine, 116, 119

transcendent (-ce), 11, 60, 64, 67, 70-3, 77-9, 81, 81, 90, 93-4, 96, 109, 118, 138, 140-1, 145-7, 153, 160-1, 167

Tree of Life, 37, 44, 51, 57, 93, 133, 169

truth, 26, 30, 37, 48, 56-7, 122, 164-5

two-slit (experiment), 15-6, 103

Tzadok Ha'Kohen, 136

Uncertainty Principle (see Heisenberg), 1, 15, 117-20, 123-5, 143, 149, 166, 169

unconscious, 6, 8, 74, 74, 83, 98-100, 129, 144-5, 166-7

unfoldment (see Bohm, David), 19-21, 24

Union (Divine, *Zivug*), 39, 95, 114

unity (*Shlaymut*), 10, 24, 33-4, 49, 55-6, 78-9, 114, 138, 158

universe, 2, 5-6, 9-11, 14-5, 17-8, 21-2, 24-5, 33, 45-9, 51, 57, 60-2, 64, 67, 78, 97-8, 103-4, 106, 121, 124, 126, 128-9, 132, 138, 149, 151, 153, 155-8, 160-1, 167, 170

Unknowable Head (*RADLA*), 107, 118, 120-130, 132-3, 137-8, 142-3, 145-7, 149, 167, 169

utopian, 159

Vazza, Franco, 47

Vessel (*Keli*), 37, 43, 59, 67, 70-1, 75, 78-80, 93-6, 99-100, 109, 146-8, 161

Void (Primordial, *Makom Panoi, Chalal*), 39-40, 56-7, 79, 95-6, 98, 157, 161

von Neumann, John, 17, 102

wave function, 16-7, 61, 64, 78, 102-3, 106-7, 121-2, 126-7, 127-8, 132-3, 142-3

Weber, Renée, 159

Weinberg, Steven, 14

Wenger, Yoel Chonon, xv

whisky, 138

Whitehead (-ian), Alfred North, 149-51

Wigner, Eugene, 14, 130

Wigner's friend paradox, 107, 130-1

Withdrawal, 79, 95-6, 98-100

World, 36-7, 39-46, 50-1, 54, 65-8, 70, 73, 75-6, 77, 79, 81-82, 92, 95, 101, 109, 120-2, 128, 136, 148, 157, 160, 169

Written Torah (Pentateuch), 26, 68

Yetzirah (World of Formation), 35, 39, 42-4, 50, 76, 128, 148

Zayin Tachtonim (Z"T; 7 bottom
'bodily' *Sefirot)*, 35, 66-7, 72,
74, 76, 78, 81-2, 98-9, 101, 106,
111-113, 115, 120, 134, 136,
144-6, 150-1, 157, 166-7
Zeir Anpin (Z"A, Partzuf), 35,

39, 41, 70, 97, 99, 115, 157
zero, 56
Zika virus, 88
Zohar, 2, 44, 120, 156, 171
Zoroastrianism, 154

IFF
BOOKS

ACADEMIC AND SPECIALIST

Iff Books publishes non-fiction. It aims to work with authors and titles
that augment our understanding of the human condition, society and
civilisation, and the world or universe in which we live.
If you have enjoyed this book, why not tell other readers by posting a
review on your preferred book site.

Recent bestsellers from Iff Books are:

Why Materialism Is Baloney
How true skeptics know there is no death and fathom answers
to life, the universe, and everything
Bernardo Kastrup
A hard-nosed, logical, and skeptic non-materialist metaphysics,
according to which the body is in mind, not mind in the body.
Paperback: 978-1-78279-362-5 ebook: 978-1-78279-361-8

The Fall
Steve Taylor
The Fall discusses human achievement versus the issues of war,
patriarchy and social inequality.
Paperback: 978-1-78535-804-3 ebook: 978-1-78535-805-0

Brief Peeks Beyond
Critical essays on metaphysics, neuroscience, free will,
skepticism and culture
Bernardo Kastrup
An incisive, original, compelling alternative to current mainstream
cultural views and assumptions.
Paperback: 978-1-78535-018-4 ebook: 978-1-78535-019-1

Framespotting
Changing how you look at things changes how
you see them
Laurence & Alison Matthews
A punchy, upbeat guide to framespotting. Spot deceptions and
hidden assumptions; swap growth for growing up. See and be free.
Paperback: 978-1-78279-689-3 ebook: 978-1-78279-822-4

Is There an Afterlife?

David Fontana

Is there an Afterlife? If so what is it like? How do Western ideas of the afterlife compare with Eastern? David Fontana presents the historical and contemporary evidence for survival of physical death.

Paperback: 978-1-90381-690-5

Nothing Matters

a book about nothing

Ronald Green

Thinking about Nothing opens the world to everything by illuminating new angles to old problems and stimulating new ways of thinking.

Paperback: 978-1-84694-707-0 ebook: 978-1-78099-016-3

Panpsychism

The Philosophy of the Sensuous Cosmos

Peter Ells

Are free will and mind chimeras? This book, anti-materialistic but respecting science, answers: No! Mind is foundational to all existence.

Paperback: 978-1-84694-505-2 ebook: 978-1-78099-018-7

Punk Science

Inside the Mind of God

Manjir Samanta-Laughton

Many have experienced unexplainable phenomena; God, psychic abilities, extraordinary healing and angelic encounters. Can cutting-edge science actually explain phenomena previously thought of as 'paranormal'?

Paperback: 978-1-90504-793-2

The Vagabond Spirit of Poetry
Edward Clarke
Spend time with the wisest poets of the modern age and of the
past, and let Edward Clarke remind you of the importance of
poetry in our industrialized world.
Paperback: 978-1-78279-370-0 ebook: 978-1-78279-369-4

Readers of ebooks can buy or view any of these bestsellers by
clicking on the live link in the title. Most titles are published in
paperback and as an ebook. Paperbacks are available in traditional
bookshops. Both print and ebook formats are available online.
Find more titles and sign up to our readers' newsletter at
http://www.johnhuntpublishing.com/non-fiction
Follow us on Facebook at
https://www.facebook.com/JHPNonFiction
and Twitter at https://twitter.com/JHPNonFiction